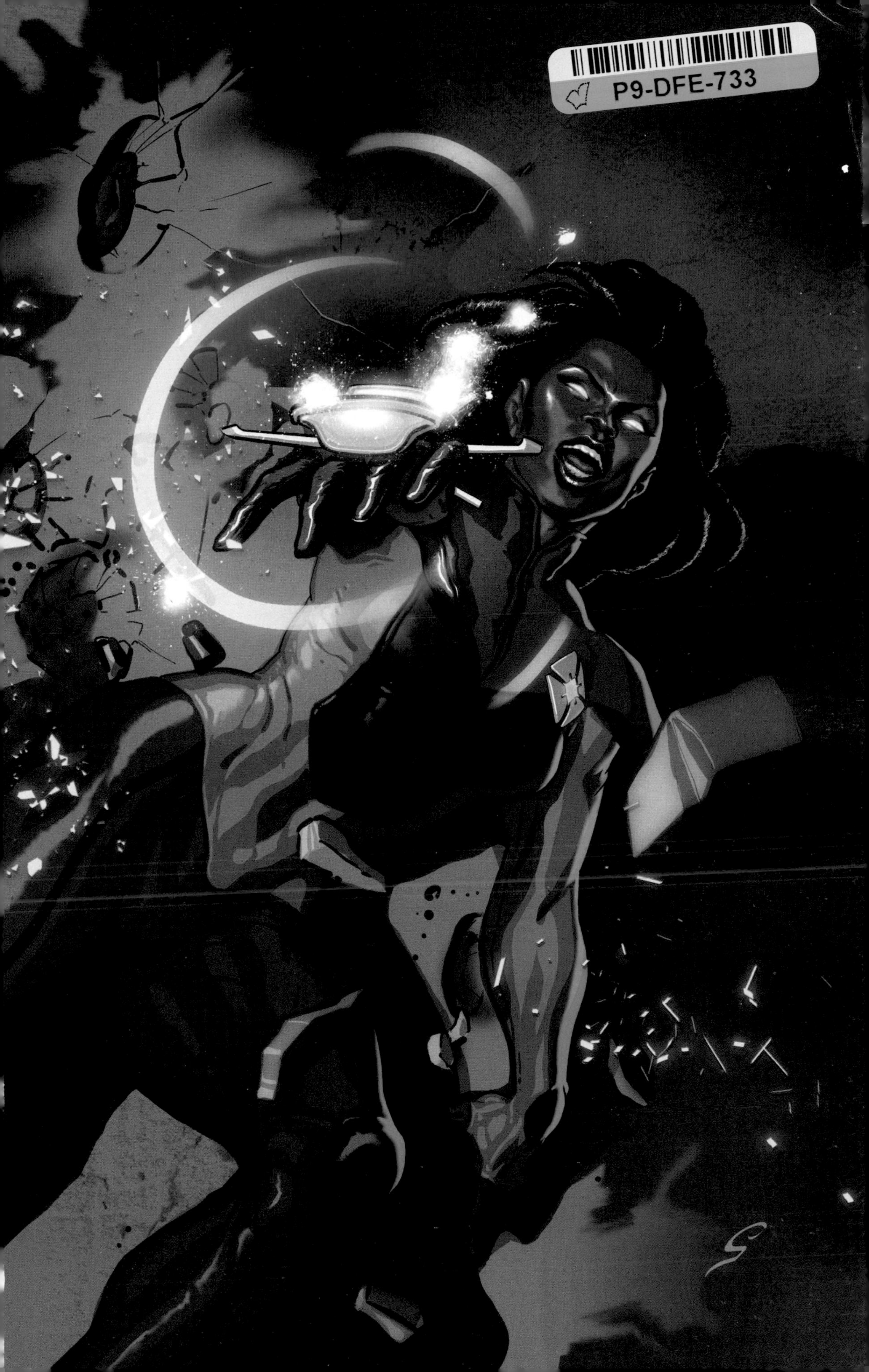

LIVEWIRE

WRITER
VITA AYALA

ARTIST
KANO

LETTERER
SAIDA TEMOFONTE

COVERS BY
KENNETH ROCAFORT

ASSOCIATE EDITOR
DAVID MENCHEL

EDITOR
HEATHER ANTOS

GALLERY
KANO
KHARY RANDOLPH
BECCA FARROW
RHAZZAH
PAUL RENAUD
JOHN K. SNYDER III
JASON WRIGHT

COLLECTION BACK COVER ART
JUAN DOE

COLLECTION COVER ART
KENNETH ROCAFORT

COLLECTION FRONT ART:
GREY WILLIAMSON
FRANCIS PORTELA
ANDREW DALHOUSE

COLLECTION EDITOR
IVAN COHEN

COLLECTION DESIGNER
STEVE BLACKWELL

DAN MINTZ Chairman **FRED PIERCE** Publisher **WALTER BLACK** VP Operations **MATTHEW KLEIN** VP Sales & Marketing **ROBERT MEYERS** Senior Editorial Director **MEL CAYLO** Director of Marketing
TRAVIS ESCARFULLERY Director of Design & Production **PETER STERN** Director of International Publishing & Merchandising **LYSA HAWKINS & HEATHER ANTOS** Editors
DAVID MENCHEL Associate Editor **DREW BAUMGARTNER** Assistant Editor **JEFF WALKER** Production & Design Manager **EMILY HECHT** Sales & Social Media Manager
KAT O'NEILL Sales & Live Events Manager **DANIELLE WARD** Sales Manager **CONNOR HILL** Sales Operations Coordinator **GREGG KATZMAN** Marketing Coordinator

RUSS BROWN President, Consumer Products, Promotions & Ad Sales **OLIVER TAYLOR** International Licensing Coordinator

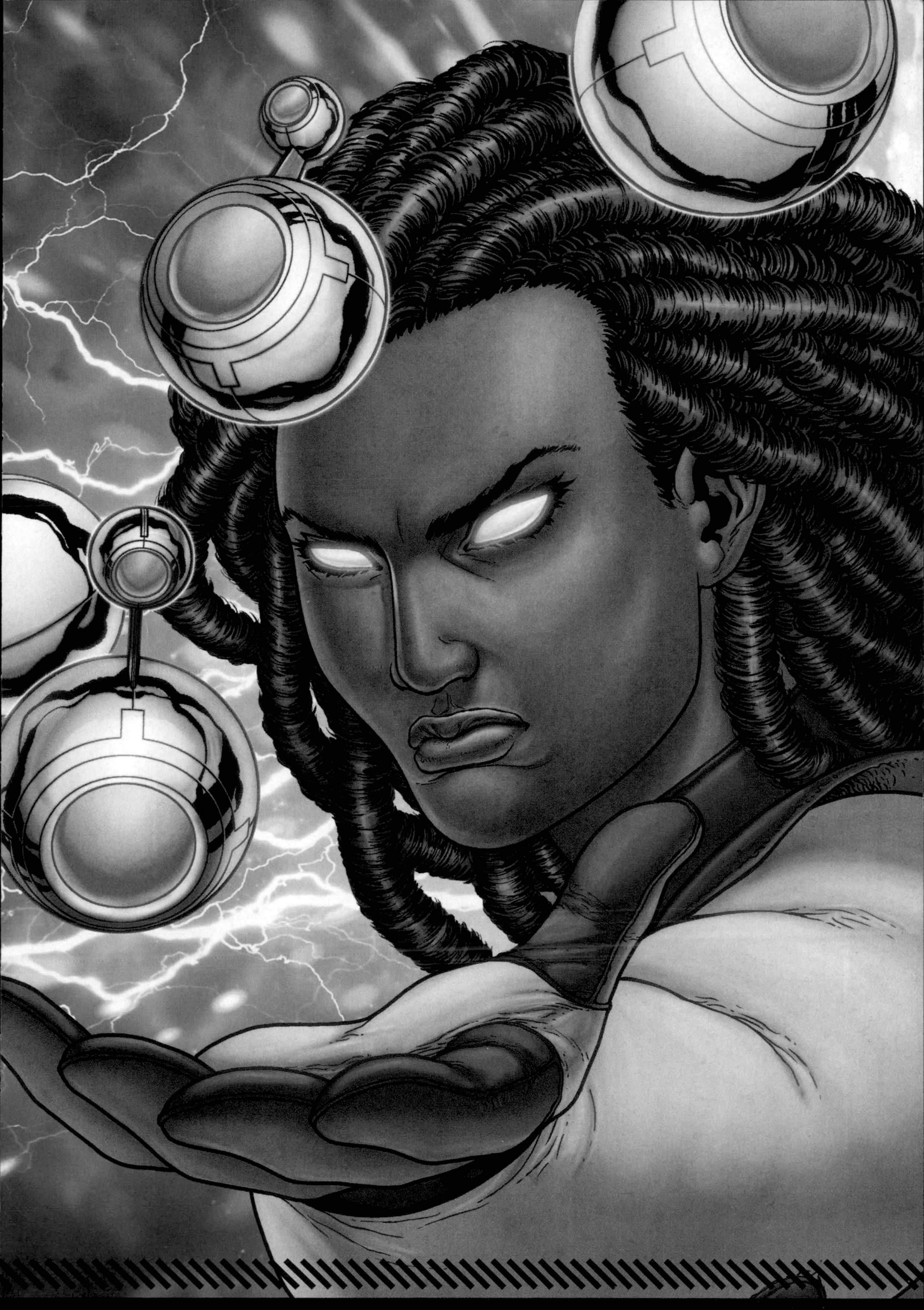

Livewire®: Guardian. Published by Valiant Entertainment LLC. Office of Publication: 350 Seventh Avenue, New York, NY 10001. Compilation copyright © 2019 Valiant Entertainment LLC. All rights reserved. Contains materials originally published in single magazine form as Livewire #5-8. Copyright © 2019 Valiant Entertainment LLC. All rights reserved. All characters, their distinctive likeness and related indicia featured in this publication are trademarks of Valiant Entertainment LLC. The stories, characters, and incidents featured in this publication are entirely fictional. Valiant Entertainment does not read or accept unsolicited submissions of ideas, stories, or artwork. Printed in the U.S.A. First Printing. ISBN: 9781682153260.

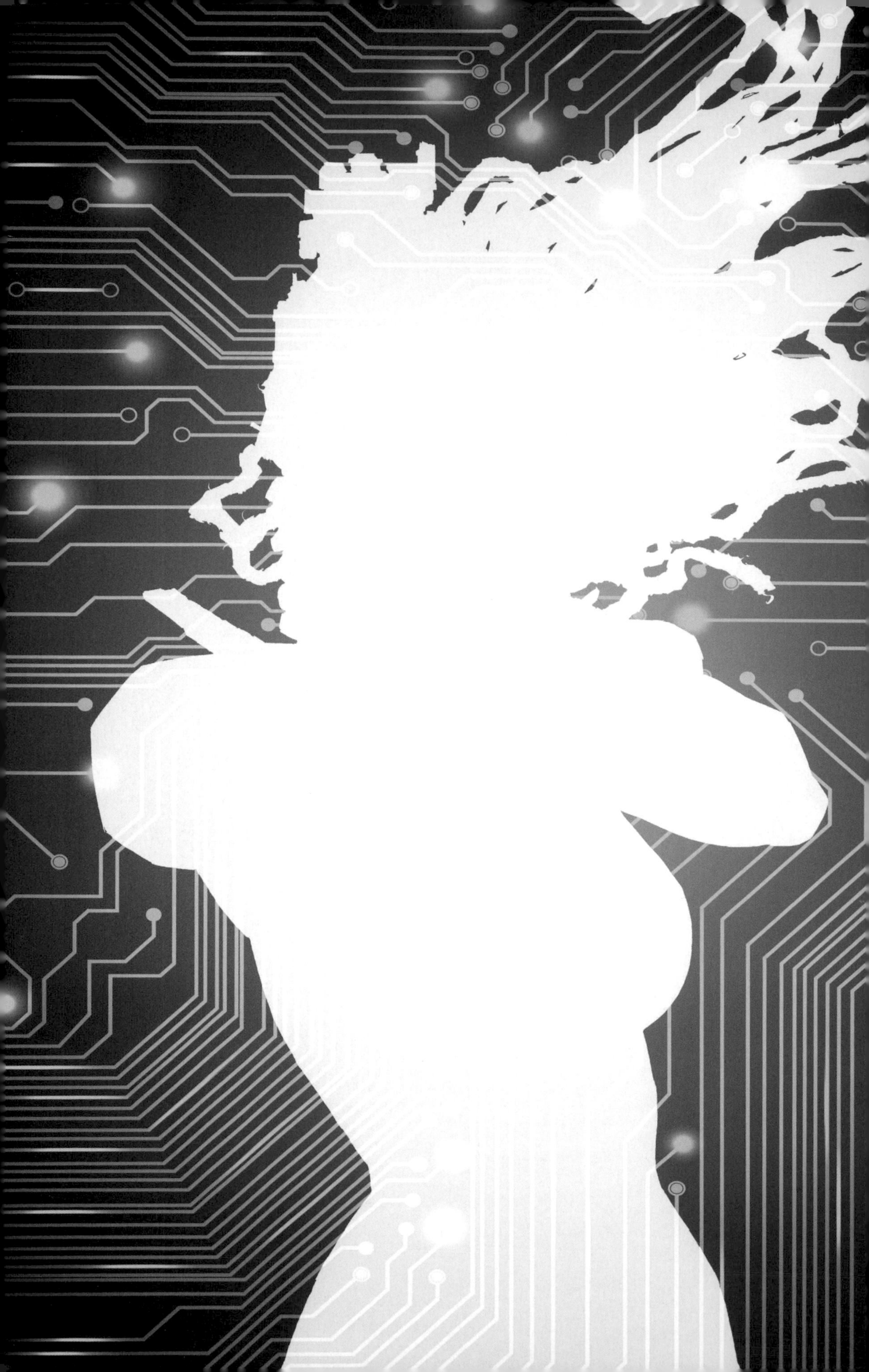

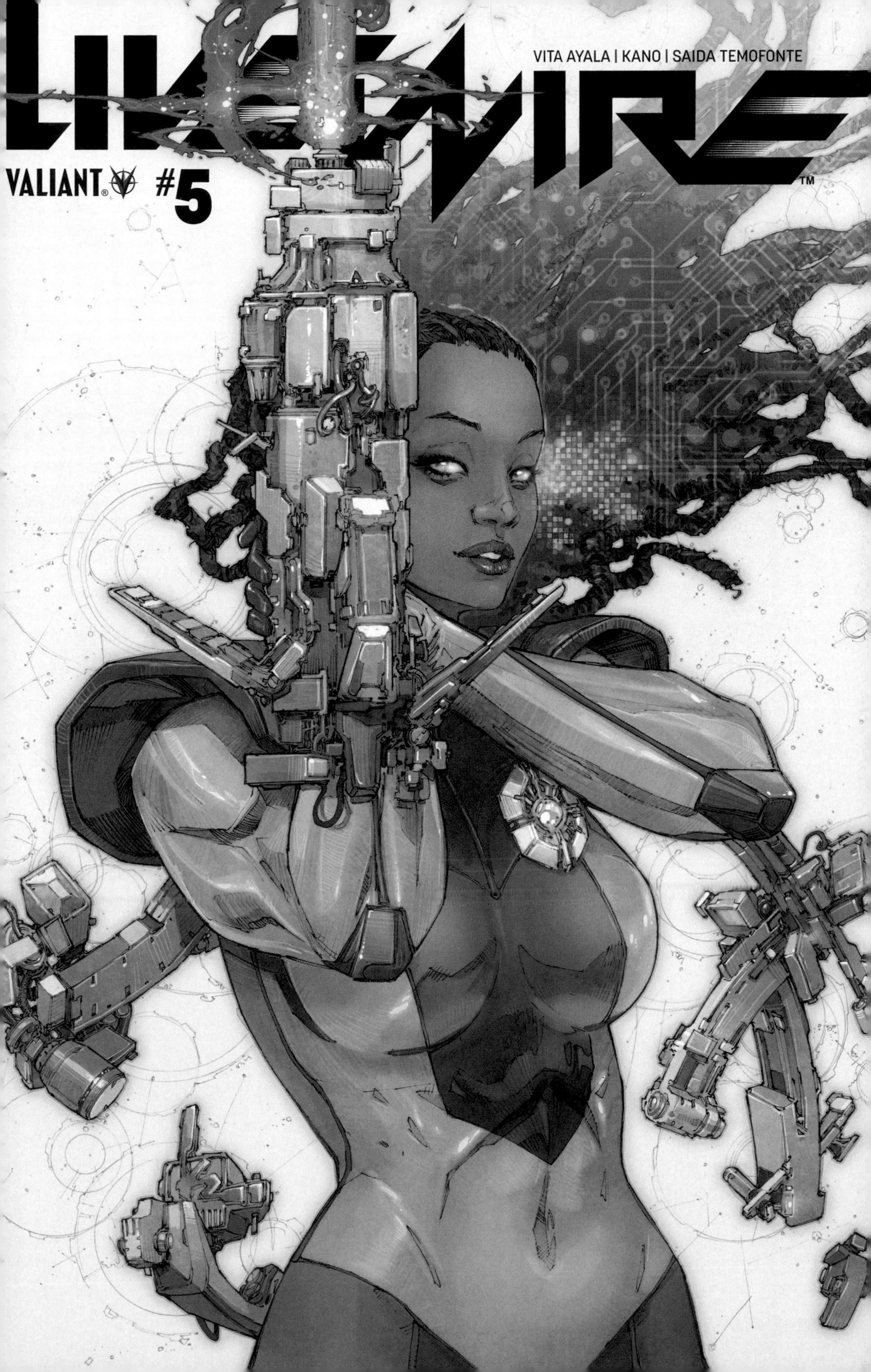
LIVEWIRE
VITA AYALA | KANO | SAIDA TEMOFONTE
VALIANT
#5

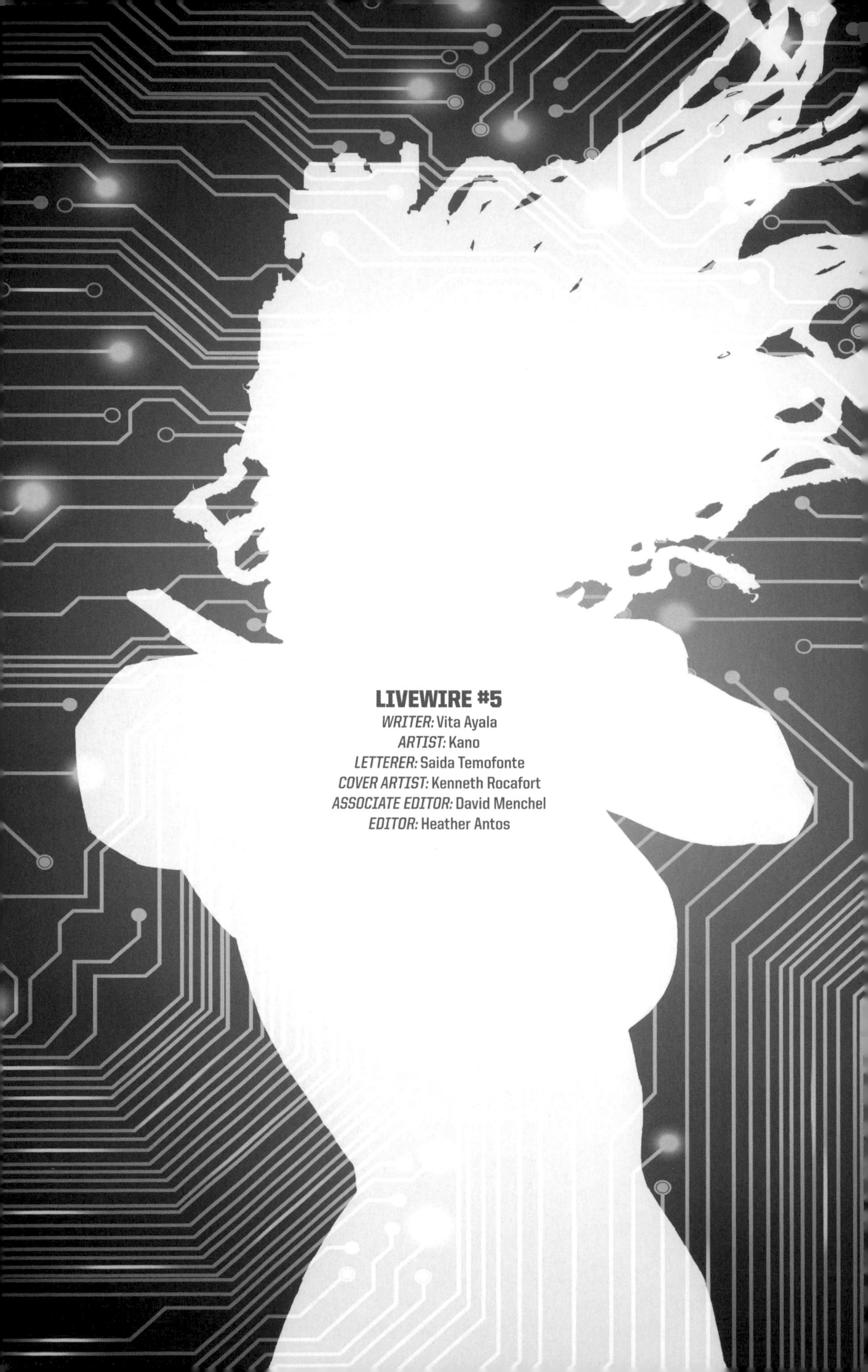

LIVEWIRE #5

WRITER: Vita Ayala
ARTIST: Kano
LETTERER: Saida Temofonte
COVER ARTIST: Kenneth Rocafort
ASSOCIATE EDITOR: David Menchel
EDITOR: Heather Antos

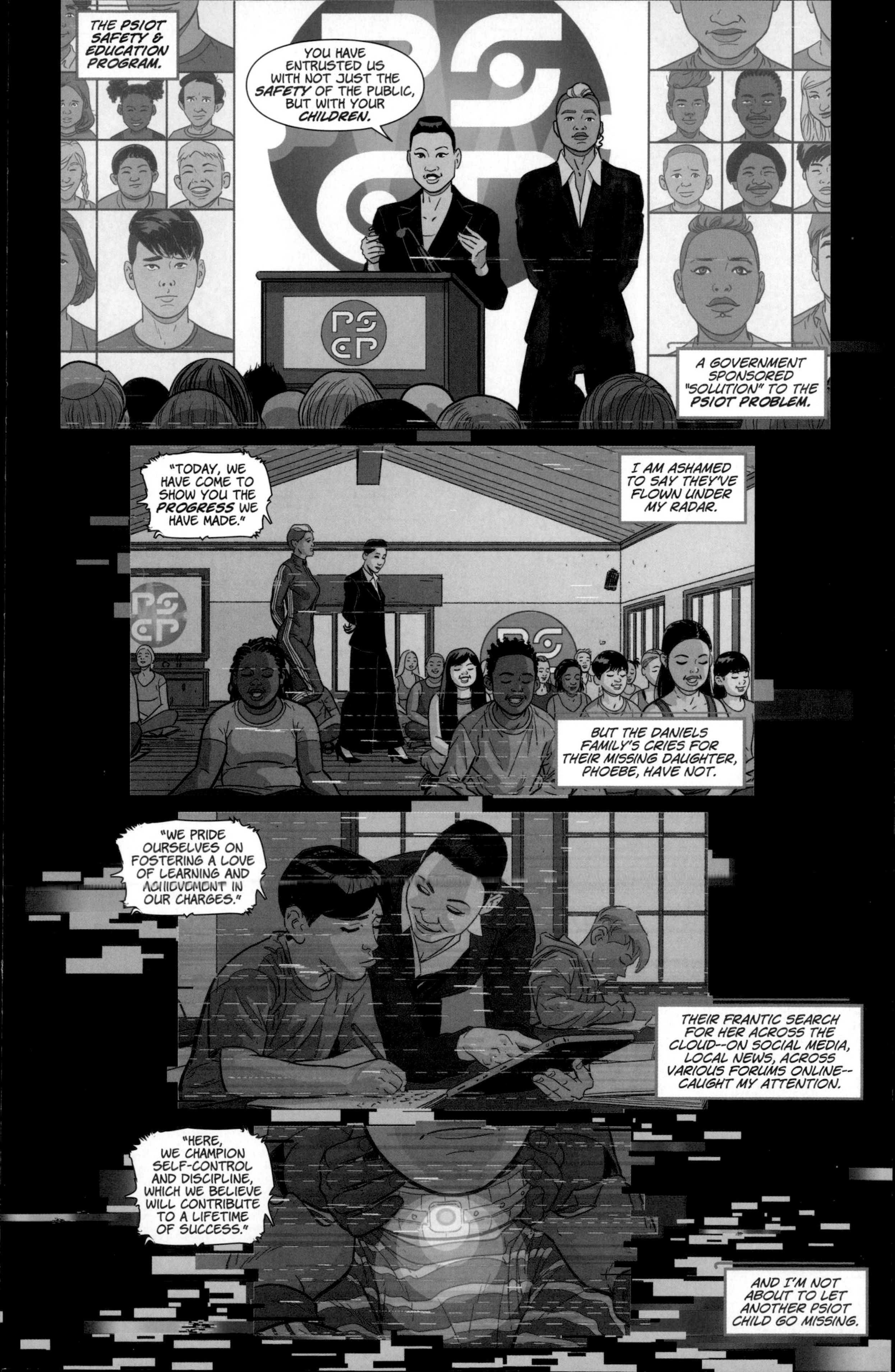
THE PSIOT SAFETY & EDUCATION PROGRAM.
YOU HAVE ENTRUSTED US WITH NOT JUST THE SAFETY OF THE PUBLIC, BUT WITH YOUR CHILDREN.
A GOVERNMENT SPONSORED "SOLUTION" TO THE PSIOT PROBLEM.
"TODAY, WE HAVE COME TO SHOW YOU THE PROGRESS WE HAVE MADE."
I AM ASHAMED TO SAY THEY'VE FLOWN UNDER MY RADAR.
BUT THE DANIELS FAMILY'S CRIES FOR THEIR MISSING DAUGHTER, PHOEBE, HAVE NOT.
"WE PRIDE OURSELVES ON FOSTERING A LOVE OF LEARNING AND ACHIEVEMENT IN OUR CHARGES."
THEIR FRANTIC SEARCH FOR HER ACROSS THE CLOUD--ON SOCIAL MEDIA, LOCAL NEWS, ACROSS VARIOUS FORUMS ONLINE--CAUGHT MY ATTENTION.
"HERE, WE CHAMPION SELF-CONTROL AND DISCIPLINE, WHICH WE BELIEVE WILL CONTRIBUTE TO A LIFETIME OF SUCCESS."
AND I'M NOT ABOUT TO LET ANOTHER PSIOT CHILD GO MISSING.

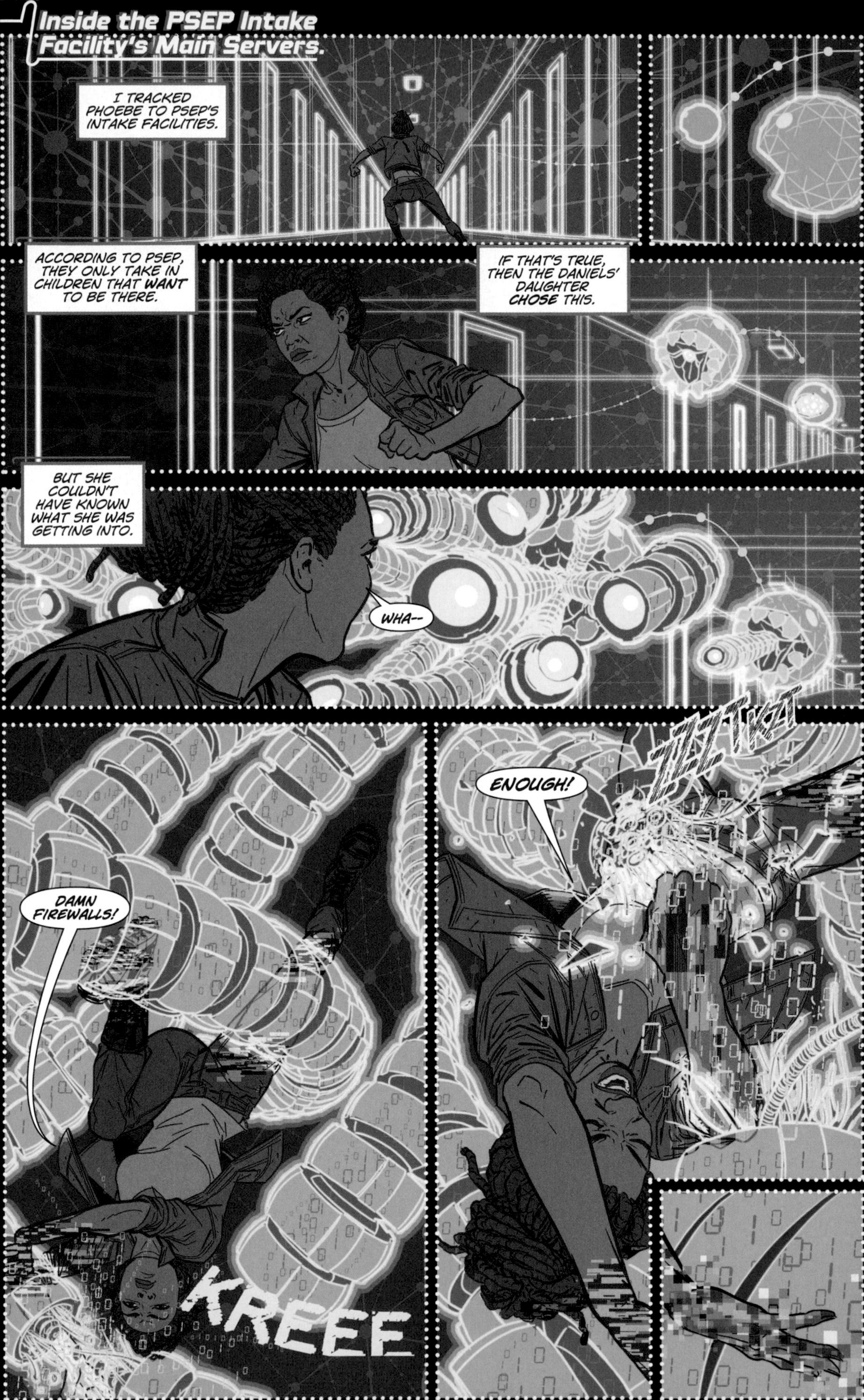
Inside the PSEP Intake Facility's Main Servers.
I TRACKED PHOEBE TO PSEP'S INTAKE FACILITIES.
ACCORDING TO PSEP, THEY ONLY TAKE IN CHILDREN THAT WANT TO BE THERE.
IF THAT'S TRUE, THEN THE DANIELS' DAUGHTER CHOSE THIS.
BUT SHE COULDN'T HAVE KNOWN WHAT SHE WAS GETTING INTO.
WHA--
DAMN FIREWALLS!
KREEE
ENOUGH!

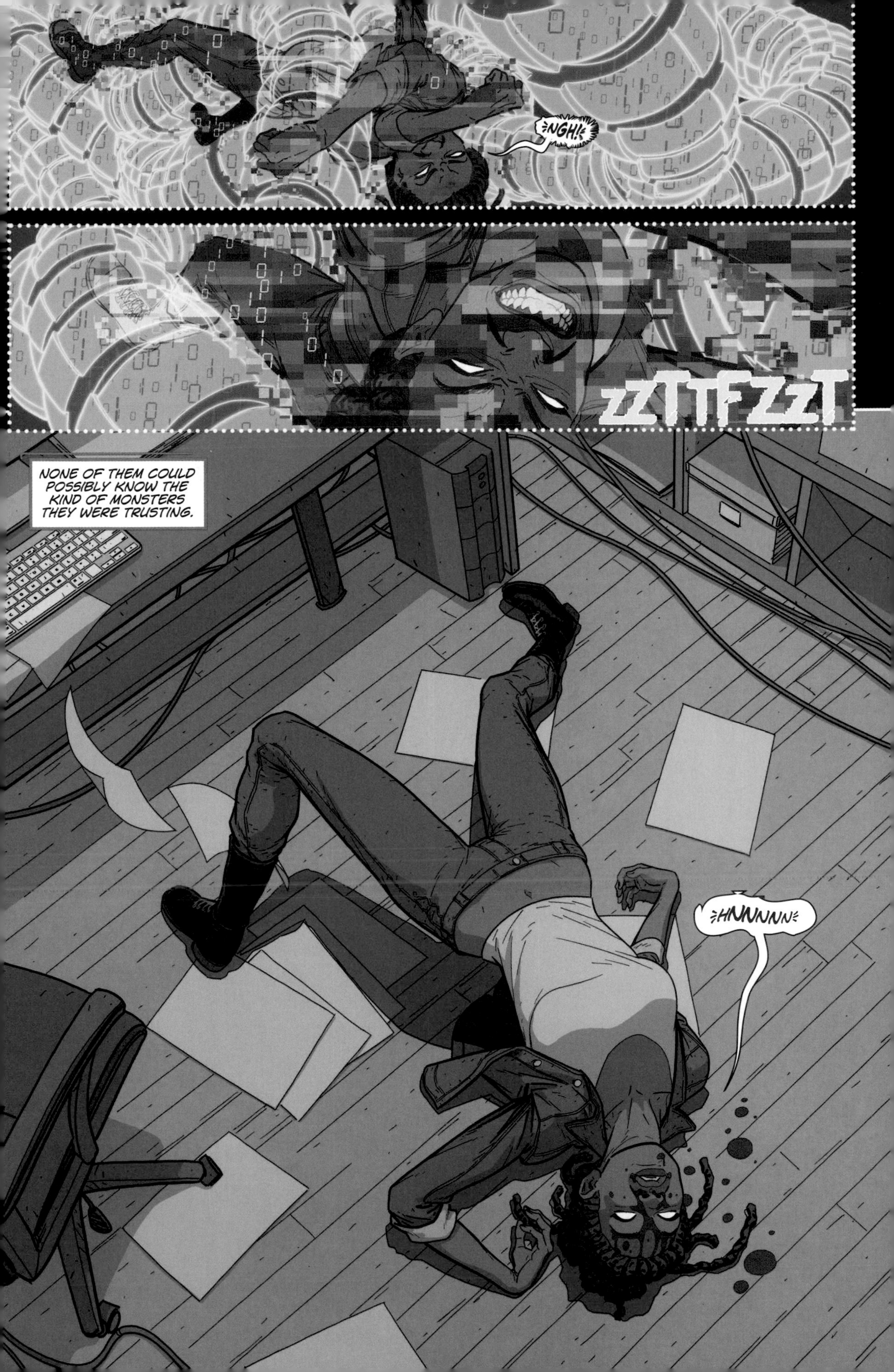
NGH!
zZTTFZzT
NONE OF THEM COULD POSSIBLY KNOW THE KIND OF MONSTERS THEY WERE TRUSTING.
HNNNNN

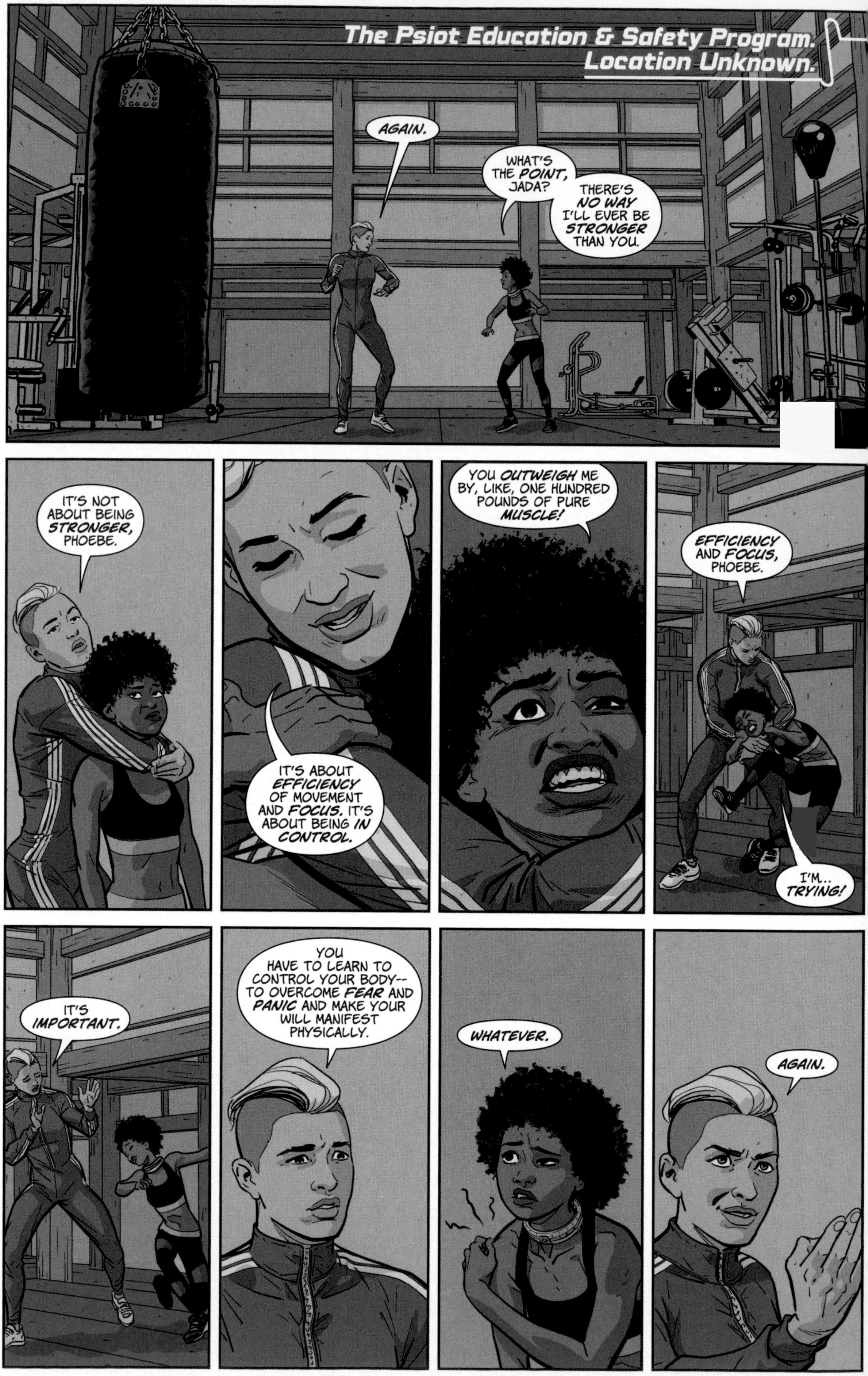
The Psiot Education & Safety Program.
Location Unknown.
AGAIN.
WHAT'S THE POINT, JADA?
THERE'S NO WAY I'LL EVER BE STRONGER THAN YOU.
IT'S NOT ABOUT BEING STRONGER, PHOEBE.
IT'S ABOUT EFFICIENCY OF MOVEMENT AND FOCUS. IT'S ABOUT BEING IN CONTROL.
YOU OUTWEIGH ME BY, LIKE, ONE HUNDRED POUNDS OF PURE MUSCLE!
EFFICIENCY AND FOCUS, PHOEBE.
I'M... TRYING!
IT'S IMPORTANT.
YOU HAVE TO LEARN TO CONTROL YOUR BODY-- TO OVERCOME FEAR AND PANIC AND MAKE YOUR WILL MANIFEST PHYSICALLY.
WHATEVER.
AGAIN.

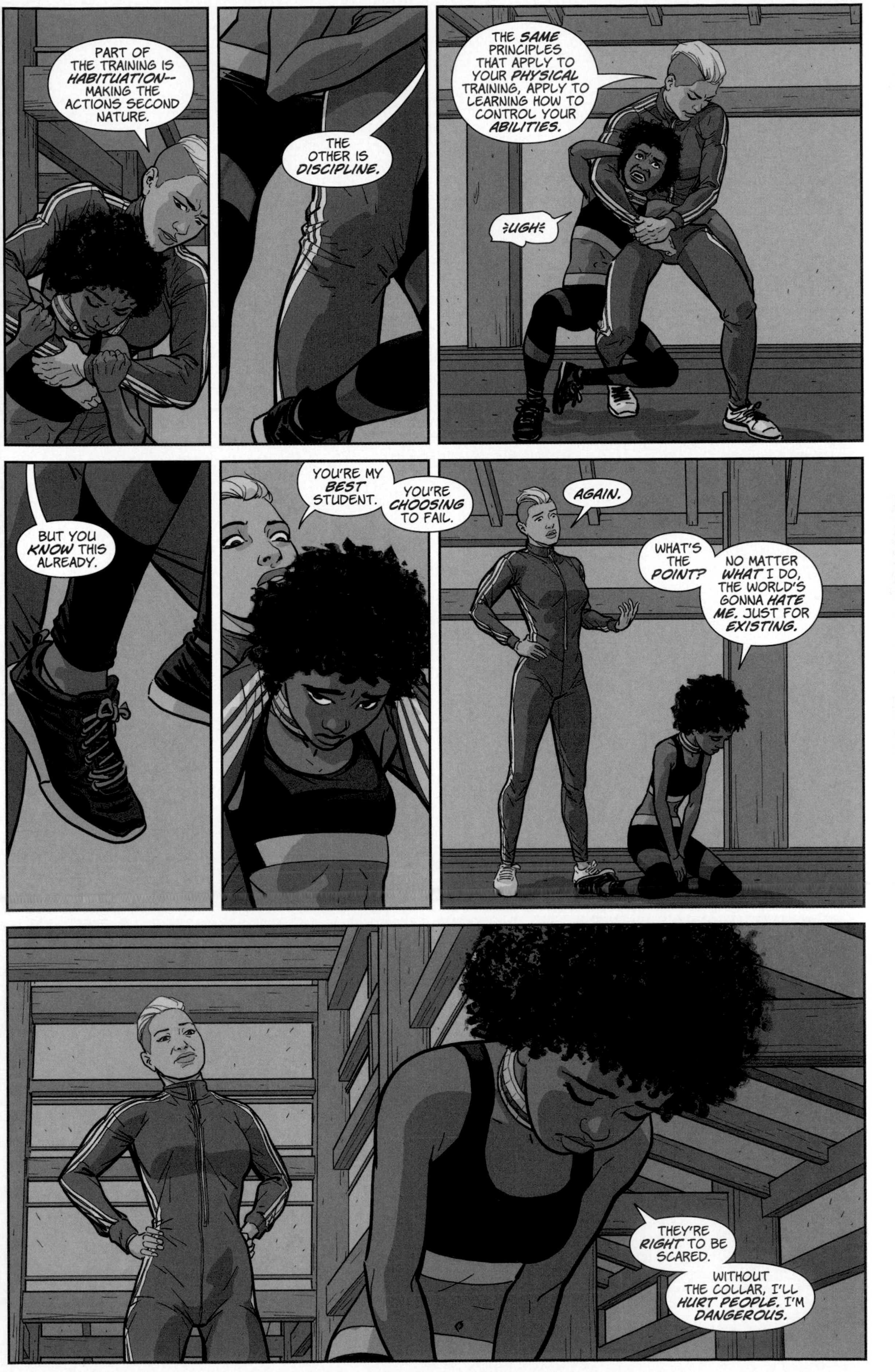
PART OF THE TRAINING IS HABITUATION-- MAKING THE ACTIONS SECOND NATURE.
THE OTHER IS DISCIPLINE.
THE SAME PRINCIPLES THAT APPLY TO YOUR PHYSICAL TRAINING, APPLY TO LEARNING HOW TO CONTROL YOUR ABILITIES.
UGH
BUT YOU KNOW THIS ALREADY.
YOU'RE MY BEST STUDENT.
YOU'RE CHOOSING TO FAIL.
AGAIN.
WHAT'S THE POINT?
NO MATTER WHAT I DO, THE WORLD'S GONNA HATE ME. JUST FOR EXISTING.
THEY'RE RIGHT TO BE SCARED.
WITHOUT THE COLLAR, I'LL HURT PEOPLE. I'M DANGEROUS.

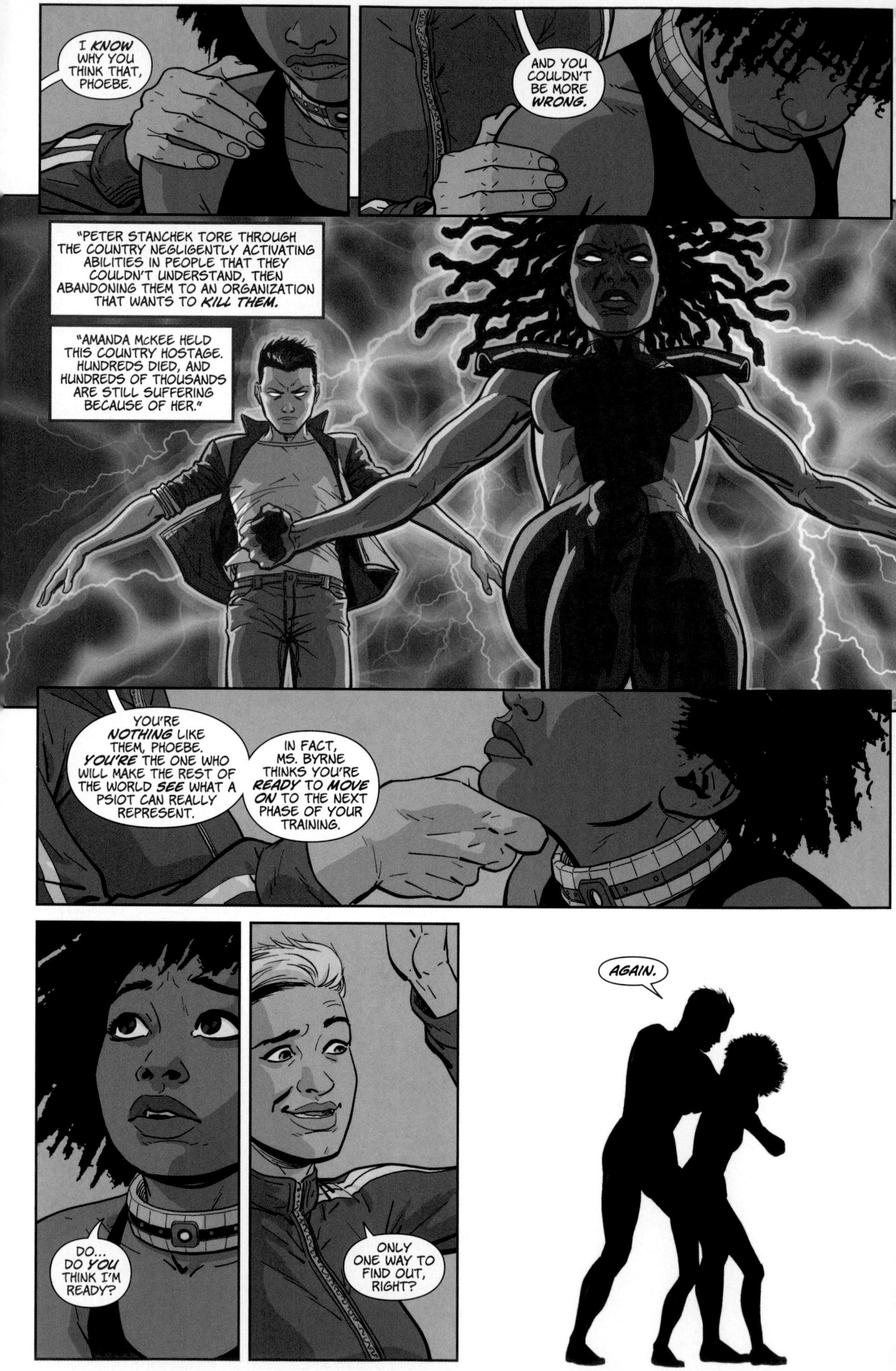
I KNOW WHY YOU THINK THAT, PHOEBE.
AND YOU COULDN'T BE MORE WRONG.
"PETER STANCHEK TORE THROUGH THE COUNTRY NEGLIGENTLY ACTIVATING ABILITIES IN PEOPLE THAT THEY COULDN'T UNDERSTAND, THEN ABANDONING THEM TO AN ORGANIZATION THAT WANTS TO KILL THEM.
"AMANDA McKEE HELD THIS COUNTRY HOSTAGE. HUNDREDS DIED, AND HUNDREDS OF THOUSANDS ARE STILL SUFFERING BECAUSE OF HER."
YOU'RE NOTHING LIKE THEM, PHOEBE. YOU'RE THE ONE WHO WILL MAKE THE REST OF THE WORLD SEE WHAT A PSIOT CAN REALLY REPRESENT.
IN FACT, MS. BYRNE THINKS YOU'RE READY TO MOVE ON TO THE NEXT PHASE OF YOUR TRAINING.
DO... DO YOU THINK I'M READY?
ONLY ONE WAY TO FIND OUT, RIGHT?
AGAIN.

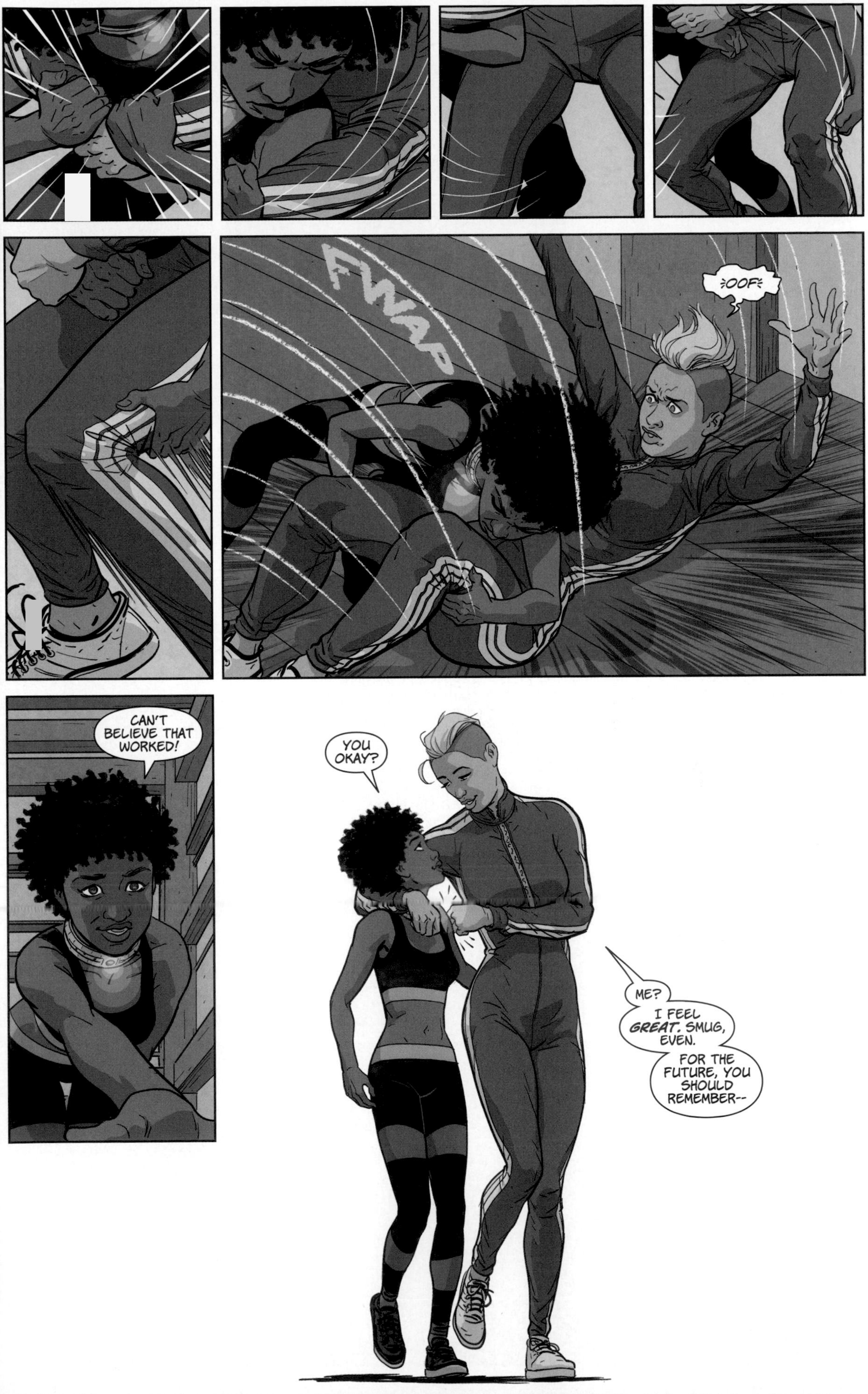
FWAP
OOF
CAN'T BELIEVE THAT WORKED!
YOU OKAY?
ME? I FEEL *GREAT.* SMUG, EVEN.
FOR THE FUTURE, YOU SHOULD REMEMBER--

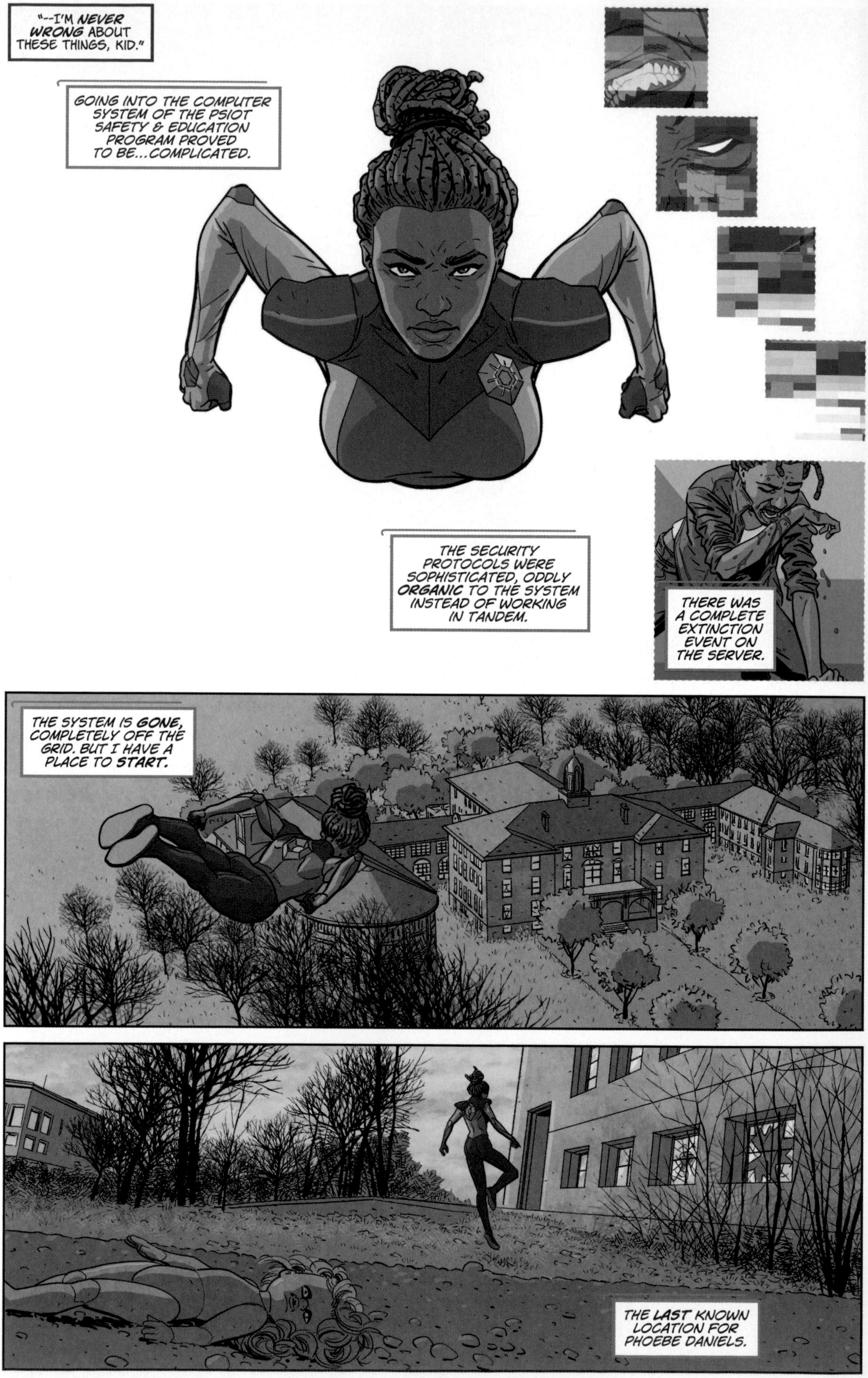
"--I'M NEVER WRONG ABOUT THESE THINGS, KID."
GOING INTO THE COMPUTER SYSTEM OF THE PSIOT SAFETY & EDUCATION PROGRAM PROVED TO BE...COMPLICATED.
THE SECURITY PROTOCOLS WERE SOPHISTICATED, ODDLY ORGANIC TO THE SYSTEM INSTEAD OF WORKING IN TANDEM.
THERE WAS A COMPLETE EXTINCTION EVENT ON THE SERVER.
THE SYSTEM IS GONE, COMPLETELY OFF THE GRID. BUT I HAVE A PLACE TO START.
THE LAST KNOWN LOCATION FOR PHOEBE DANIELS.

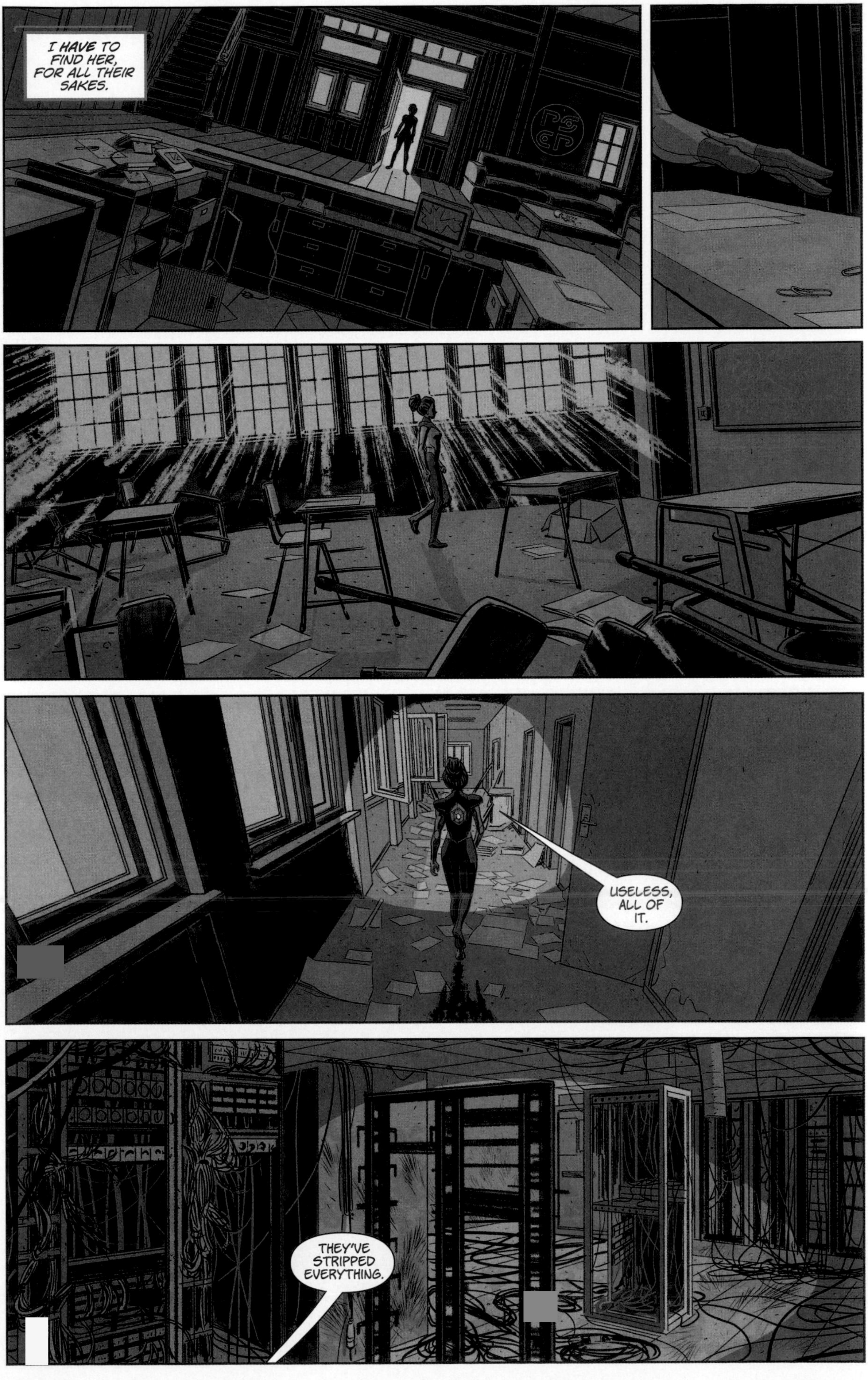
I HAVE TO FIND HER, FOR ALL THEIR SAKES.
USELESS, ALL OF IT.
THEY'VE STRIPPED EVERYTHING.

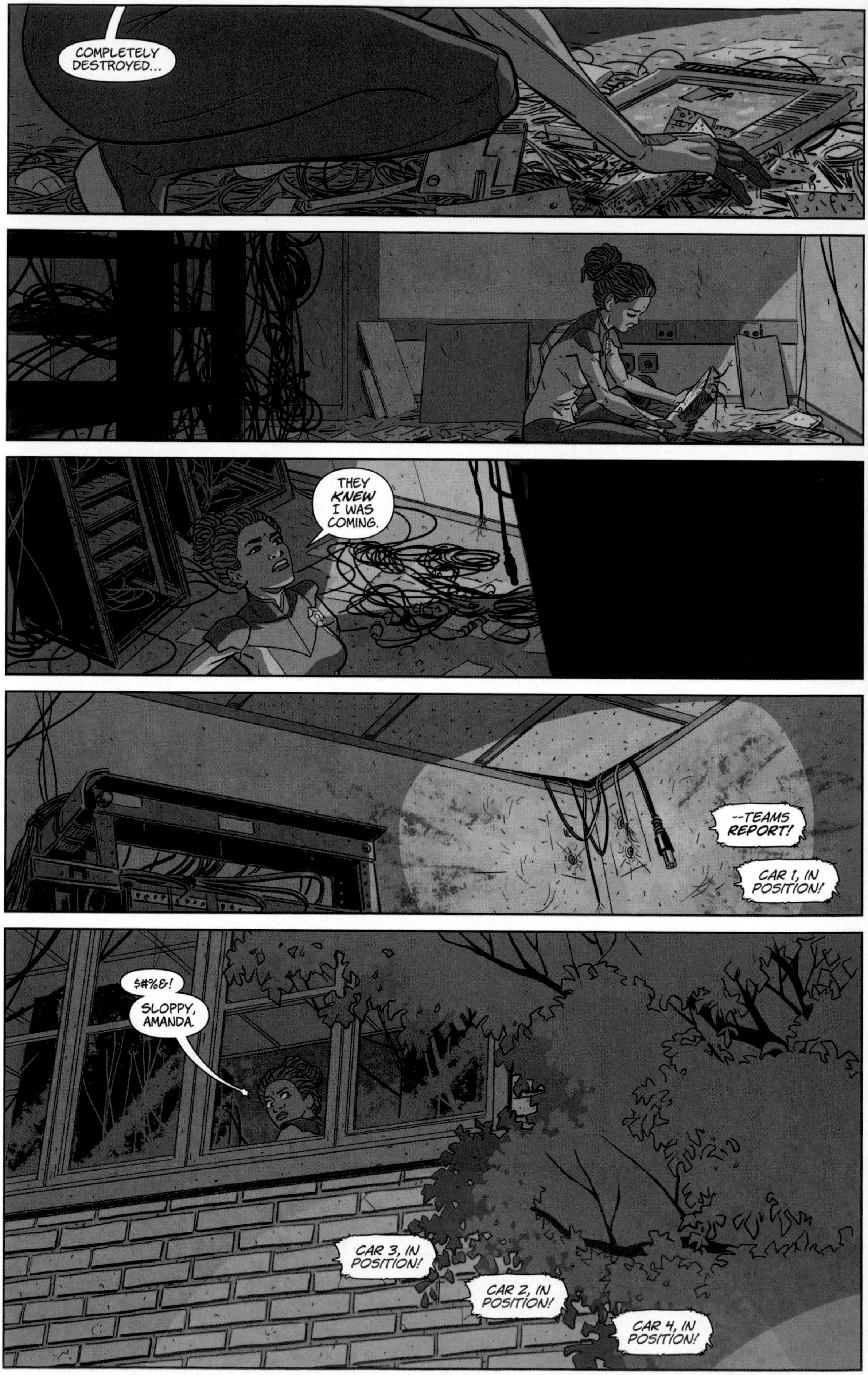

COMPLETELY DESTROYED...
THEY KNEW I WAS COMING.
--TEAMS REPORT!
CAR 1, IN POSITION!
$#%&! SLOPPY, AMANDA.
CAR 3, IN POSITION!
CAR 2, IN POSITION!
CAR 4, IN POSITION!

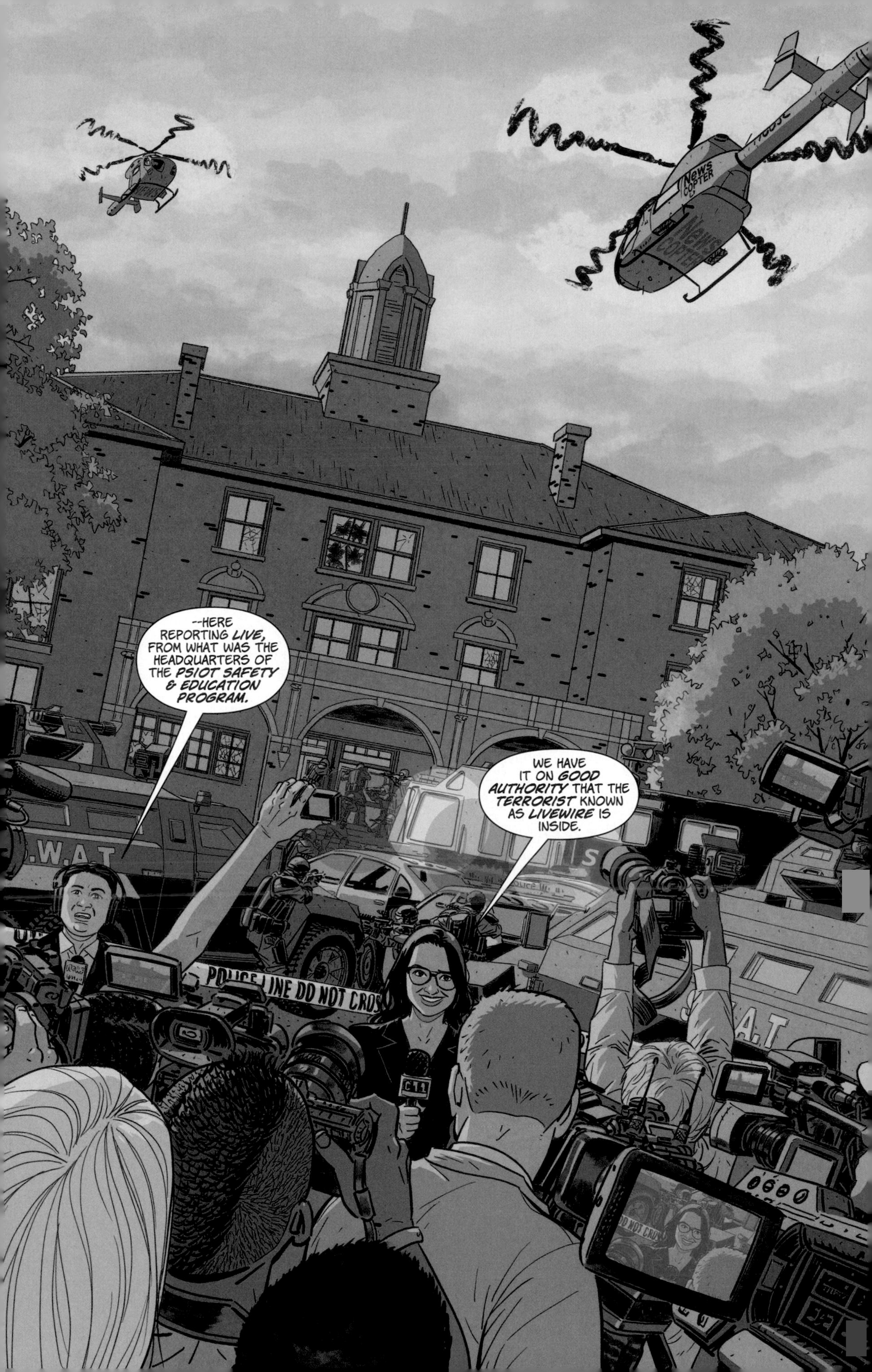

--HERE REPORTING *LIVE,* FROM WHAT WAS THE HEADQUARTERS OF THE *PSIOT SAFETY & EDUCATION PROGRAM.*
WE HAVE IT ON *GOOD AUTHORITY* THAT THE *TERRORIST* KNOWN AS *LIVEWIRE* IS INSIDE.
POLICE LINE DO NOT CROS

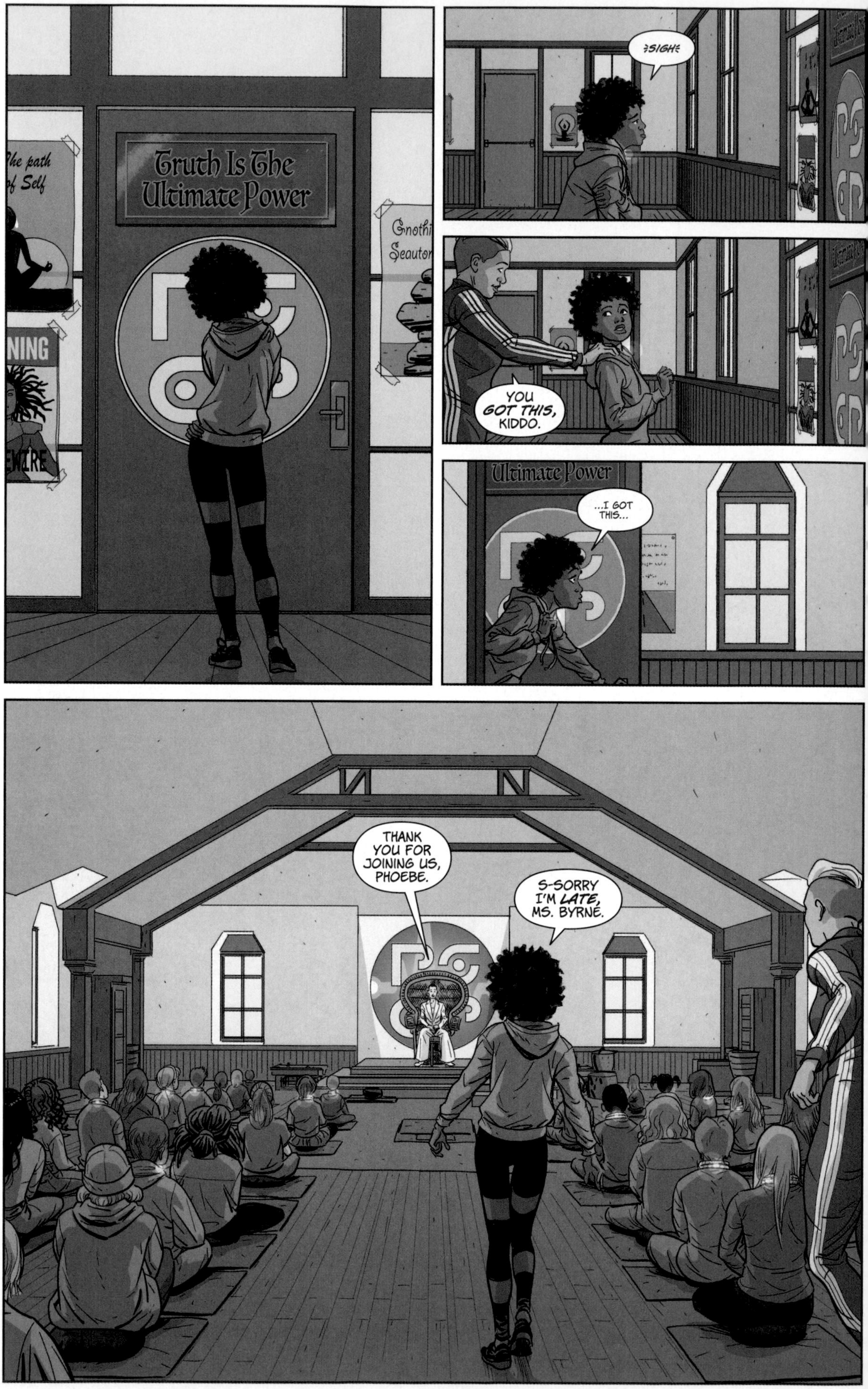
Truth Is The Ultimate Power
SIGH
YOU *GOT THIS,* KIDDO.
Ultimate Power
...I GOT THIS...
THANK YOU FOR JOINING US, PHOEBE.
S-SORRY I'M *LATE,* MS. BYRNE.

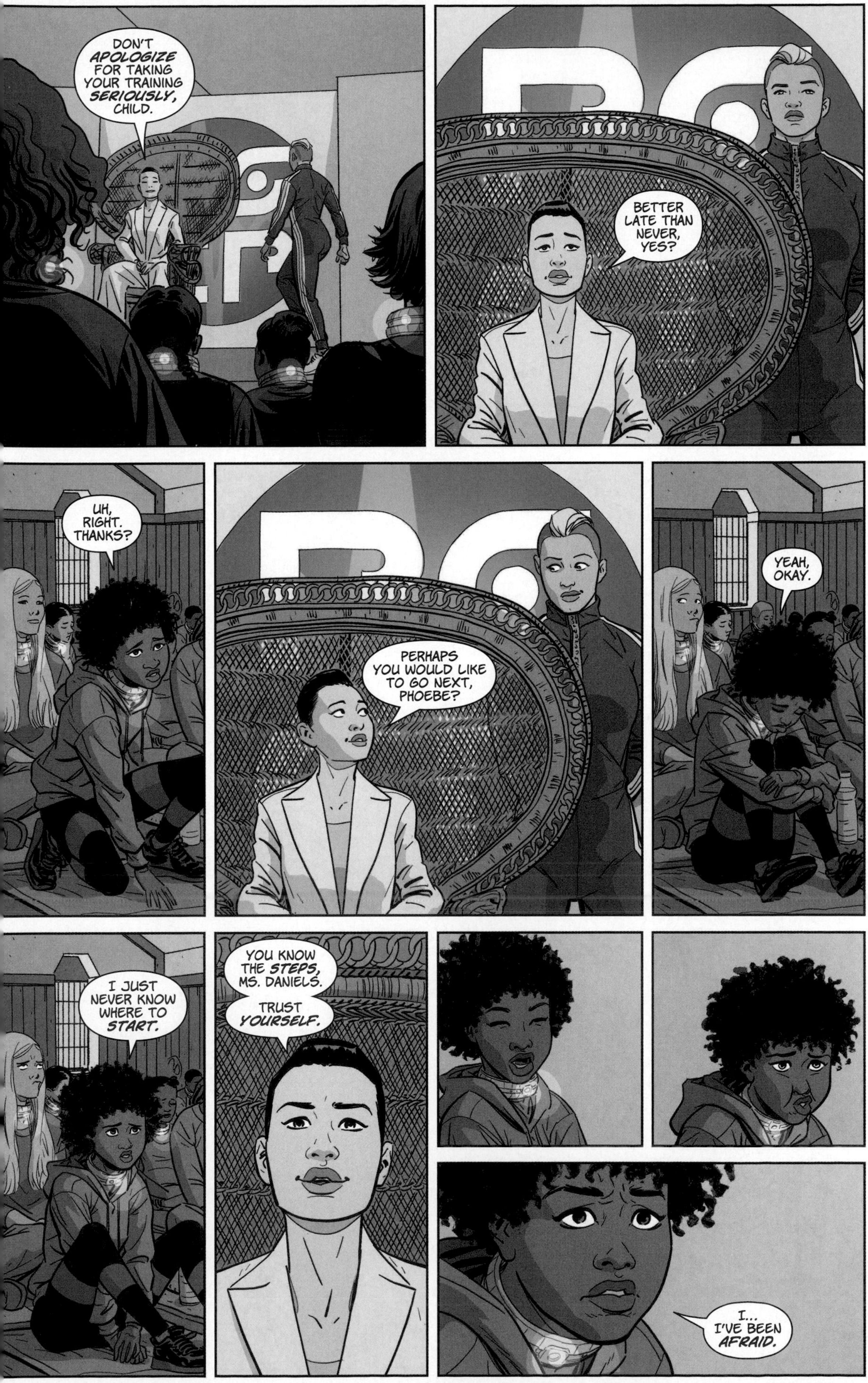
DON'T APOLOGIZE FOR TAKING YOUR TRAINING SERIOUSLY, CHILD.
BETTER LATE THAN NEVER, YES?
UH, RIGHT. THANKS?
PERHAPS YOU WOULD LIKE TO GO NEXT, PHOEBE?
YEAH, OKAY.
I JUST NEVER KNOW WHERE TO START.
YOU KNOW THE STEPS, MS. DANIELS.
TRUST YOURSELF.
I... I'VE BEEN AFRAID.

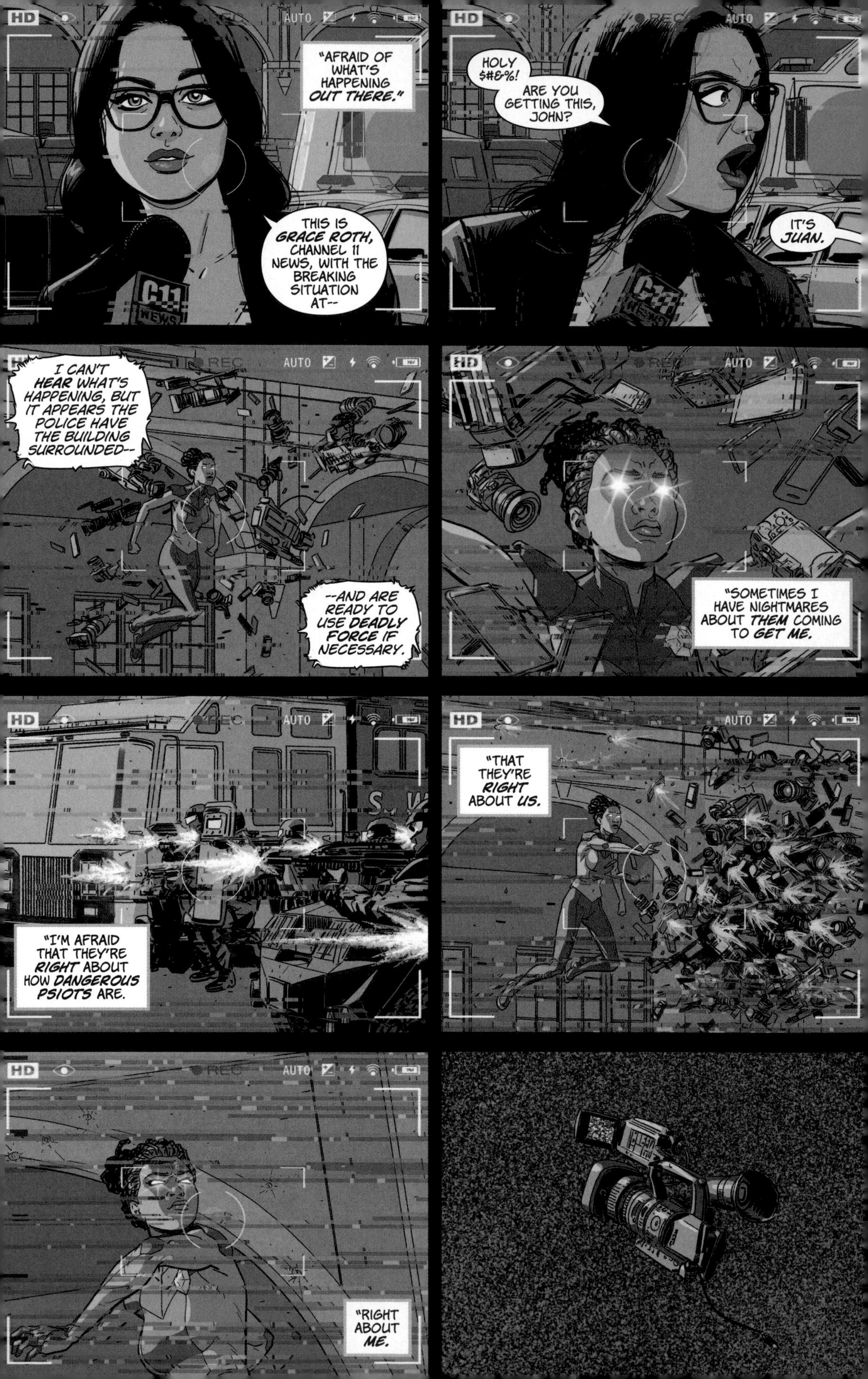

HD
AUTO
"AFRAID OF WHAT'S HAPPENING OUT THERE."
THIS IS GRACE ROTH, CHANNEL 11 NEWS, WITH THE BREAKING SITUATION AT--
C11 NEWS
HOLY $#&%!
ARE YOU GETTING THIS, JOHN?
IT'S JUAN.
I CAN'T HEAR WHAT'S HAPPENING, BUT IT APPEARS THE POLICE HAVE THE BUILDING SURROUNDED--
--AND ARE READY TO USE DEADLY FORCE IF NECESSARY.
"SOMETIMES I HAVE NIGHTMARES ABOUT THEM COMING TO GET ME.
"I'M AFRAID THAT THEY'RE RIGHT ABOUT HOW DANGEROUS PSIOTS ARE.
"THAT THEY'RE RIGHT ABOUT US.
"RIGHT ABOUT ME.

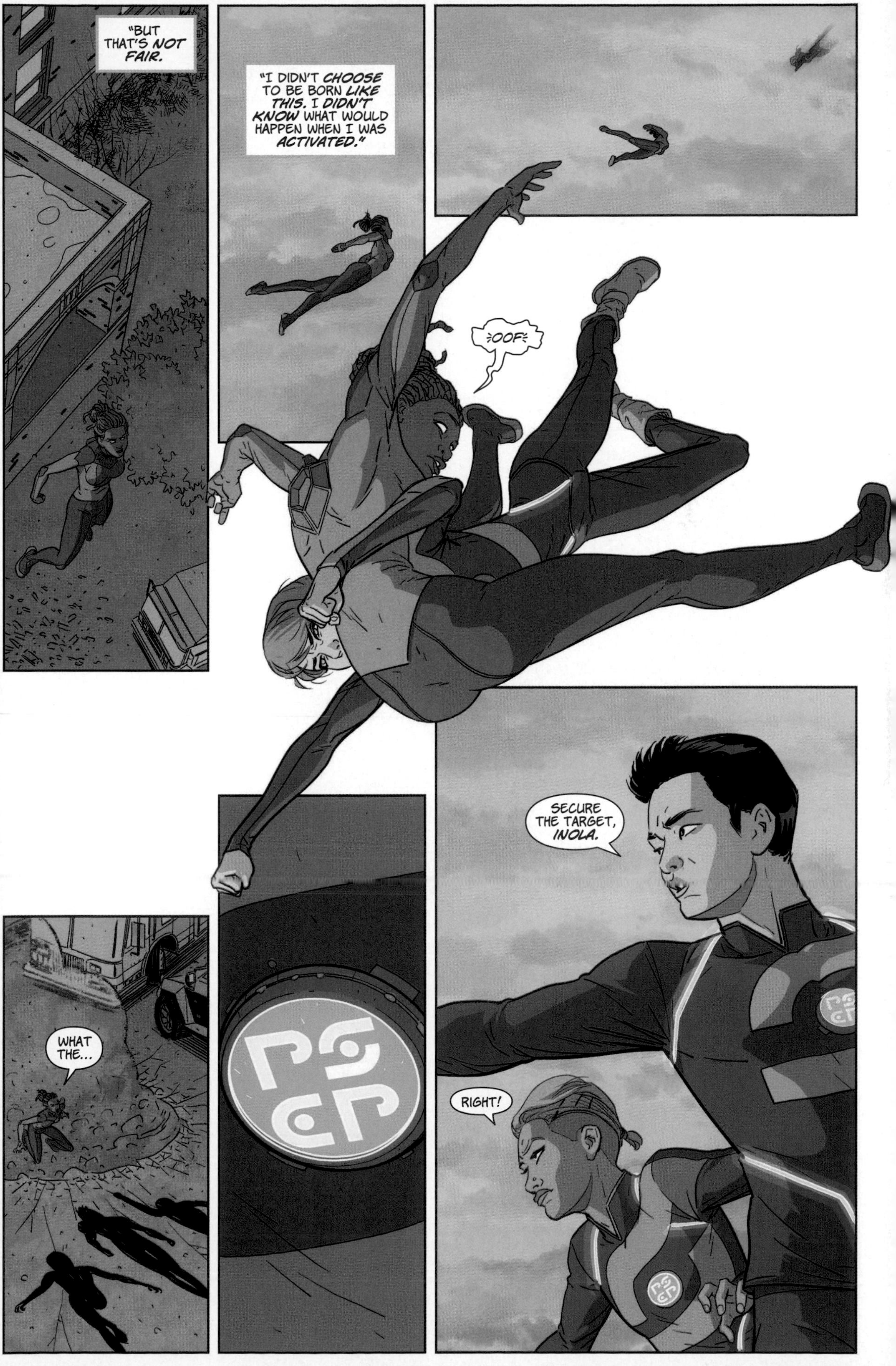
"BUT THAT'S NOT FAIR.
"I DIDN'T CHOOSE TO BE BORN LIKE THIS. I DIDN'T KNOW WHAT WOULD HAPPEN WHEN I WAS ACTIVATED."
OOF
WHAT THE...
SECURE THE TARGET, INOLA.
RIGHT!

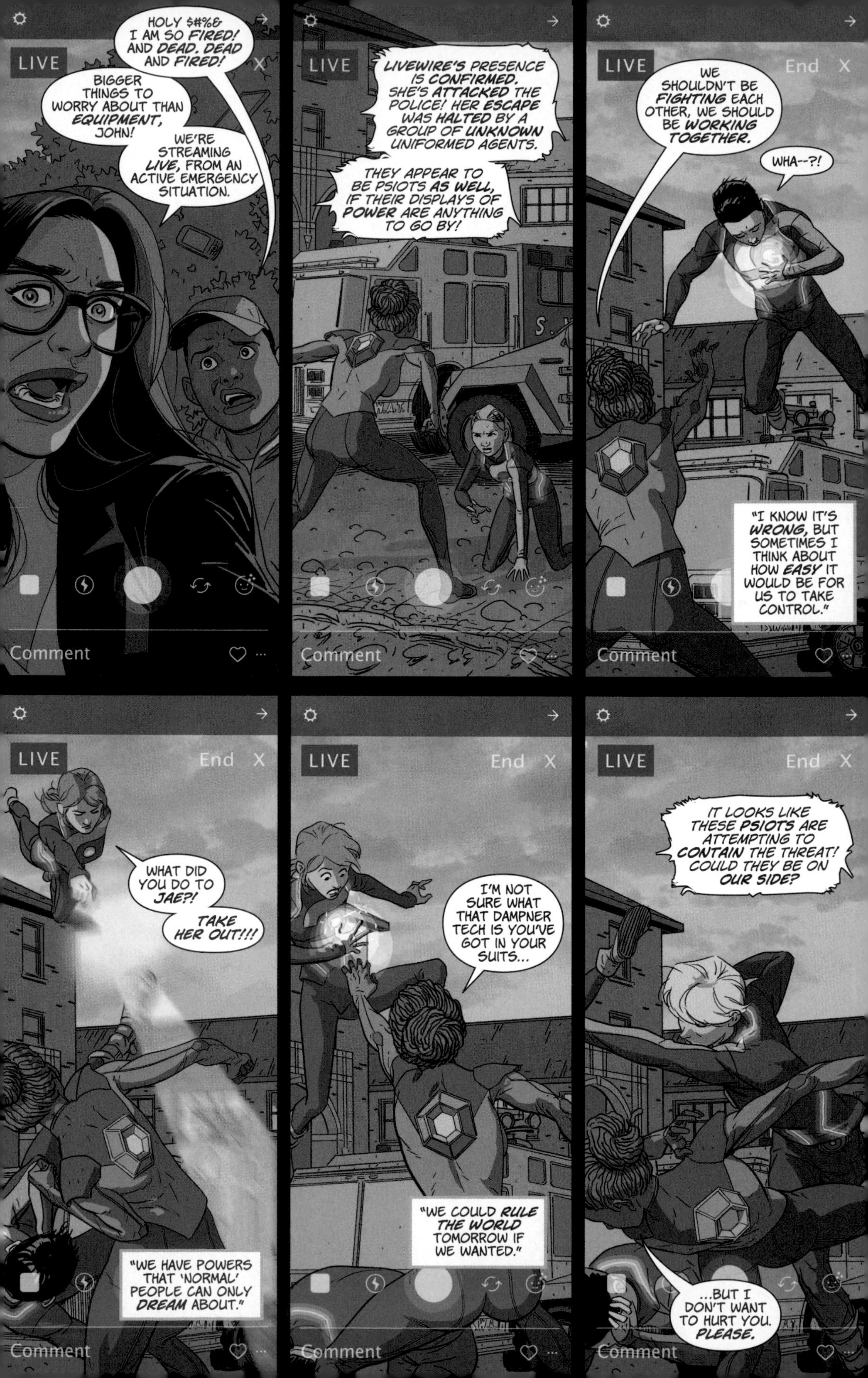
LIVE
HOLY $#%& I AM SO FIRED! AND DEAD. DEAD AND FIRED!
BIGGER THINGS TO WORRY ABOUT THAN EQUIPMENT, JOHN!
WE'RE STREAMING LIVE, FROM AN ACTIVE EMERGENCY SITUATION.
Comment
LIVE
LIVEWIRE'S PRESENCE IS CONFIRMED. SHE'S ATTACKED THE POLICE! HER ESCAPE WAS HALTED BY A GROUP OF UNKNOWN UNIFORMED AGENTS.
THEY APPEAR TO BE PSIOTS AS WELL, IF THEIR DISPLAYS OF POWER ARE ANYTHING TO GO BY!
Comment
LIVE
End
WE SHOULDN'T BE FIGHTING EACH OTHER, WE SHOULD BE WORKING TOGETHER.
WHA--?!
"I KNOW IT'S WRONG, BUT SOMETIMES I THINK ABOUT HOW EASY IT WOULD BE FOR US TO TAKE CONTROL."
Comment
LIVE
End
WHAT DID YOU DO TO JAE?!
TAKE HER OUT!!!
"WE HAVE POWERS THAT 'NORMAL' PEOPLE CAN ONLY DREAM ABOUT."
Comment
LIVE
End
I'M NOT SURE WHAT THAT DAMPNER TECH IS YOU'VE GOT IN YOUR SUITS...
"WE COULD RULE THE WORLD TOMORROW IF WE WANTED."
Comment
LIVE
End
IT LOOKS LIKE THESE PSIOTS ARE ATTEMPTING TO CONTAIN THE THREAT! COULD THEY BE ON OUR SIDE?
...BUT I DON'T WANT TO HURT YOU. PLEASE.
Comment

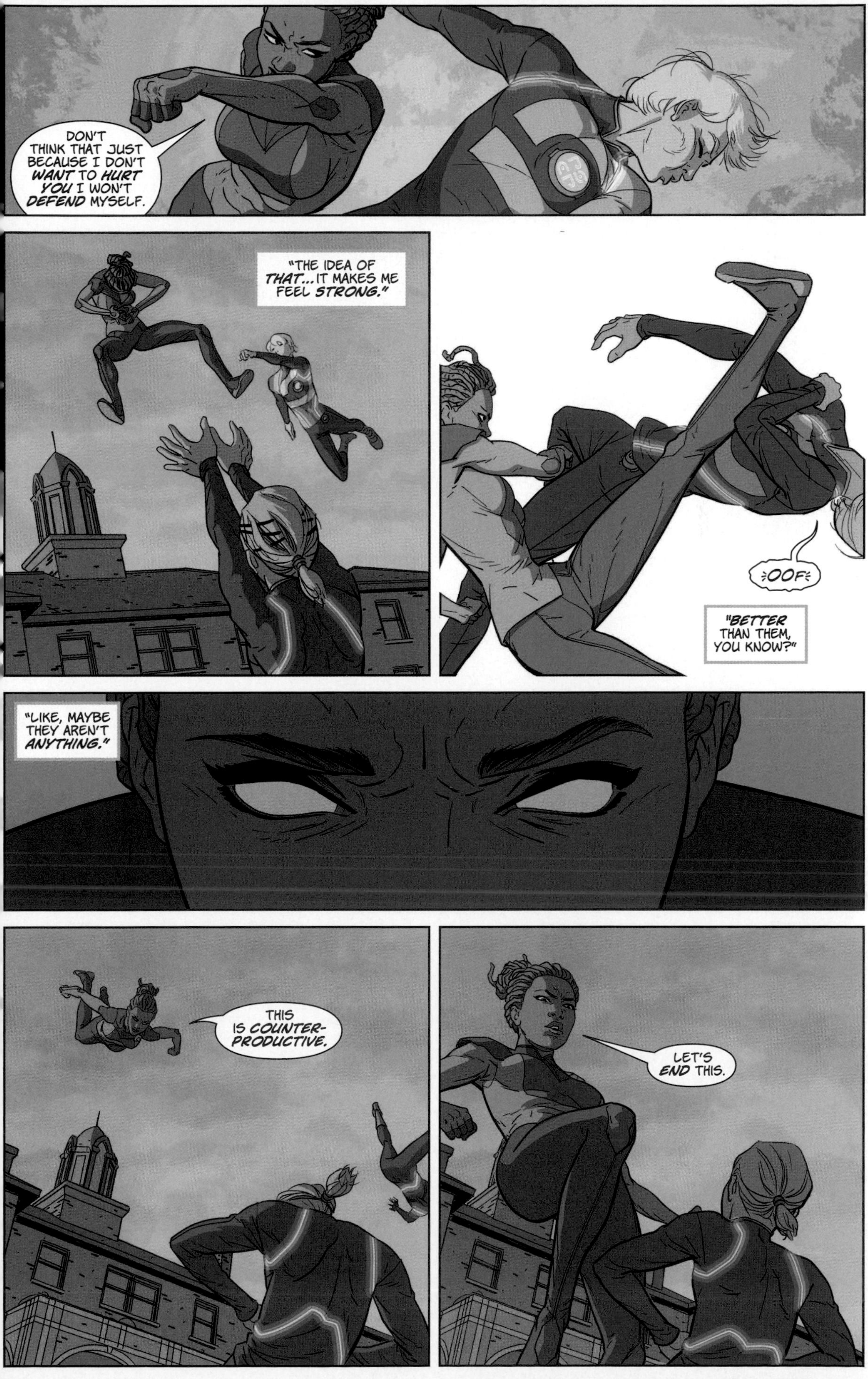
DON'T THINK THAT JUST BECAUSE I DON'T WANT TO HURT YOU I WON'T DEFEND MYSELF.
"THE IDEA OF THAT... IT MAKES ME FEEL STRONG."
OOF
"BETTER THAN THEM, YOU KNOW?"
"LIKE, MAYBE THEY AREN'T ANYTHING."
THIS IS COUNTER-PRODUCTIVE.
LET'S END THIS.

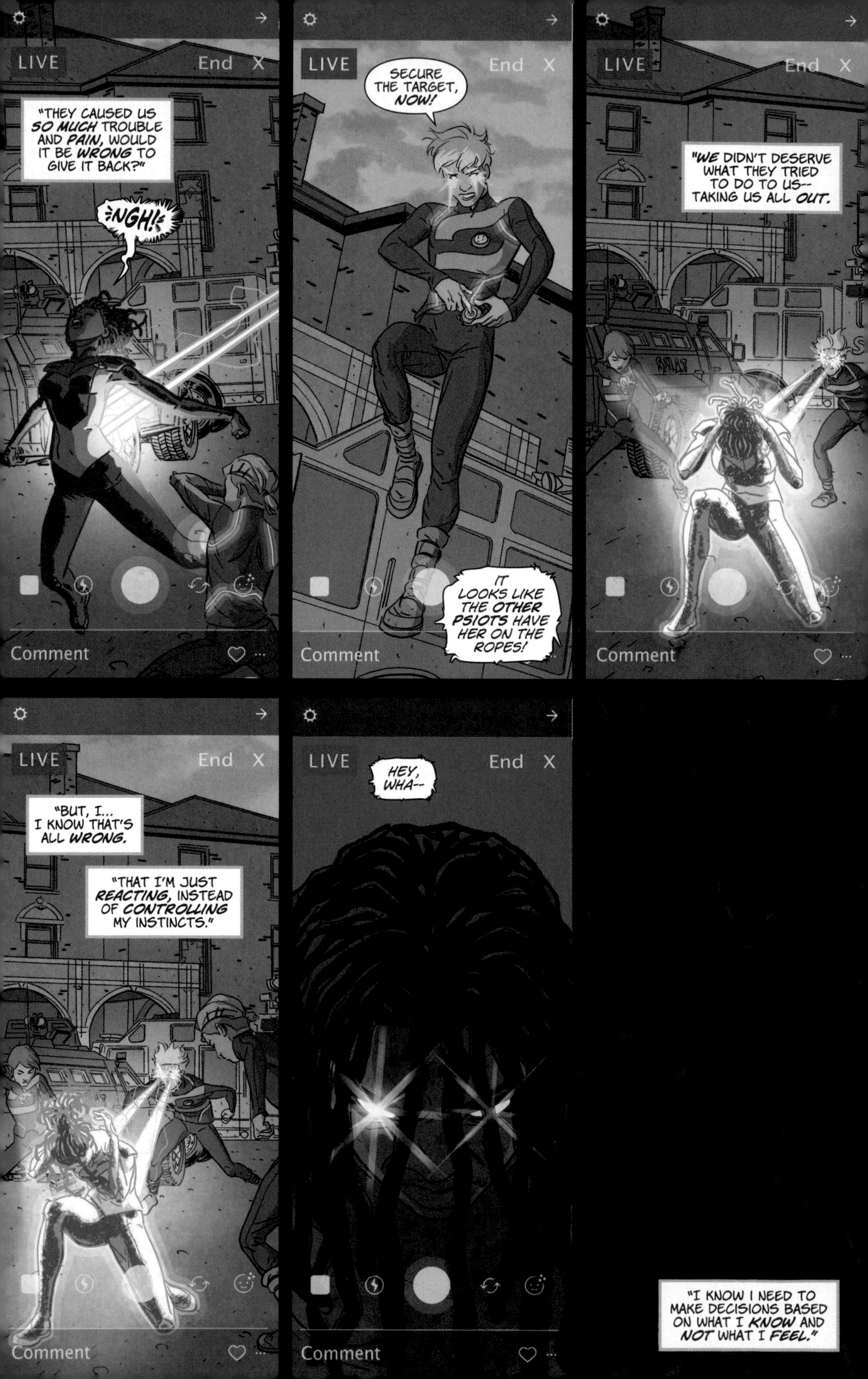
LIVE
End X
"THEY CAUSED US SO MUCH TROUBLE AND PAIN, WOULD IT BE WRONG TO GIVE IT BACK?"
NGH!
Comment
LIVE
End X
SECURE THE TARGET, NOW!
IT LOOKS LIKE THE OTHER PSIOTS HAVE HER ON THE ROPES!
Comment
LIVE
End X
"WE DIDN'T DESERVE WHAT THEY TRIED TO DO TO US-- TAKING US ALL OUT.
Comment
LIVE
End X
"BUT, I... I KNOW THAT'S ALL WRONG.
"THAT I'M JUST REACTING, INSTEAD OF CONTROLLING MY INSTINCTS."
Comment
LIVE
End X
HEY, WHA--
Comment
"I KNOW I NEED TO MAKE DECISIONS BASED ON WHAT I KNOW AND NOT WHAT I FEEL."

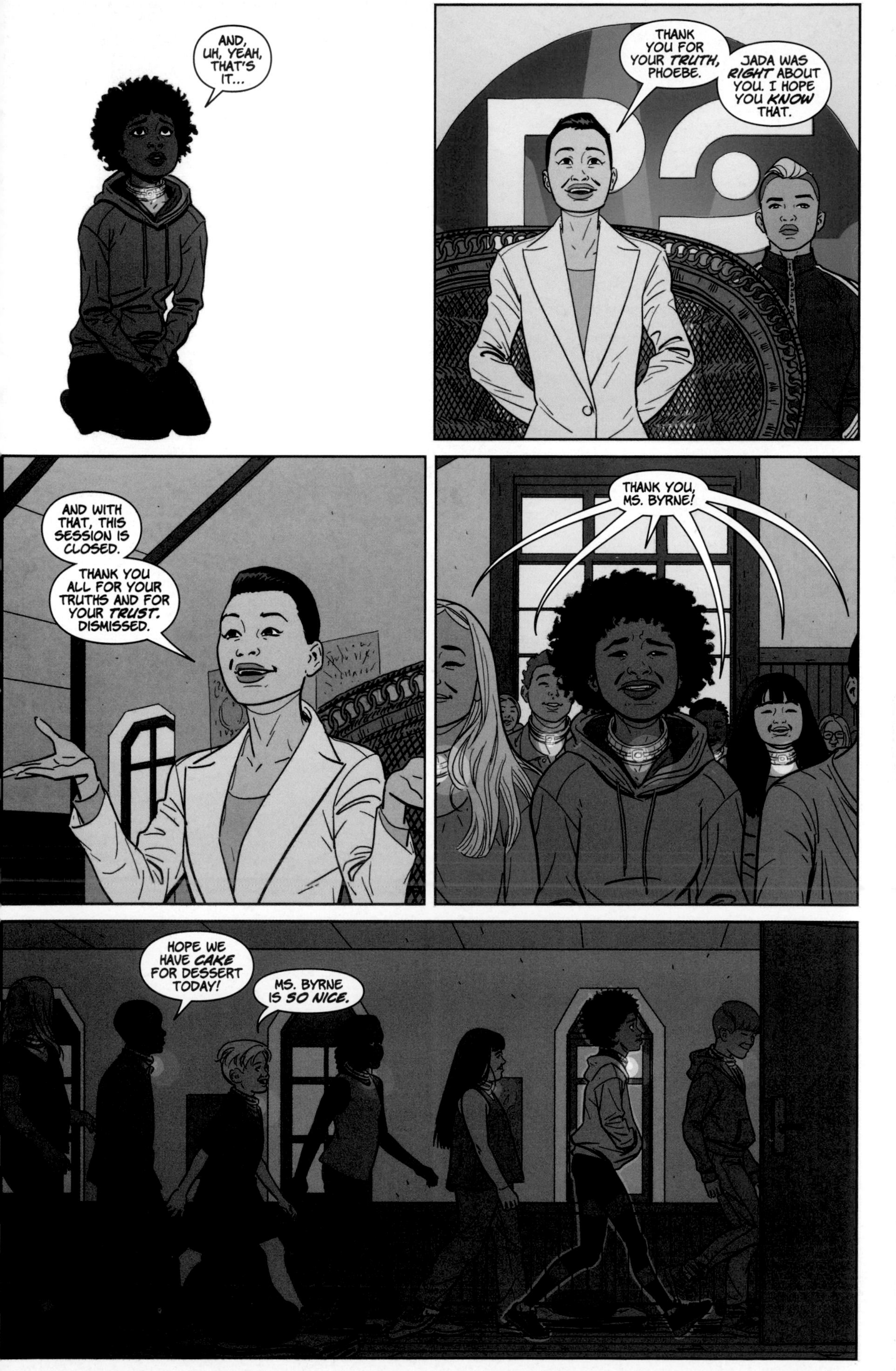
AND, UH, YEAH, THAT'S IT...
THANK YOU FOR YOUR TRUTH, PHOEBE.
JADA WAS RIGHT ABOUT YOU. I HOPE YOU KNOW THAT.
AND WITH THAT, THIS SESSION IS CLOSED.
THANK YOU ALL FOR YOUR TRUTHS AND FOR YOUR TRUST. DISMISSED.
THANK YOU, MS. BYRNE!
HOPE WE HAVE CAKE FOR DESSERT TODAY!
MS. BYRNE IS SO NICE.

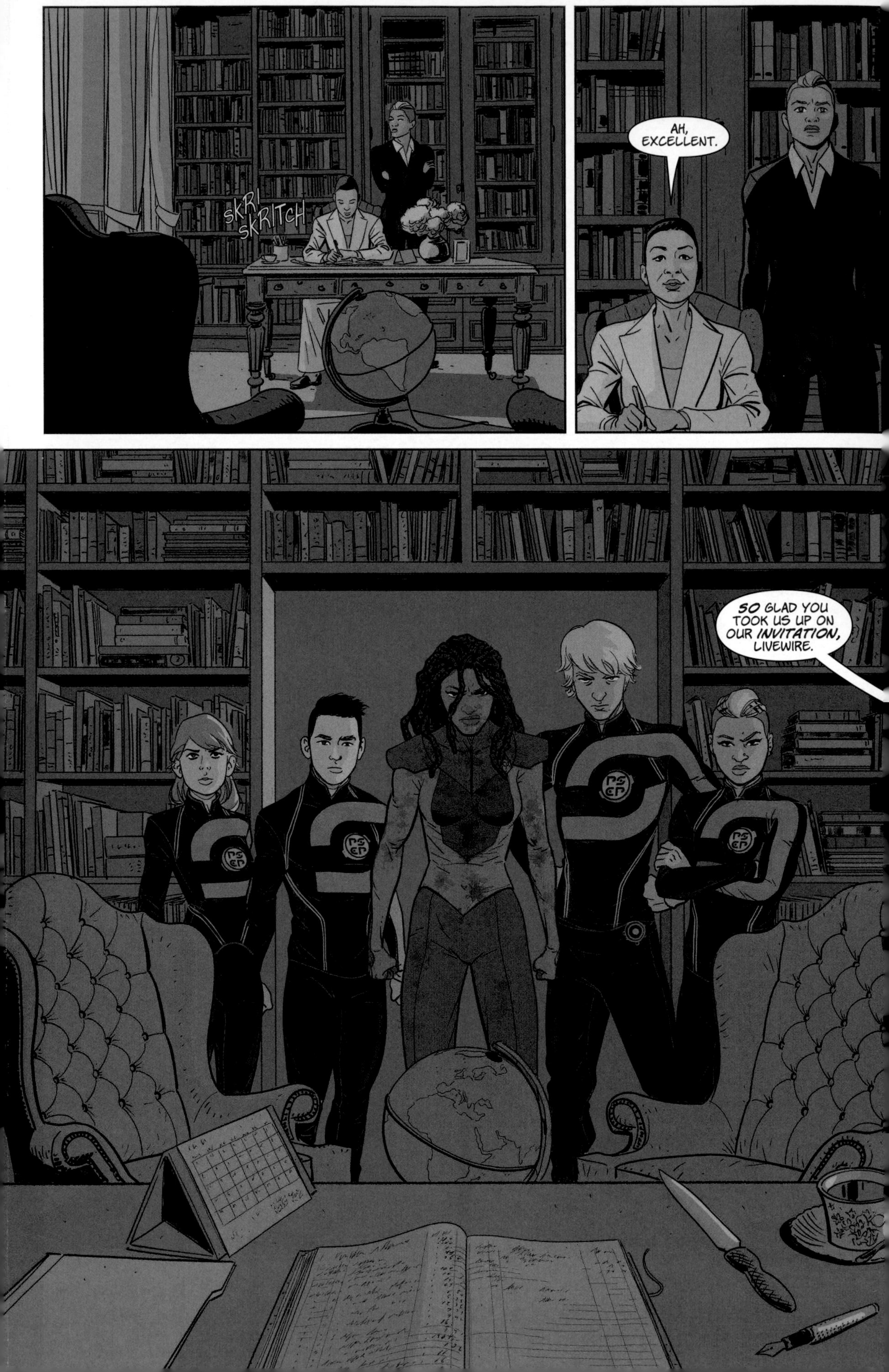
SKRI SKRITCH
AH, EXCELLENT.
SO GLAD YOU TOOK US UP ON OUR INVITATION, LIVEWIRE.

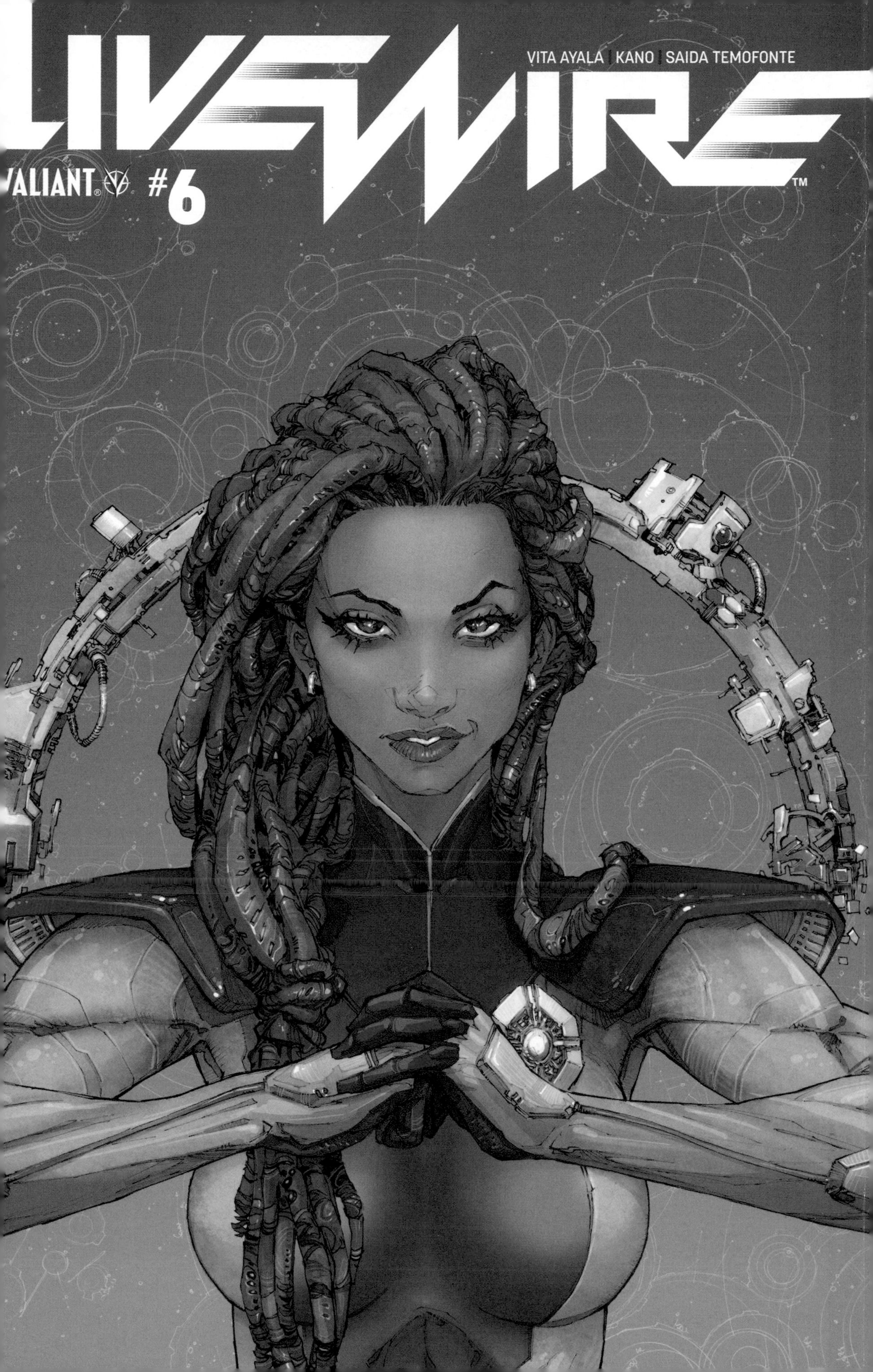
VITA AYALA | KANO | SAIDA TEMOFONTE
LIVEWIRE
VALIANT
#6

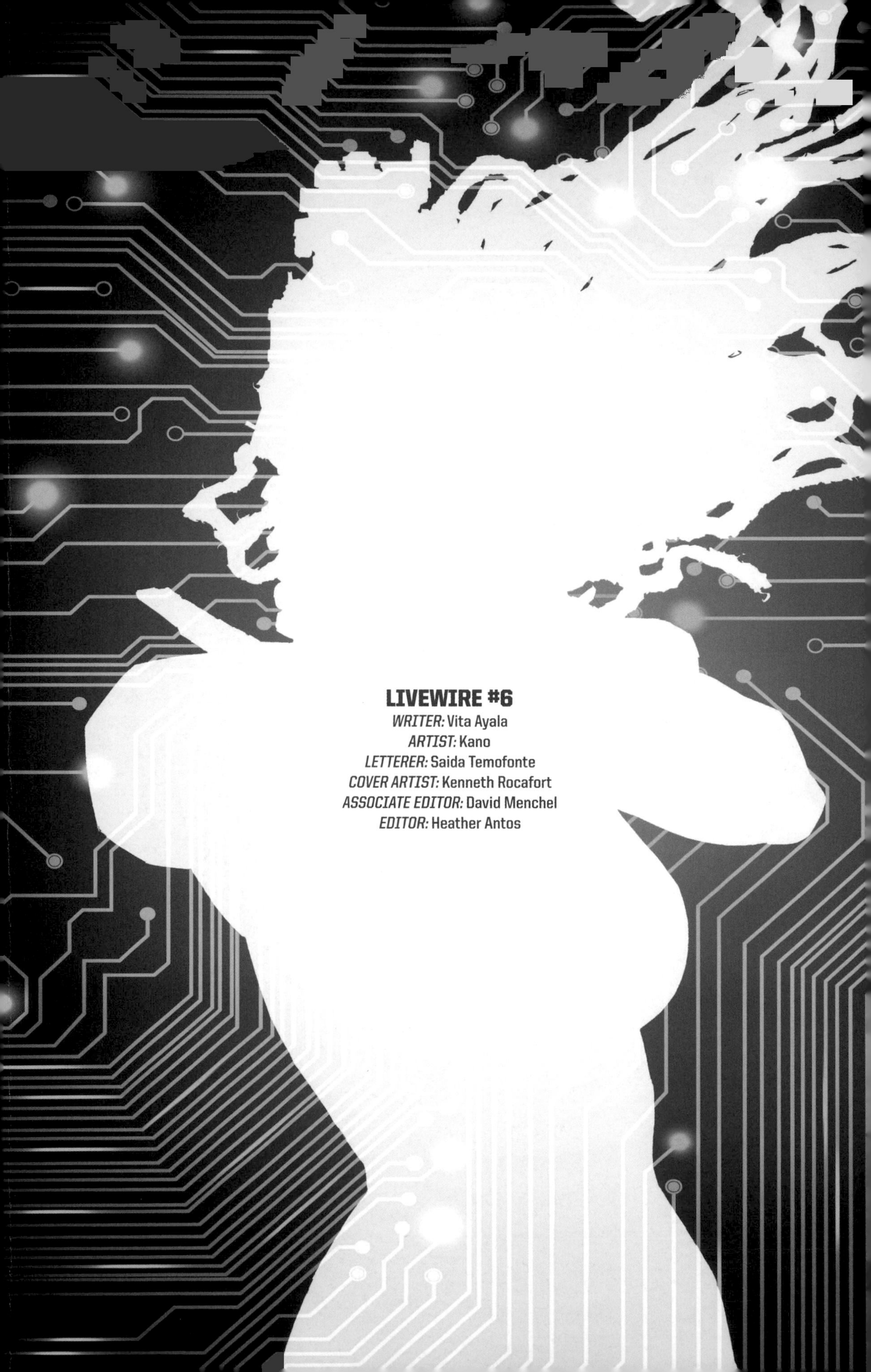
LIVEWIRE #6
WRITER: Vita Ayala
ARTIST: Kano
LETTERER: Saida Temofonte
COVER ARTIST: Kenneth Rocafort
ASSOCIATE EDITOR: David Menchel
EDITOR: Heather Antos

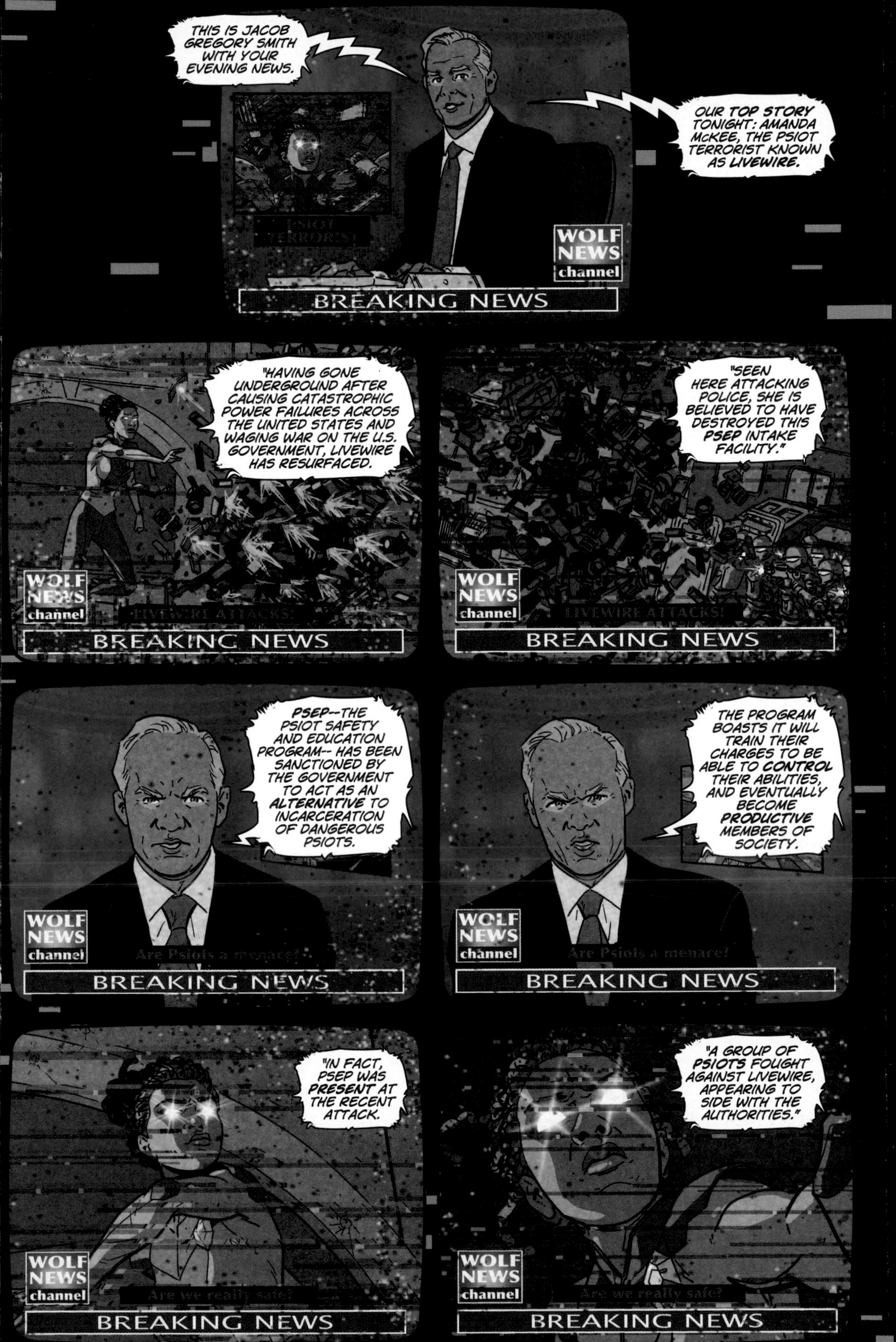
THIS IS JACOB GREGORY SMITH WITH YOUR EVENING NEWS.
OUR TOP STORY TONIGHT: AMANDA McKEE, THE PSIOT TERRORIST KNOWN AS LIVEWIRE.
PSIOT TERRORIST
WOLF NEWS channel
BREAKING NEWS
"HAVING GONE UNDERGROUND AFTER CAUSING CATASTROPHIC POWER FAILURES ACROSS THE UNITED STATES AND WAGING WAR ON THE U.S. GOVERNMENT, LIVEWIRE HAS RESURFACED.
WOLF NEWS channel
LIVEWIRE ATTACKS!
BREAKING NEWS
"SEEN HERE ATTACKING POLICE, SHE IS BELIEVED TO HAVE DESTROYED THIS PSEP INTAKE FACILITY."
WOLF NEWS channel
LIVEWIRE ATTACKS!
BREAKING NEWS
PSEP--THE PSIOT SAFETY AND EDUCATION PROGRAM-- HAS BEEN SANCTIONED BY THE GOVERNMENT TO ACT AS AN ALTERNATIVE TO INCARCERATION OF DANGEROUS PSIOTS.
WOLF NEWS channel
Are Psiots a menace?
BREAKING NEWS
THE PROGRAM BOASTS IT WILL TRAIN THEIR CHARGES TO BE ABLE TO CONTROL THEIR ABILITIES, AND EVENTUALLY BECOME PRODUCTIVE MEMBERS OF SOCIETY.
WOLF NEWS channel
Are Psiots a menace?
BREAKING NEWS
"IN FACT, PSEP WAS PRESENT AT THE RECENT ATTACK.
WOLF NEWS channel
Are we really safe?
BREAKING NEWS
"A GROUP OF PSIOTS FOUGHT AGAINST LIVEWIRE, APPEARING TO SIDE WITH THE AUTHORITIES."
WOLF NEWS channel
Are we really safe?
BREAKING NEWS

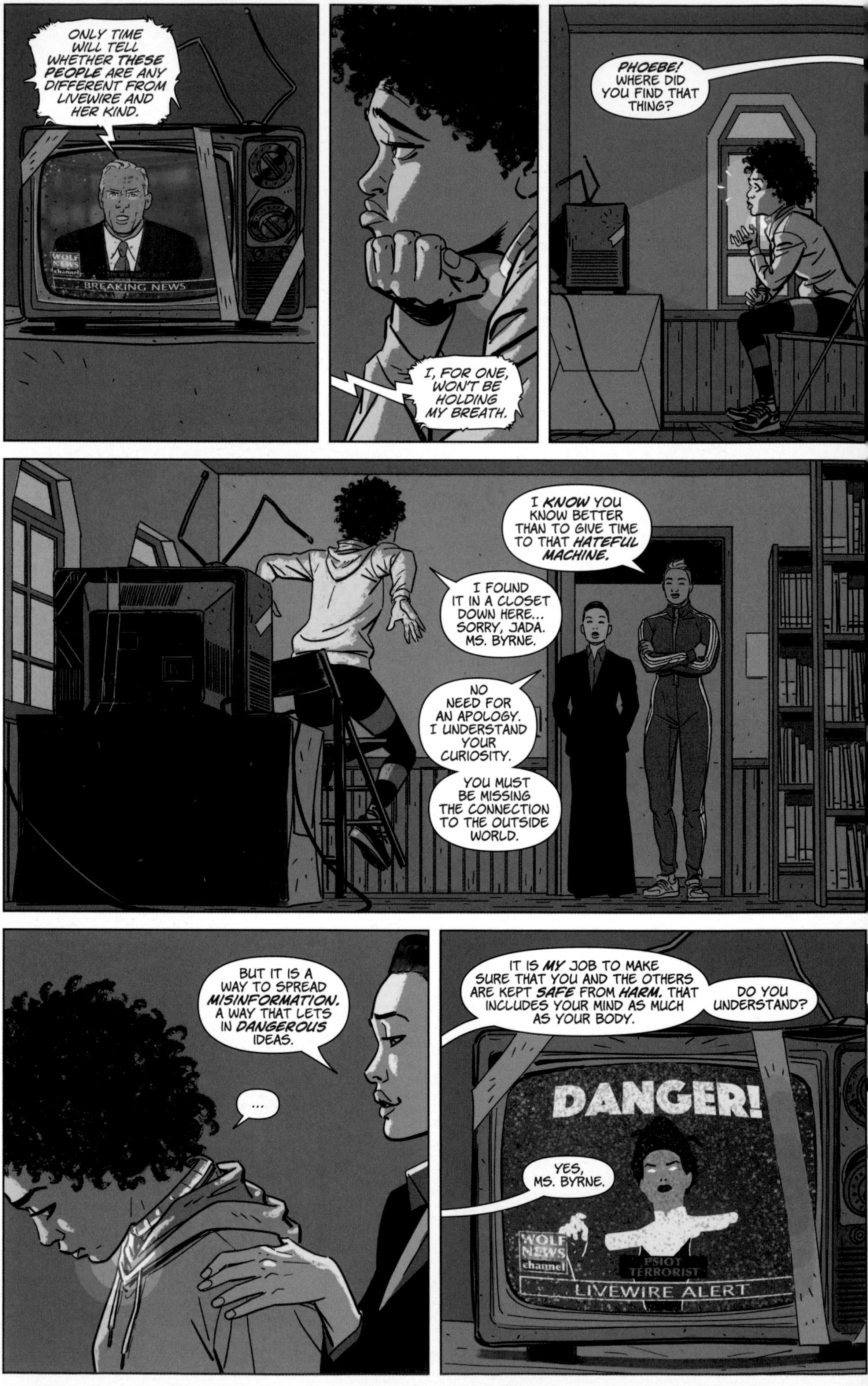
ONLY TIME WILL TELL WHETHER THESE PEOPLE ARE ANY DIFFERENT FROM LIVEWIRE AND HER KIND.
WOLF NEWS channel
BREAKING NEWS
I, FOR ONE, WON'T BE HOLDING MY BREATH.
PHOEBE! WHERE DID YOU FIND THAT THING?
I KNOW YOU KNOW BETTER THAN TO GIVE TIME TO THAT HATEFUL MACHINE.
I FOUND IT IN A CLOSET DOWN HERE... SORRY, JADA. MS. BYRNE.
NO NEED FOR AN APOLOGY. I UNDERSTAND YOUR CURIOSITY.
YOU MUST BE MISSING THE CONNECTION TO THE OUTSIDE WORLD.
BUT IT IS A WAY TO SPREAD MISINFORMATION. A WAY THAT LETS IN DANGEROUS IDEAS.
...
IT IS MY JOB TO MAKE SURE THAT YOU AND THE OTHERS ARE KEPT SAFE FROM HARM. THAT INCLUDES YOUR MIND AS MUCH AS YOUR BODY.
DO YOU UNDERSTAND?
DANGER!
YES, MS. BYRNE.
WOLF NEWS channel
PSIOT TERRORIST
LIVEWIRE ALERT

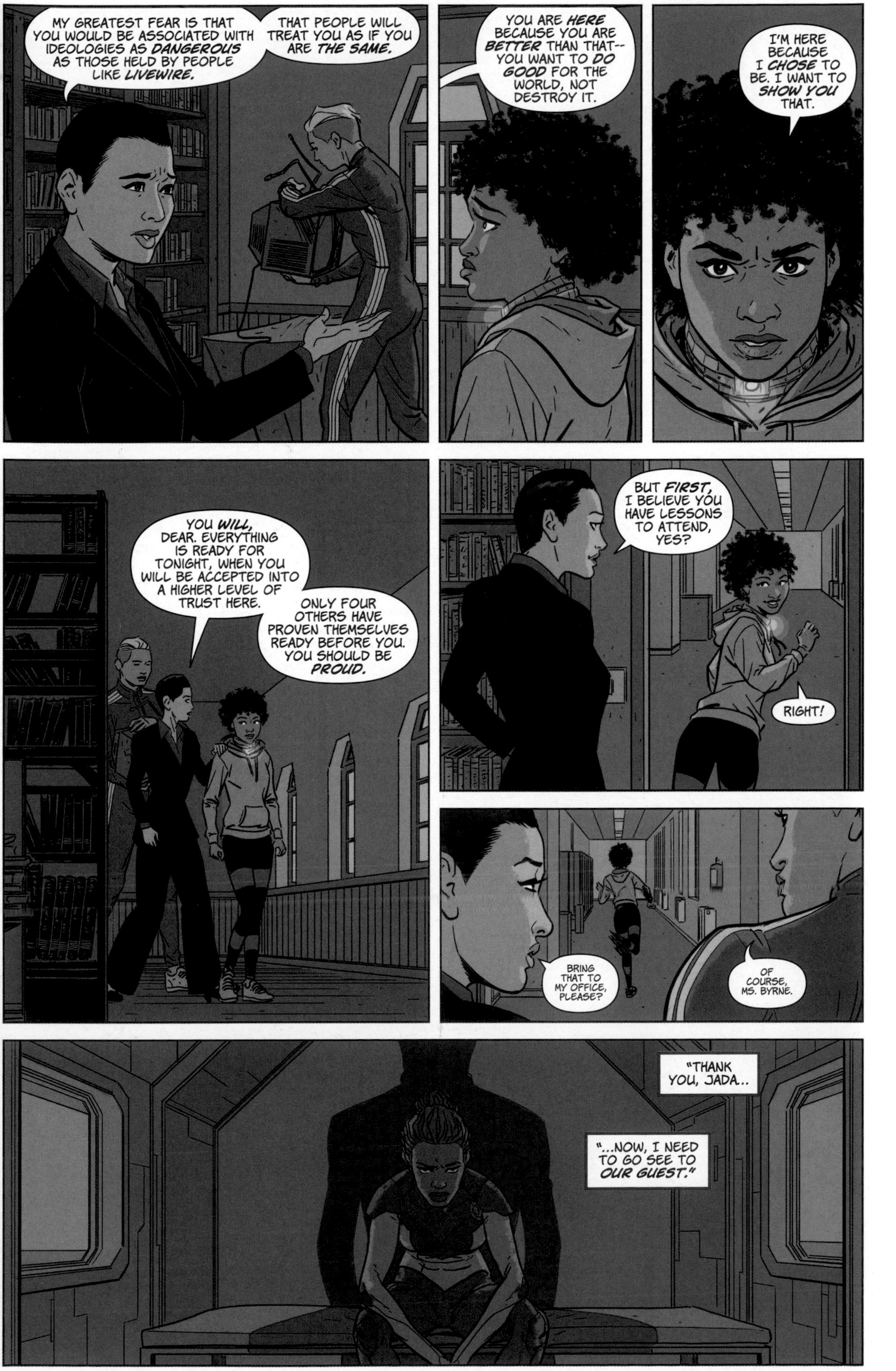

MY GREATEST FEAR IS THAT YOU WOULD BE ASSOCIATED WITH IDEOLOGIES AS DANGEROUS AS THOSE HELD BY PEOPLE LIKE LIVEWIRE.
THAT PEOPLE WILL TREAT YOU AS IF YOU ARE THE SAME.
YOU ARE HERE BECAUSE YOU ARE BETTER THAN THAT-- YOU WANT TO DO GOOD FOR THE WORLD, NOT DESTROY IT.
I'M HERE BECAUSE I CHOSE TO BE. I WANT TO SHOW YOU THAT.
YOU WILL, DEAR. EVERYTHING IS READY FOR TONIGHT, WHEN YOU WILL BE ACCEPTED INTO A HIGHER LEVEL OF TRUST HERE.
ONLY FOUR OTHERS HAVE PROVEN THEMSELVES READY BEFORE YOU. YOU SHOULD BE PROUD.
BUT FIRST, I BELIEVE YOU HAVE LESSONS TO ATTEND, YES?
RIGHT!
BRING THAT TO MY OFFICE, PLEASE?
OF COURSE, MS. BYRNE.
"THANK YOU, JADA...
"...NOW, I NEED TO GO SEE TO OUR GUEST."

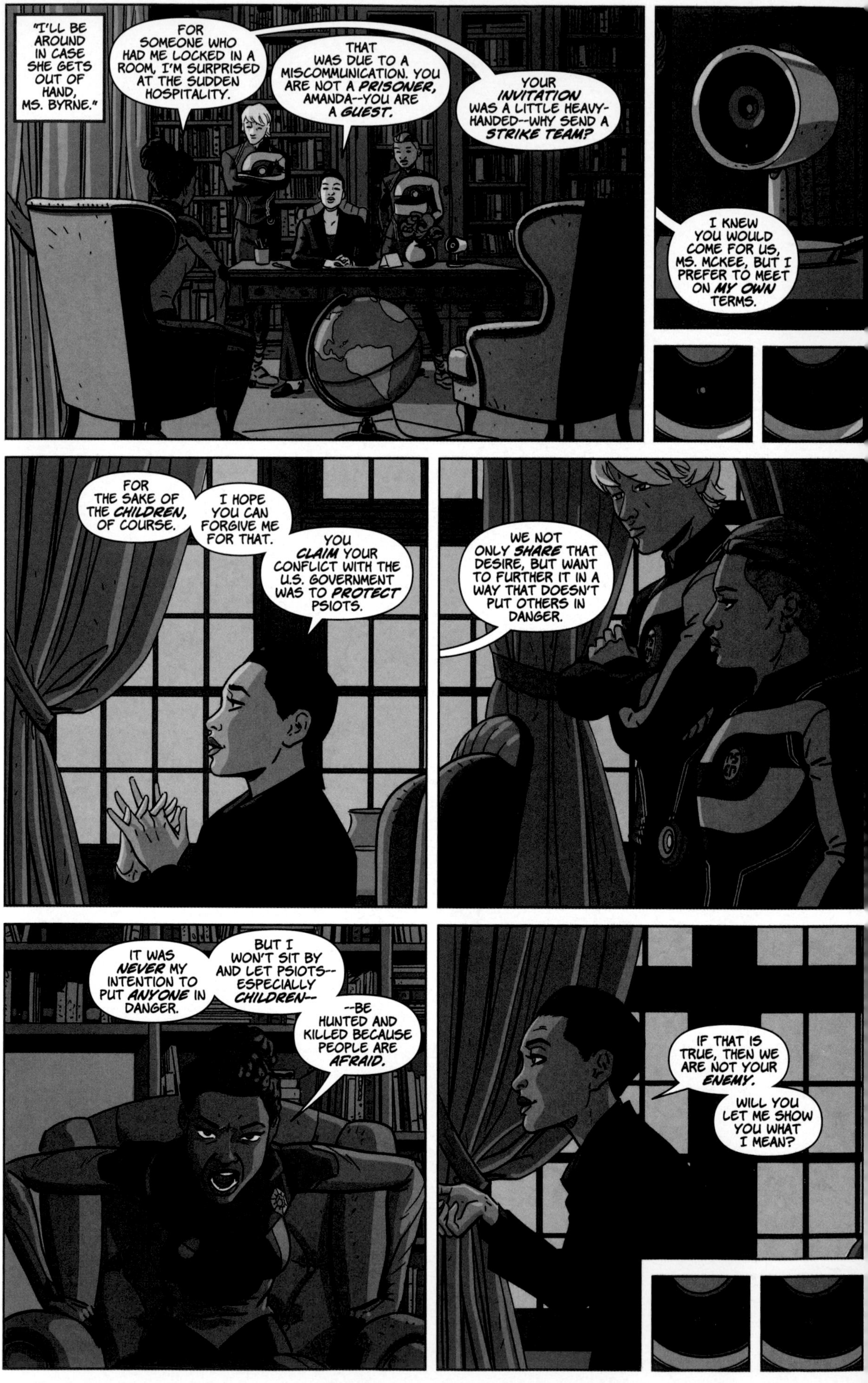
"I'LL BE AROUND IN CASE SHE GETS OUT OF HAND, MS. BYRNE."
FOR SOMEONE WHO HAD ME LOCKED IN A ROOM, I'M SURPRISED AT THE SUDDEN HOSPITALITY.
THAT WAS DUE TO A MISCOMMUNICATION. YOU ARE NOT A PRISONER, AMANDA--YOU ARE A GUEST.
YOUR INVITATION WAS A LITTLE HEAVY-HANDED--WHY SEND A STRIKE TEAM?
I KNEW YOU WOULD COME FOR US, MS. MCKEE, BUT I PREFER TO MEET ON MY OWN TERMS.
FOR THE SAKE OF THE CHILDREN, OF COURSE.
I HOPE YOU CAN FORGIVE ME FOR THAT.
YOU CLAIM YOUR CONFLICT WITH THE U.S. GOVERNMENT WAS TO PROTECT PSIOTS.
WE NOT ONLY SHARE THAT DESIRE, BUT WANT TO FURTHER IT IN A WAY THAT DOESN'T PUT OTHERS IN DANGER.
IT WAS NEVER MY INTENTION TO PUT ANYONE IN DANGER.
BUT I WON'T SIT BY AND LET PSIOTS--ESPECIALLY CHILDREN--
--BE HUNTED AND KILLED BECAUSE PEOPLE ARE AFRAID.
IF THAT IS TRUE, THEN WE ARE NOT YOUR ENEMY.
WILL YOU LET ME SHOW YOU WHAT I MEAN?

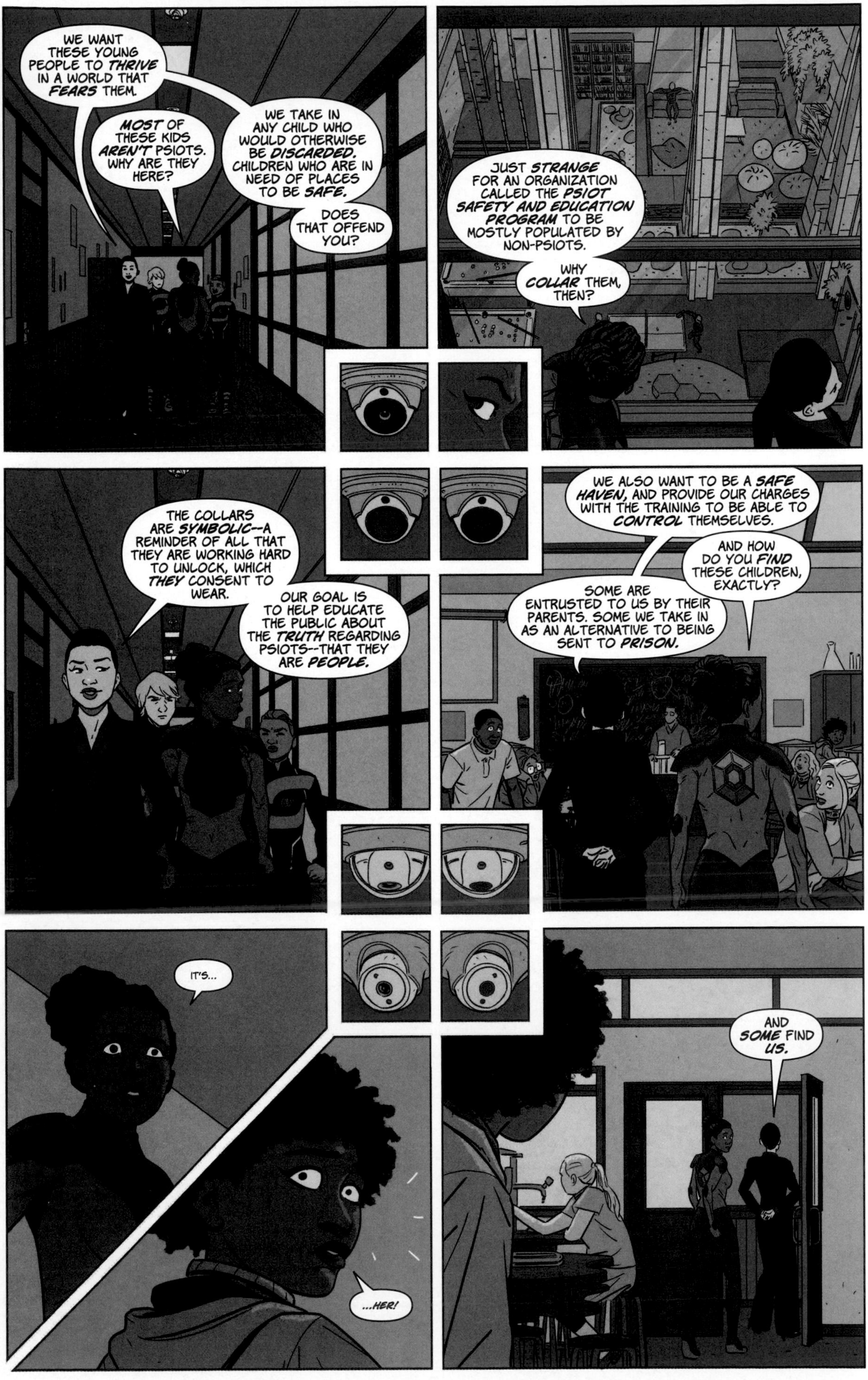
WE WANT THESE YOUNG PEOPLE TO THRIVE IN A WORLD THAT FEARS THEM.
MOST OF THESE KIDS AREN'T PSIOTS. WHY ARE THEY HERE?
WE TAKE IN ANY CHILD WHO WOULD OTHERWISE BE DISCARDED. CHILDREN WHO ARE IN NEED OF PLACES TO BE SAFE.
DOES THAT OFFEND YOU?
JUST STRANGE FOR AN ORGANIZATION CALLED THE PSIOT SAFETY AND EDUCATION PROGRAM TO BE MOSTLY POPULATED BY NON-PSIOTS.
WHY COLLAR THEM, THEN?
THE COLLARS ARE SYMBOLIC--A REMINDER OF ALL THAT THEY ARE WORKING HARD TO UNLOCK, WHICH THEY CONSENT TO WEAR.
OUR GOAL IS TO HELP EDUCATE THE PUBLIC ABOUT THE TRUTH REGARDING PSIOTS--THAT THEY ARE PEOPLE.
WE ALSO WANT TO BE A SAFE HAVEN, AND PROVIDE OUR CHARGES WITH THE TRAINING TO BE ABLE TO CONTROL THEMSELVES.
AND HOW DO YOU FIND THESE CHILDREN, EXACTLY?
SOME ARE ENTRUSTED TO US BY THEIR PARENTS. SOME WE TAKE IN AS AN ALTERNATIVE TO BEING SENT TO PRISON.
IT'S...
...HER!
AND SOME FIND US.

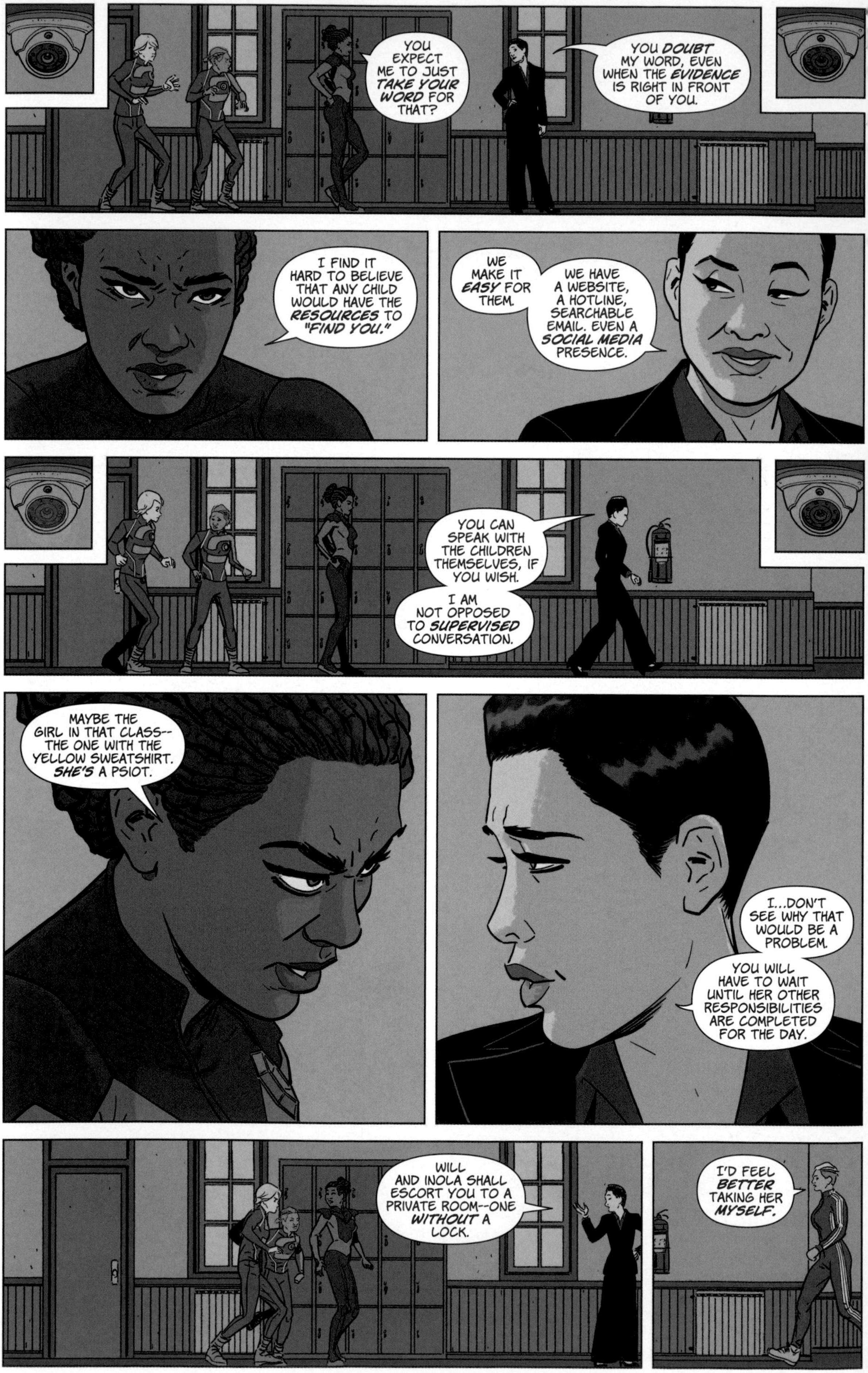
YOU EXPECT ME TO JUST TAKE YOUR WORD FOR THAT?
YOU DOUBT MY WORD, EVEN WHEN THE EVIDENCE IS RIGHT IN FRONT OF YOU.
I FIND IT HARD TO BELIEVE THAT ANY CHILD WOULD HAVE THE RESOURCES TO "FIND YOU."
WE MAKE IT EASY FOR THEM.
WE HAVE A WEBSITE, A HOTLINE, SEARCHABLE EMAIL. EVEN A SOCIAL MEDIA PRESENCE.
YOU CAN SPEAK WITH THE CHILDREN THEMSELVES, IF YOU WISH.
I AM NOT OPPOSED TO SUPERVISED CONVERSATION.
MAYBE THE GIRL IN THAT CLASS-- THE ONE WITH THE YELLOW SWEATSHIRT. SHE'S A PSIOT.
I...DON'T SEE WHY THAT WOULD BE A PROBLEM.
YOU WILL HAVE TO WAIT UNTIL HER OTHER RESPONSIBILITIES ARE COMPLETED FOR THE DAY.
WILL AND INOLA SHALL ESCORT YOU TO A PRIVATE ROOM--ONE WITHOUT A LOCK.
I'D FEEL BETTER TAKING HER MYSELF.

I'LL SEND SOMEONE WITH A MEAL FOR YOU WHEN IT IS TIME.

THE CHILDREN KNOW WHO YOU ARE. I WOULD APPRECIATE IT IF YOU DID *NOT* WANDER AROUND ALONE, AS IT COULD UPSET THEM.

I'LL MAKE SURE SHE KNOWS WHERE SHE'S SUPPOSED TO BE.

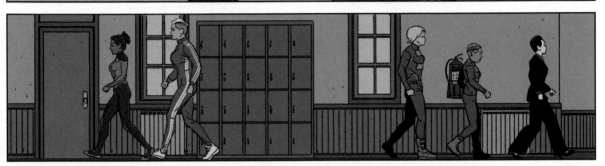

I'M GOING TO GO OUT ON A LIMB AND SAY THIS *ISN'T* MY ROOM.

I SAW HOW YOU PUT YOUR *HANDS* ON MY STUDENTS WHEN THEY CAME FOR YOU.

I HOPE YOU KNOW I WOULD NEVER REALLY HURT THEM, EVEN TO DEFEND MYSELF.

AND, YET, I ICED THEIR BRUISES *MYSELF.*

LET'S SEE HOW YOU DO AGAINST SOMEONE *YOUR* OWN SIZE.

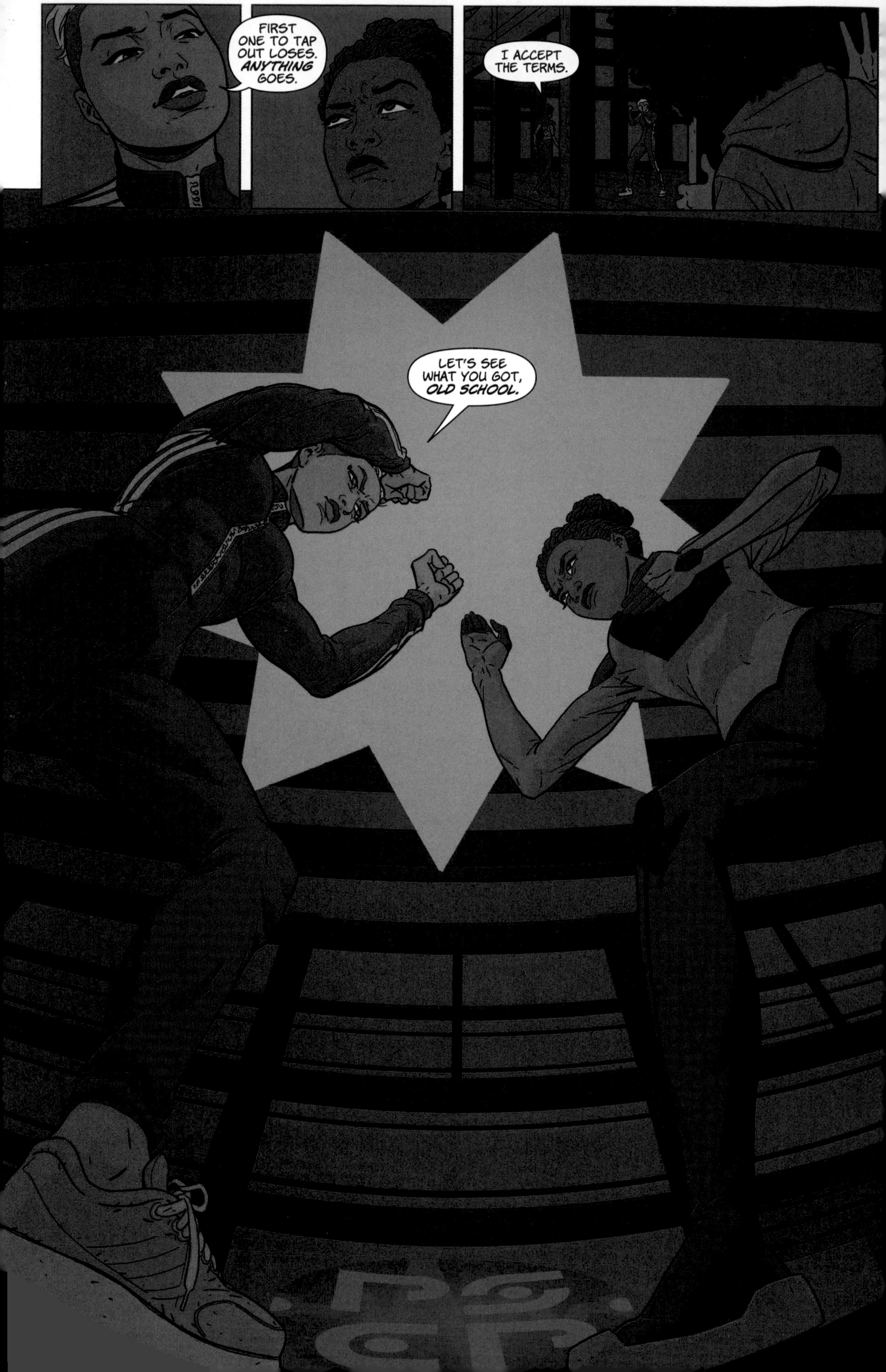
FIRST ONE TO TAP OUT LOSES. ANYTHING GOES.
I ACCEPT THE TERMS.
LET'S SEE WHAT YOU GOT, OLD SCHOOL.

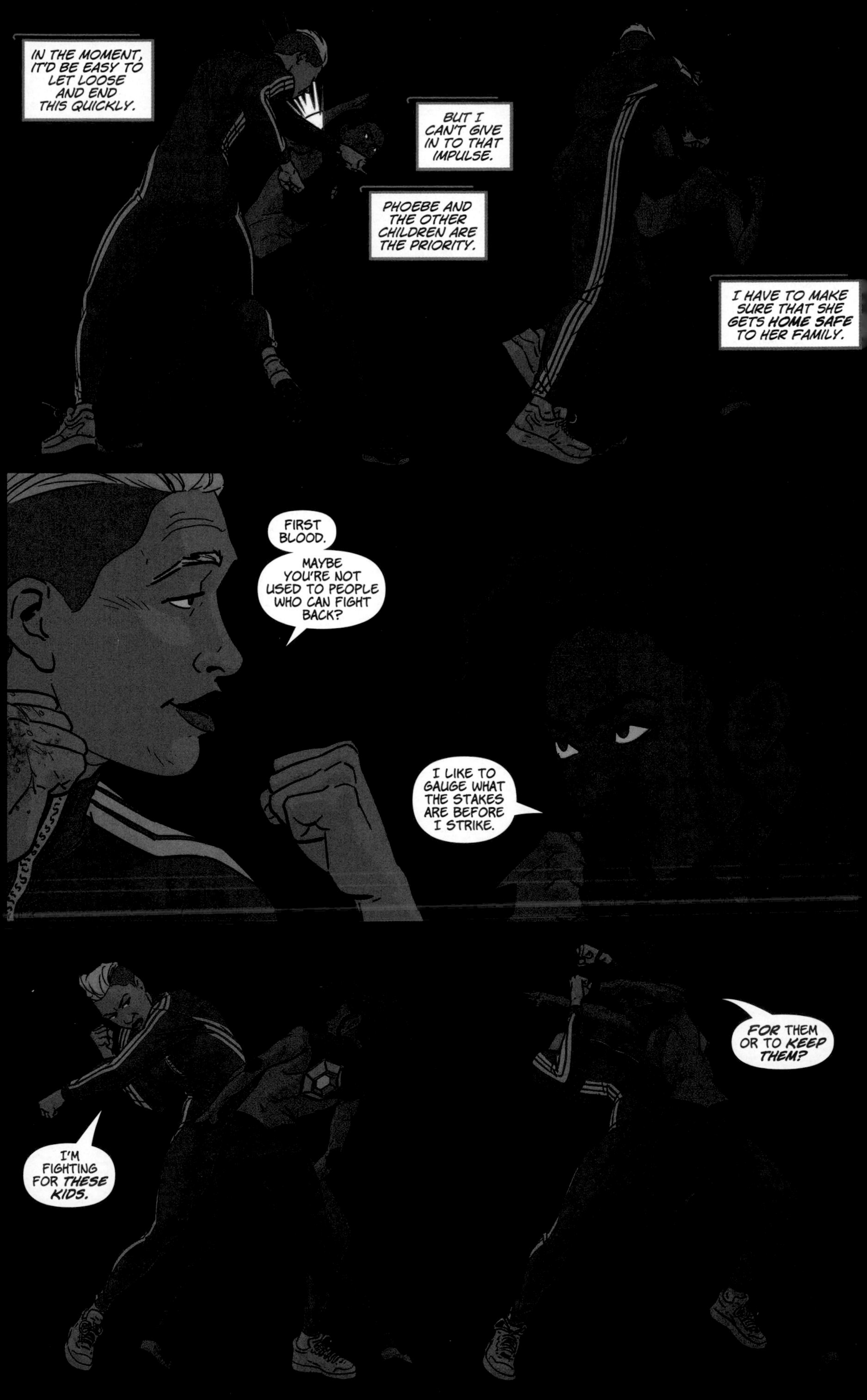
IN THE MOMENT, IT'D BE EASY TO LET LOOSE AND END THIS QUICKLY.
BUT I CAN'T GIVE IN TO THAT IMPULSE.
PHOEBE AND THE OTHER CHILDREN ARE THE PRIORITY.
I HAVE TO MAKE SURE THAT SHE GETS HOME SAFE TO HER FAMILY.
FIRST BLOOD.
MAYBE YOU'RE NOT USED TO PEOPLE WHO CAN FIGHT BACK?
I LIKE TO GAUGE WHAT THE STAKES ARE BEFORE I STRIKE.
I'M FIGHTING FOR THESE KIDS.
FOR THEM OR TO KEEP THEM?

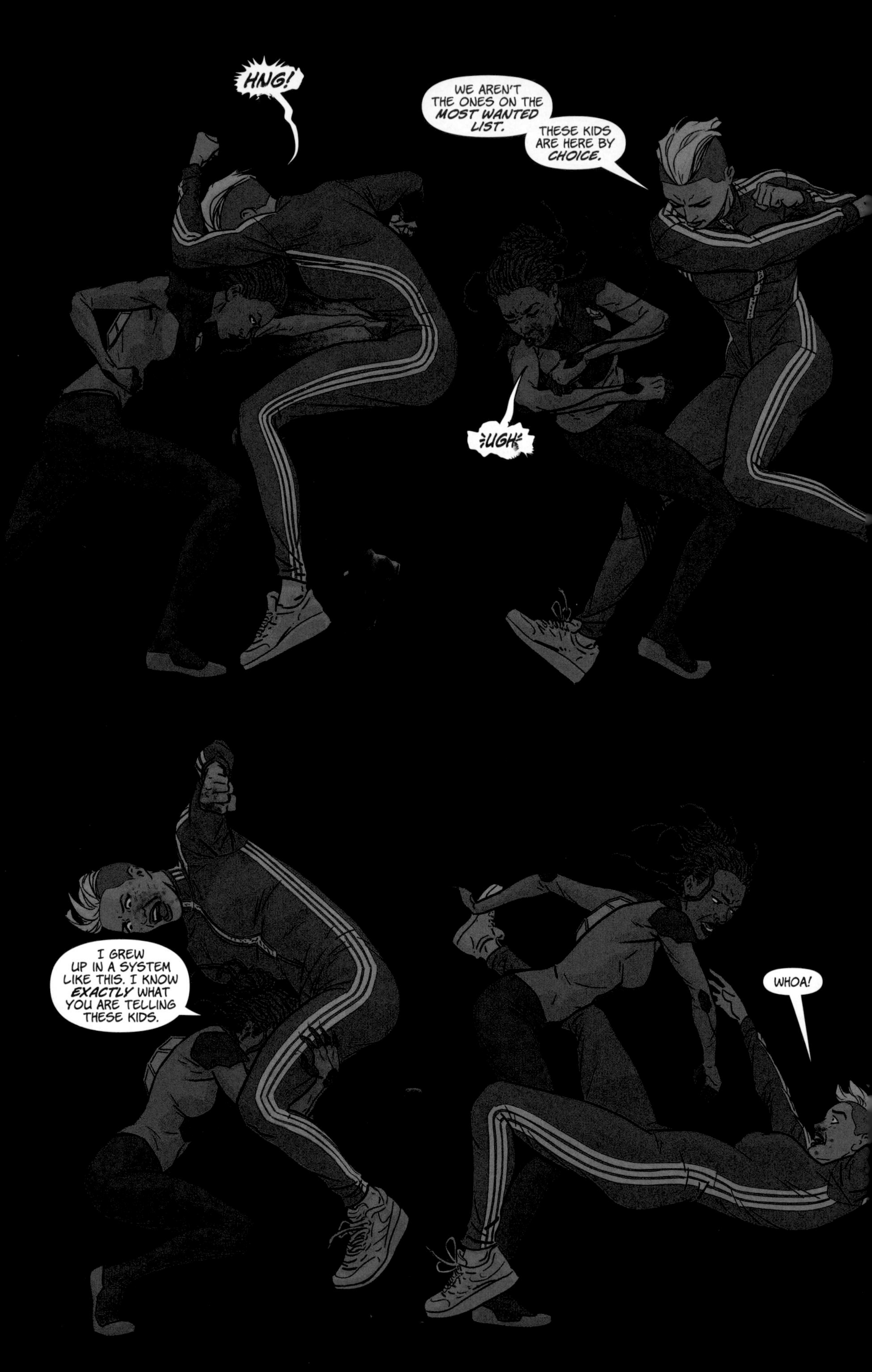
HNG!
WE AREN'T THE ONES ON THE MOST WANTED LIST.
THESE KIDS ARE HERE BY CHOICE.
UGH
I GREW UP IN A SYSTEM LIKE THIS. I KNOW EXACTLY WHAT YOU ARE TELLING THESE KIDS.
WHOA!

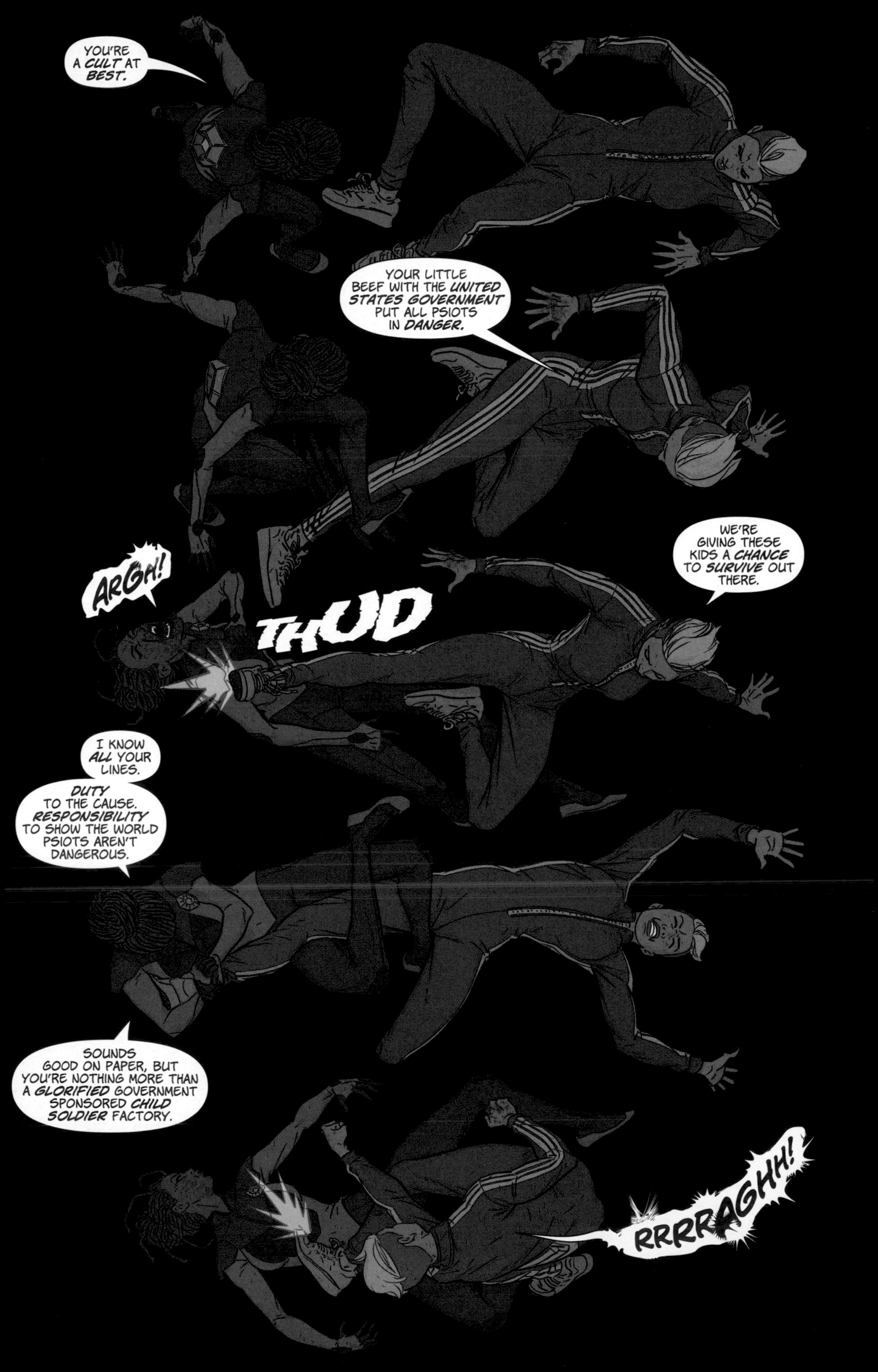

YOU'RE A CULT AT BEST.
YOUR LITTLE BEEF WITH THE UNITED STATES GOVERNMENT PUT ALL PSIOTS IN DANGER.
WE'RE GIVING THESE KIDS A CHANCE TO SURVIVE OUT THERE.
ARGH!
THUD
I KNOW ALL YOUR LINES.
DUTY TO THE CAUSE. RESPONSIBILITY TO SHOW THE WORLD PSIOTS AREN'T DANGEROUS.
SOUNDS GOOD ON PAPER, BUT YOU'RE NOTHING MORE THAN A GLORIFIED GOVERNMENT SPONSORED CHILD SOLDIER FACTORY.
RRRRAGHH!

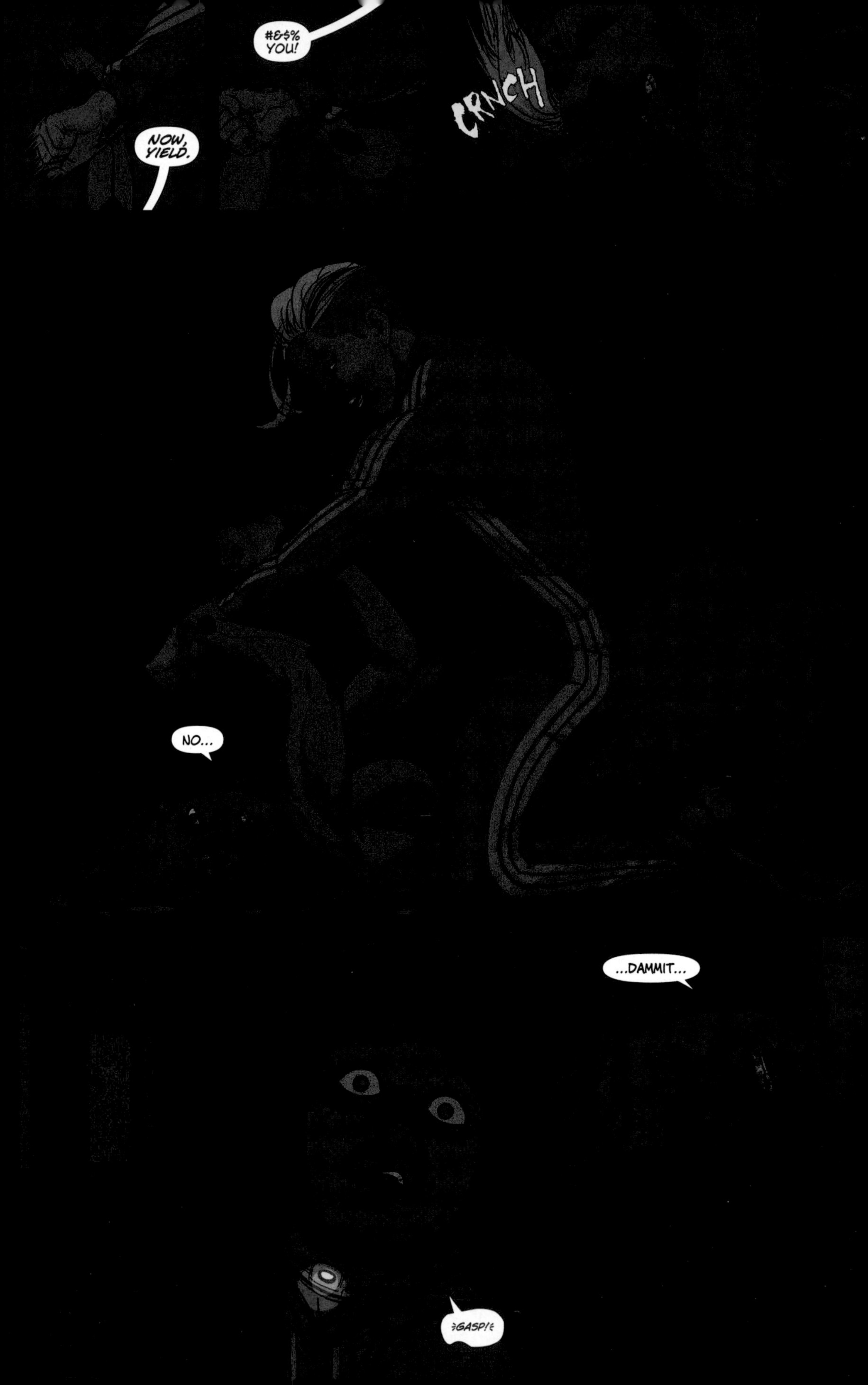
#&$% YOU!
NOW, YIELD.
CRNCH
NO...
...DAMMIT...
GASP!

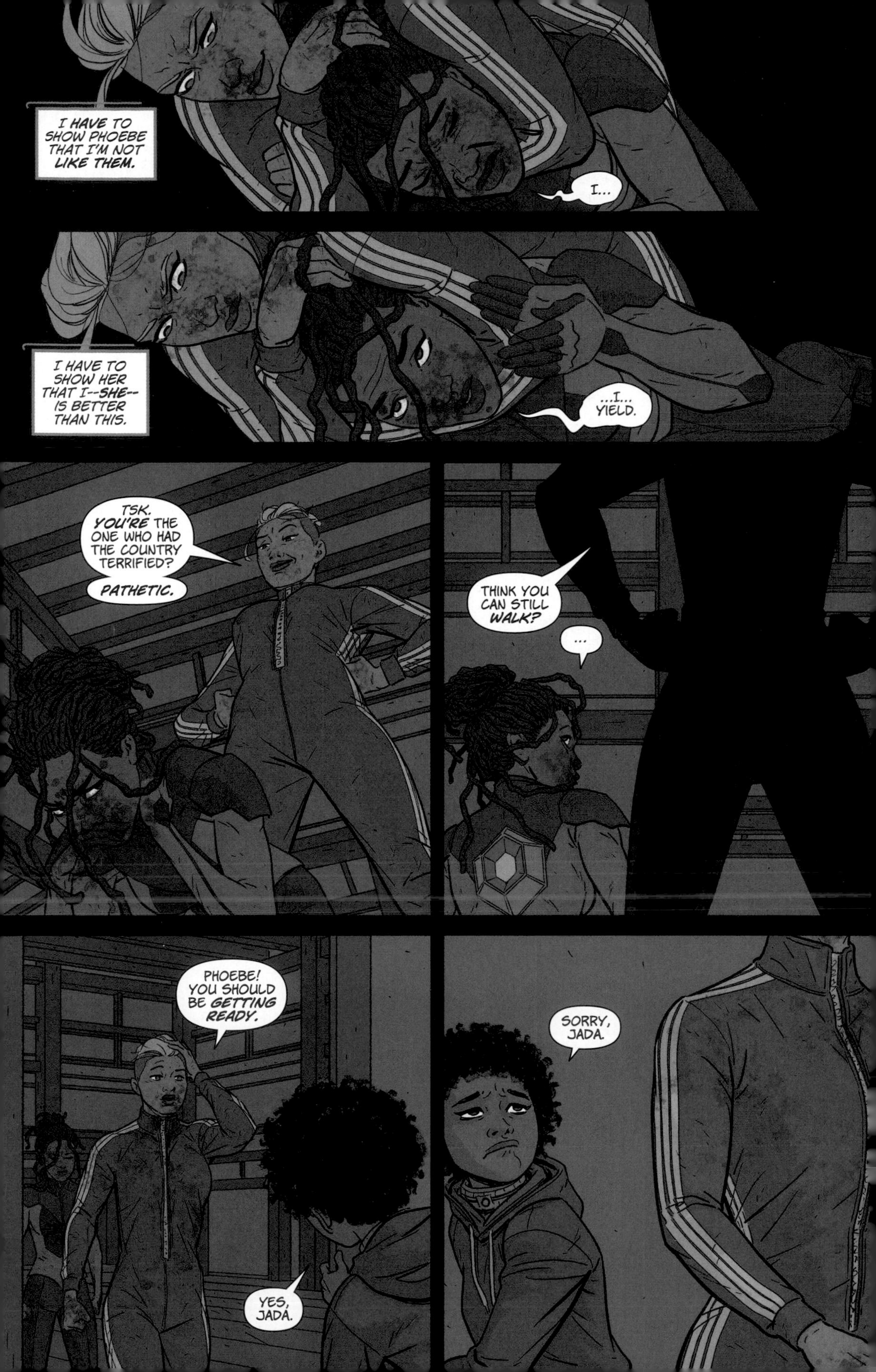
I HAVE TO SHOW PHOEBE THAT I'M NOT LIKE THEM.
I...
I HAVE TO SHOW HER THAT I--SHE-- IS BETTER THAN THIS.
...I... YIELD.
TSK. YOU'RE THE ONE WHO HAD THE COUNTRY TERRIFIED?
PATHETIC.
THINK YOU CAN STILL WALK?
...
PHOEBE! YOU SHOULD BE GETTING READY.
YES, JADA.
SORRY, JADA.

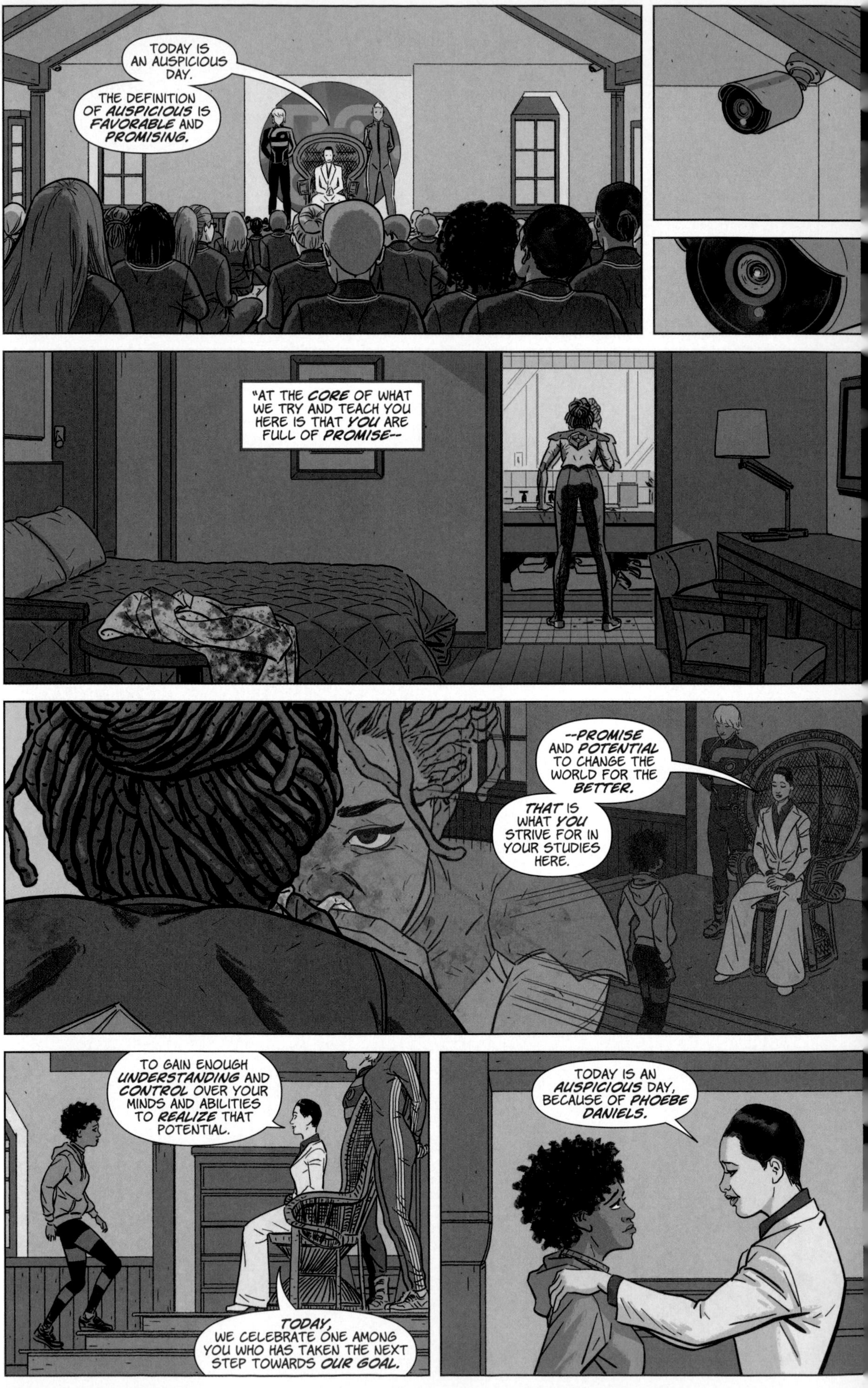
TODAY IS AN AUSPICIOUS DAY.
THE DEFINITION OF AUSPICIOUS IS FAVORABLE AND PROMISING.
"AT THE CORE OF WHAT WE TRY AND TEACH YOU HERE IS THAT YOU ARE FULL OF PROMISE--
--PROMISE AND POTENTIAL TO CHANGE THE WORLD FOR THE BETTER.
THAT IS WHAT YOU STRIVE FOR IN YOUR STUDIES HERE.
TO GAIN ENOUGH UNDERSTANDING AND CONTROL OVER YOUR MINDS AND ABILITIES TO REALIZE THAT POTENTIAL.
TODAY, WE CELEBRATE ONE AMONG YOU WHO HAS TAKEN THE NEXT STEP TOWARDS OUR GOAL.
TODAY IS AN AUSPICIOUS DAY, BECAUSE OF PHOEBE DANIELS.

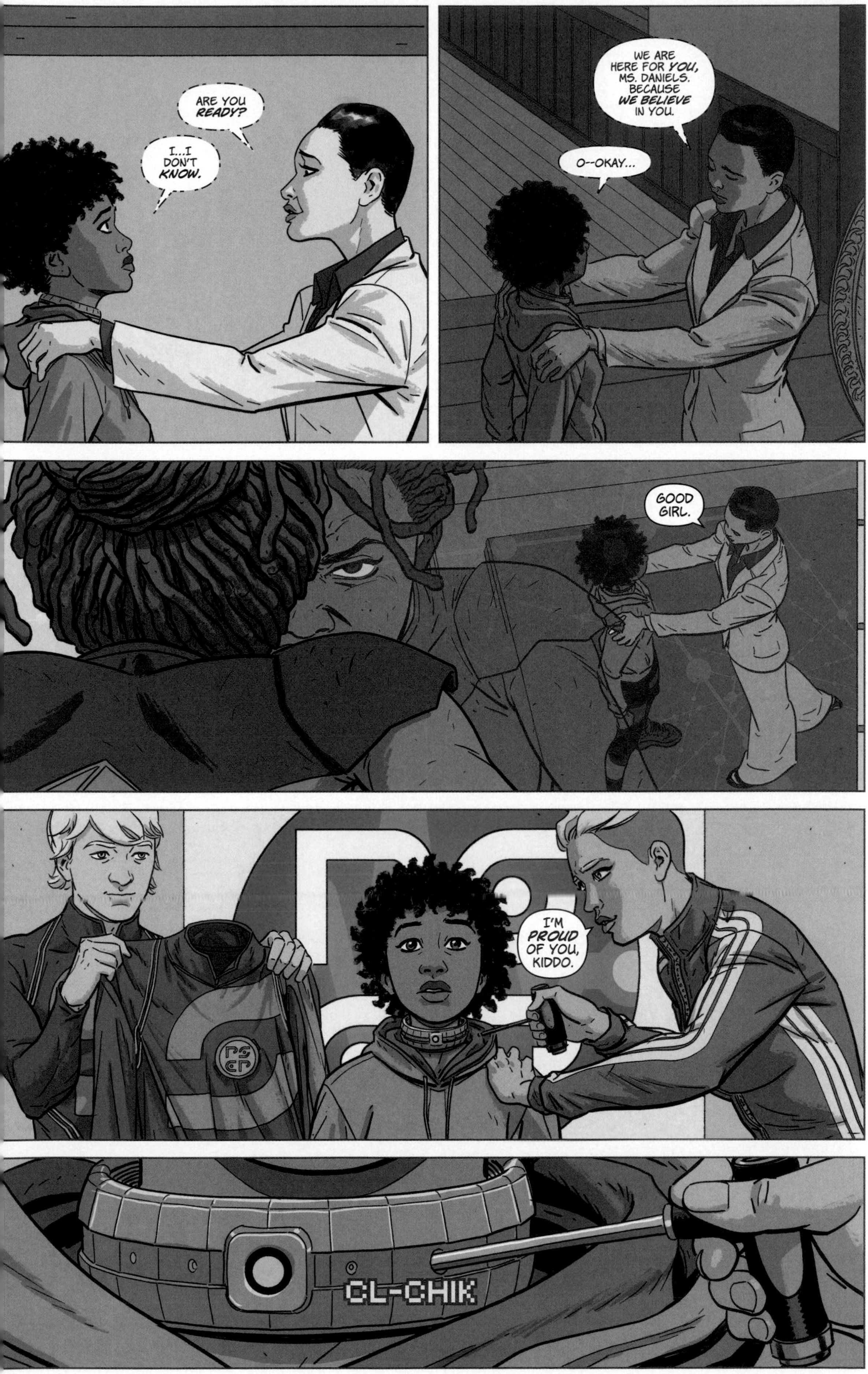
ARE YOU READY?
I...I DON'T KNOW.
WE ARE HERE FOR YOU, MS. DANIELS. BECAUSE WE BELIEVE IN YOU.
O--OKAY...
GOOD GIRL.
I'M PROUD OF YOU, KIDDO.
CL-CHIK

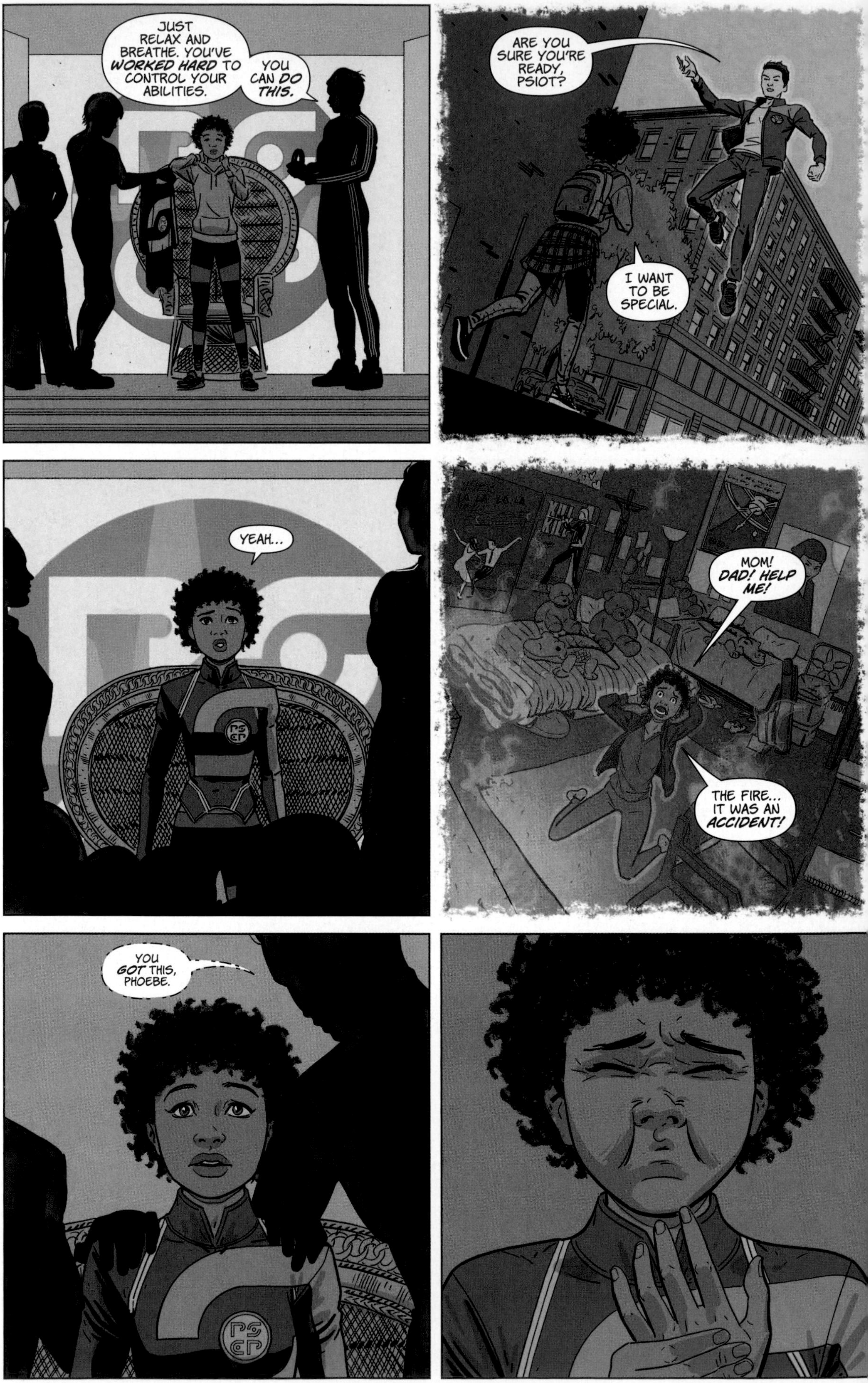
JUST RELAX AND BREATHE. YOU'VE WORKED HARD TO CONTROL YOUR ABILITIES.
YOU CAN DO THIS.
ARE YOU SURE YOU'RE READY, PSIOT?
I WANT TO BE SPECIAL.
YEAH...
MOM! DAD! HELP ME!
THE FIRE... IT WAS AN ACCIDENT!
YOU GOT THIS, PHOEBE.

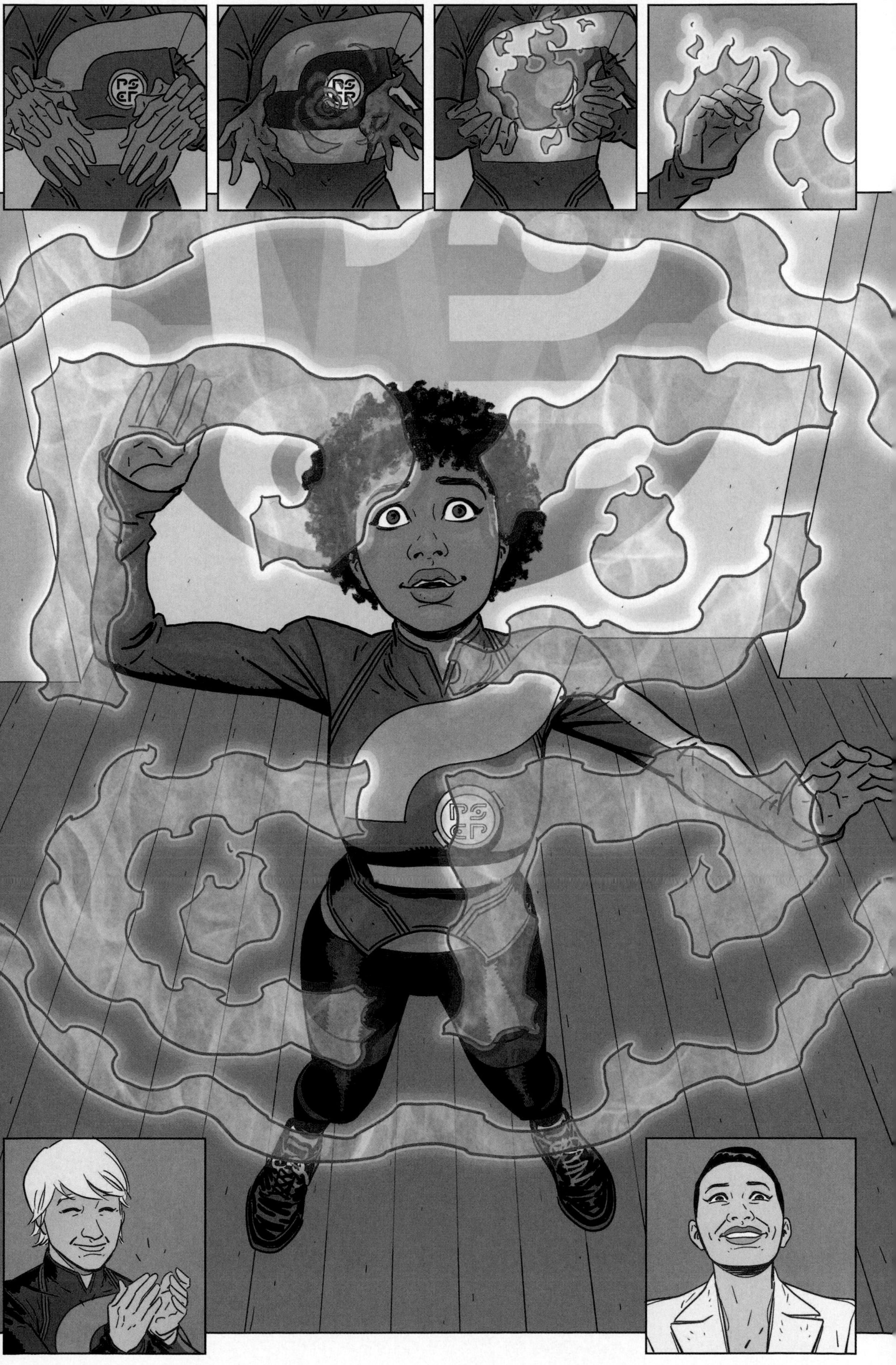

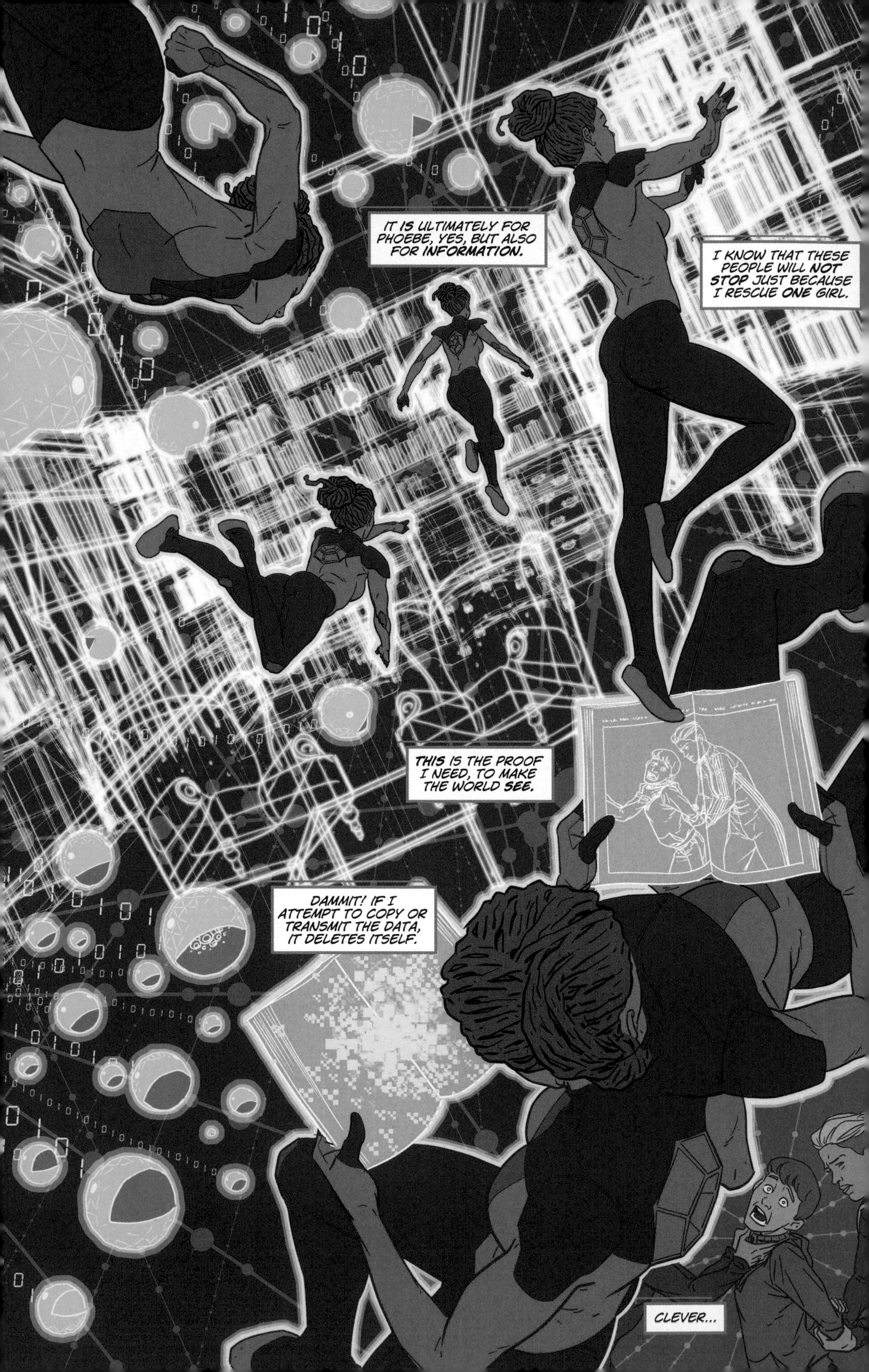
IT IS ULTIMATELY FOR PHOEBE, YES, BUT ALSO FOR INFORMATION.
I KNOW THAT THESE PEOPLE WILL NOT STOP JUST BECAUSE I RESCUE ONE GIRL.
THIS IS THE PROOF I NEED, TO MAKE THE WORLD SEE.
DAMMIT! IF I ATTEMPT TO COPY OR TRANSMIT THE DATA, IT DELETES ITSELF.
CLEVER...

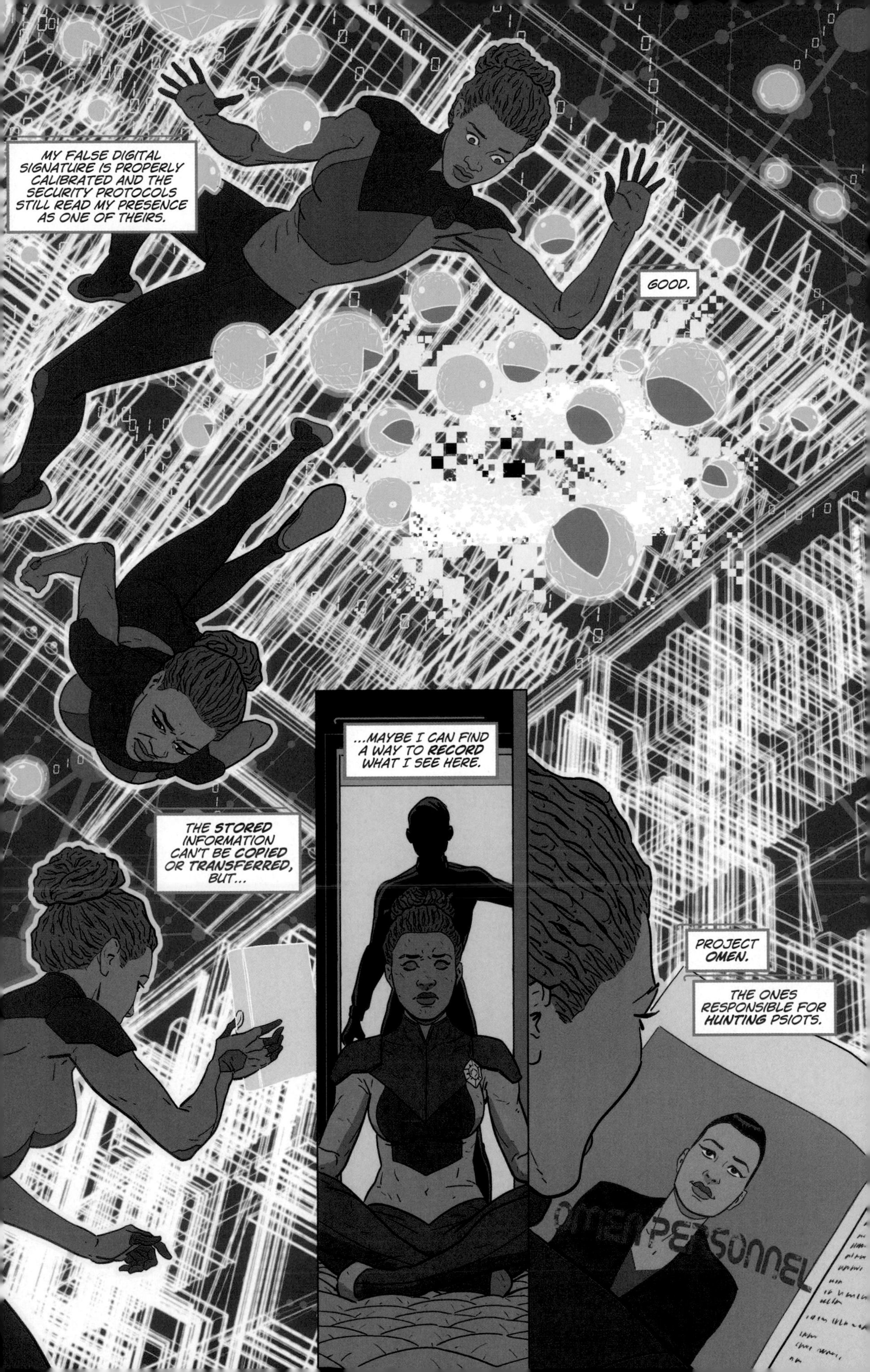
MY FALSE DIGITAL SIGNATURE IS PROPERLY CALIBRATED AND THE SECURITY PROTOCOLS STILL READ MY PRESENCE AS ONE OF THEIRS.
GOOD.
THE STORED INFORMATION CAN'T BE COPIED OR TRANSFERRED, BUT...
...MAYBE I CAN FIND A WAY TO RECORD WHAT I SEE HERE.
PROJECT OMEN.
THE ONES RESPONSIBLE FOR HUNTING PSIOTS.
OMEN PERSONNEL

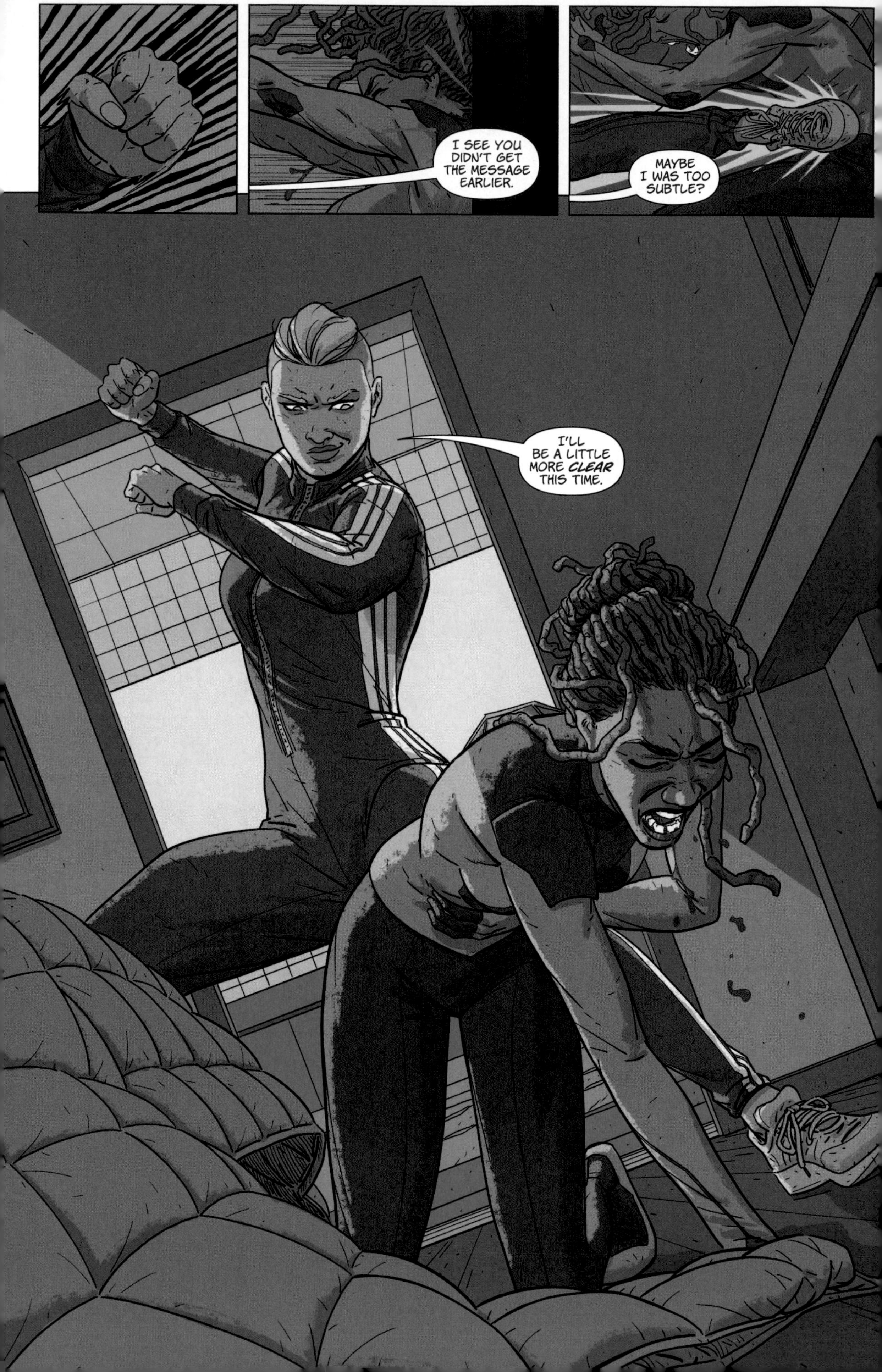
I SEE YOU DIDN'T GET THE MESSAGE EARLIER.
MAYBE I WAS TOO SUBTLE?
I'LL BE A LITTLE MORE *CLEAR* THIS TIME.

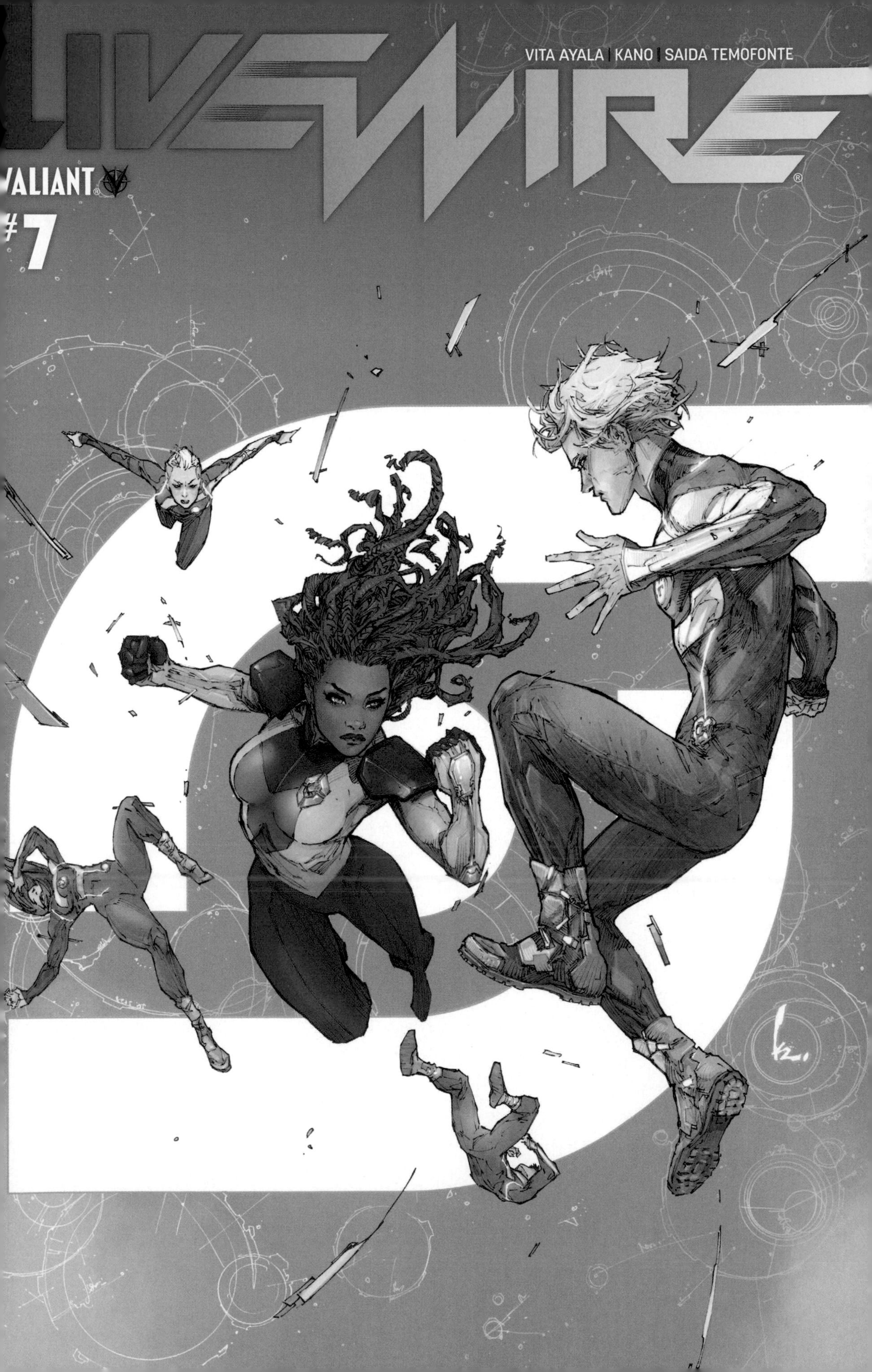
LIVEWIRE
VITA AYALA | KANO | SAIDA TEMOFONTE
VALIANT
#7

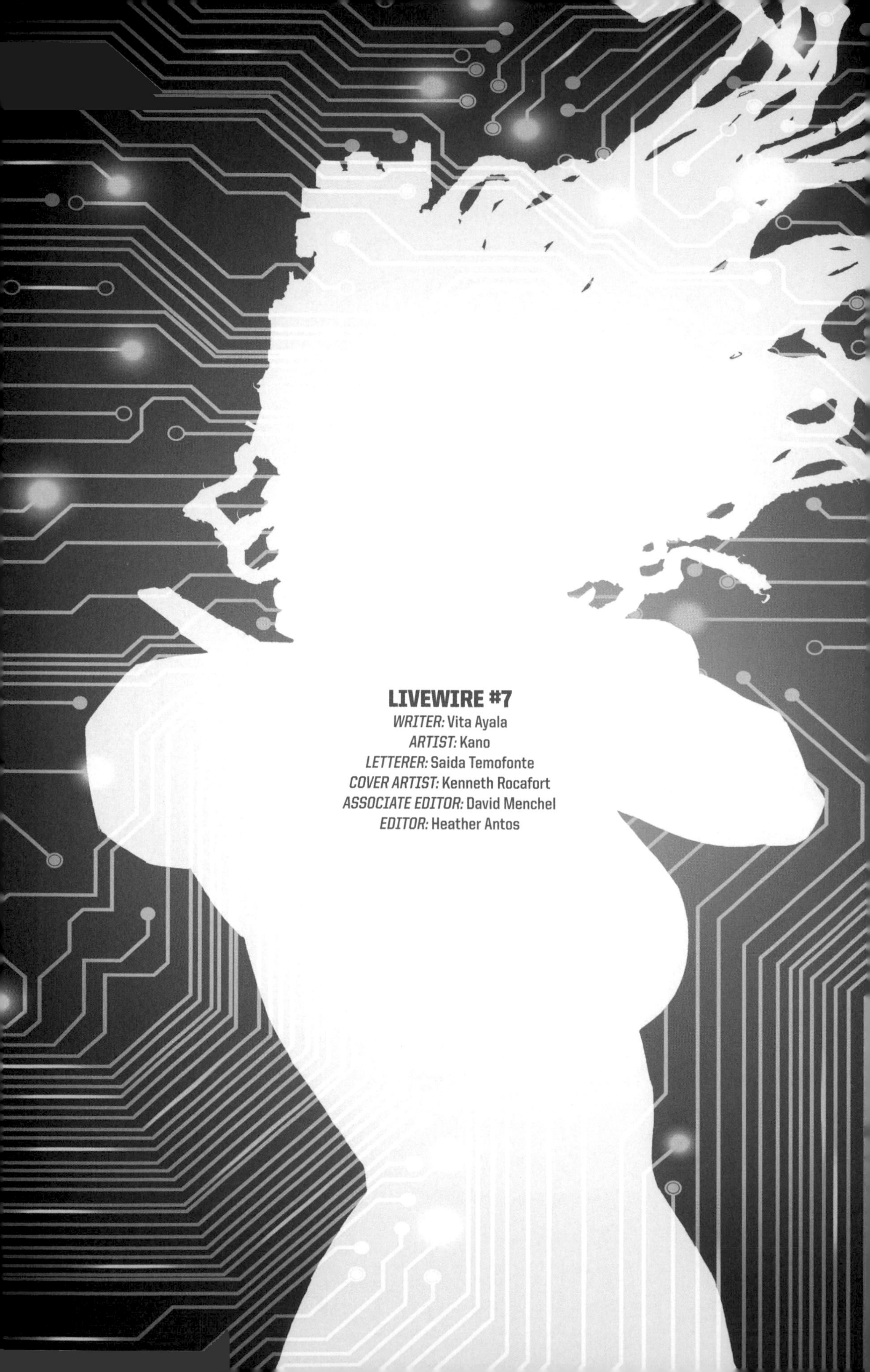

LIVEWIRE #7

WRITER: Vita Ayala
ARTIST: Kano
LETTERER: Saida Temofonte
COVER ARTIST: Kenneth Rocafort
ASSOCIATE EDITOR: David Menchel
EDITOR: Heather Antos

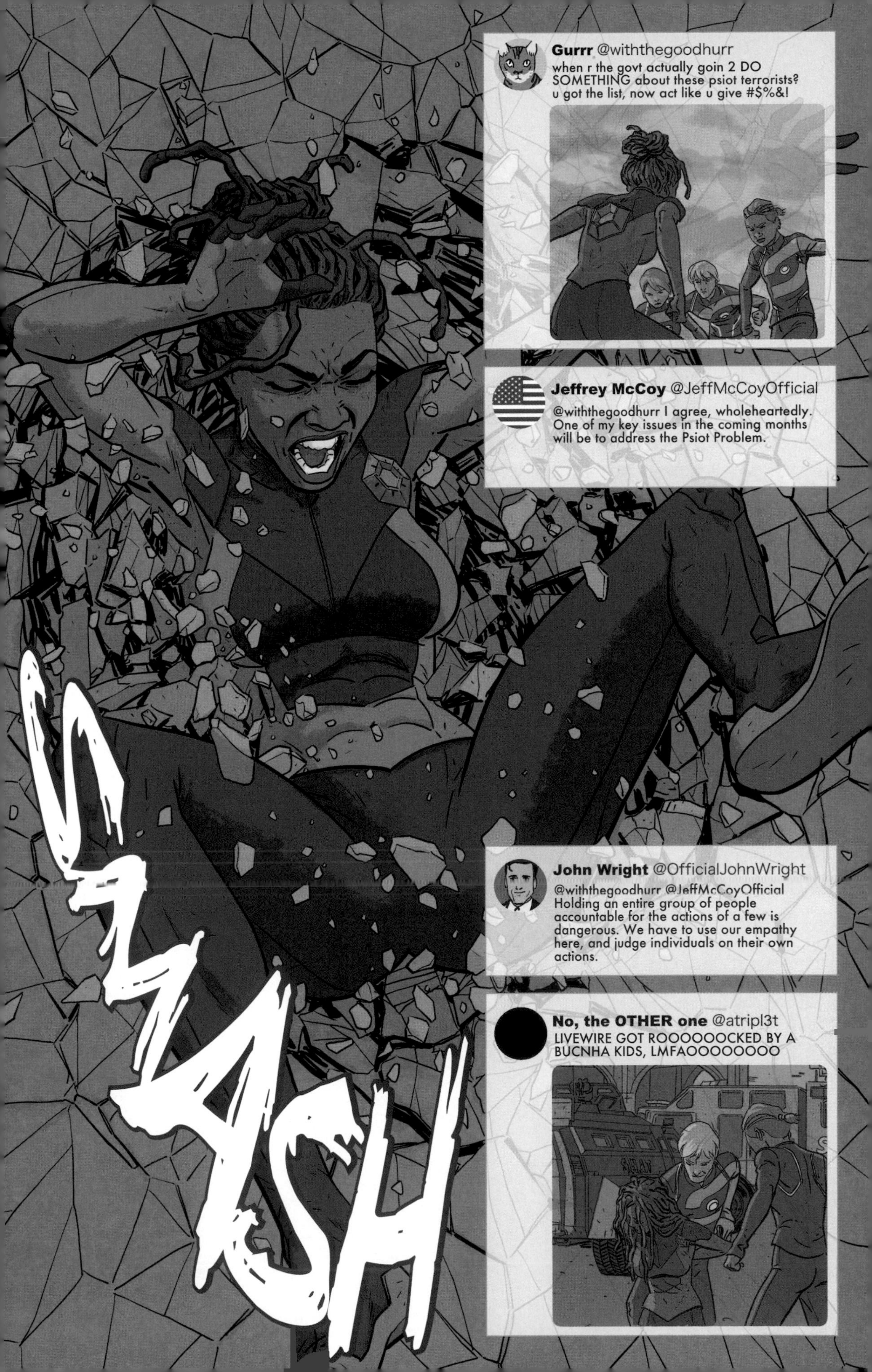
Gurrr @withthegoodhurr
when r the govt actually goin 2 DO SOMETHING about these psiot terrorists? u got the list, now act like u give #$%&!
Jeffrey McCoy @JeffMcCoyOfficial
@withthegoodhurr I agree, wholeheartedly. One of my key issues in the coming months will be to address the Psiot Problem.
SMASH
John Wright @OfficialJohnWright
@withthegoodhurr @JeffMcCoyOfficial Holding an entire group of people accountable for the actions of a few is dangerous. We have to use our empathy here, and judge individuals on their own actions.
No, the OTHER one @atripl3t
LIVEWIRE GOT ROOOOOOCKED BY A BUCNHA KIDS, LMFAOOOOOOOO

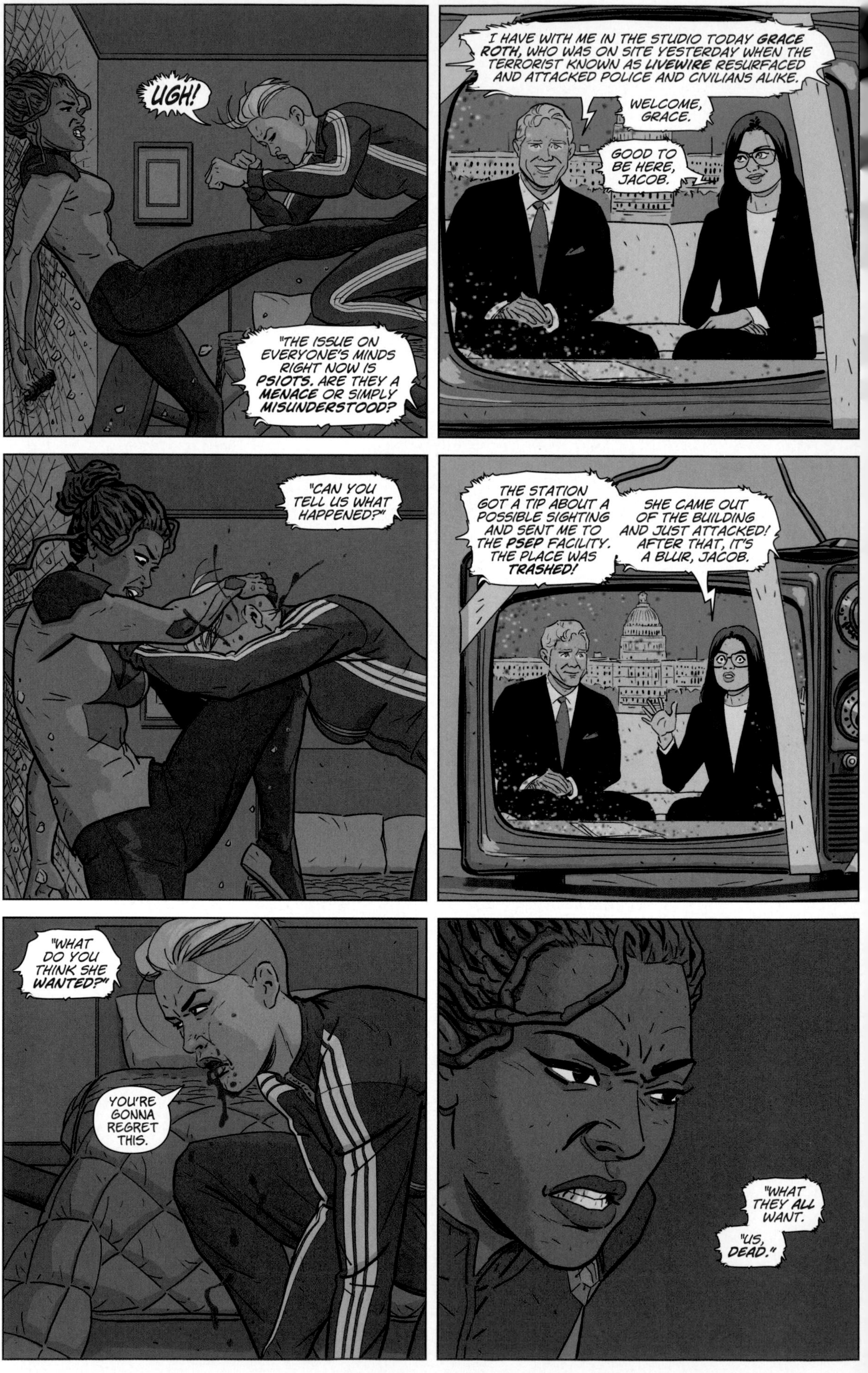
UGH!
I HAVE WITH ME IN THE STUDIO TODAY GRACE ROTH, WHO WAS ON SITE YESTERDAY WHEN THE TERRORIST KNOWN AS LIVEWIRE RESURFACED AND ATTACKED POLICE AND CIVILIANS ALIKE.
WELCOME, GRACE.
GOOD TO BE HERE, JACOB.
"THE ISSUE ON EVERYONE'S MINDS RIGHT NOW IS PSIOTS. ARE THEY A MENACE OR SIMPLY MISUNDERSTOOD?
"CAN YOU TELL US WHAT HAPPENED?"
THE STATION GOT A TIP ABOUT A POSSIBLE SIGHTING AND SENT ME TO THE PSEP FACILITY. THE PLACE WAS TRASHED!
SHE CAME OUT OF THE BUILDING AND JUST ATTACKED! AFTER THAT, IT'S A BLUR, JACOB.
"WHAT DO YOU THINK SHE WANTED?"
YOU'RE GONNA REGRET THIS.
"WHAT THEY ALL WANT.
"US, DEAD."

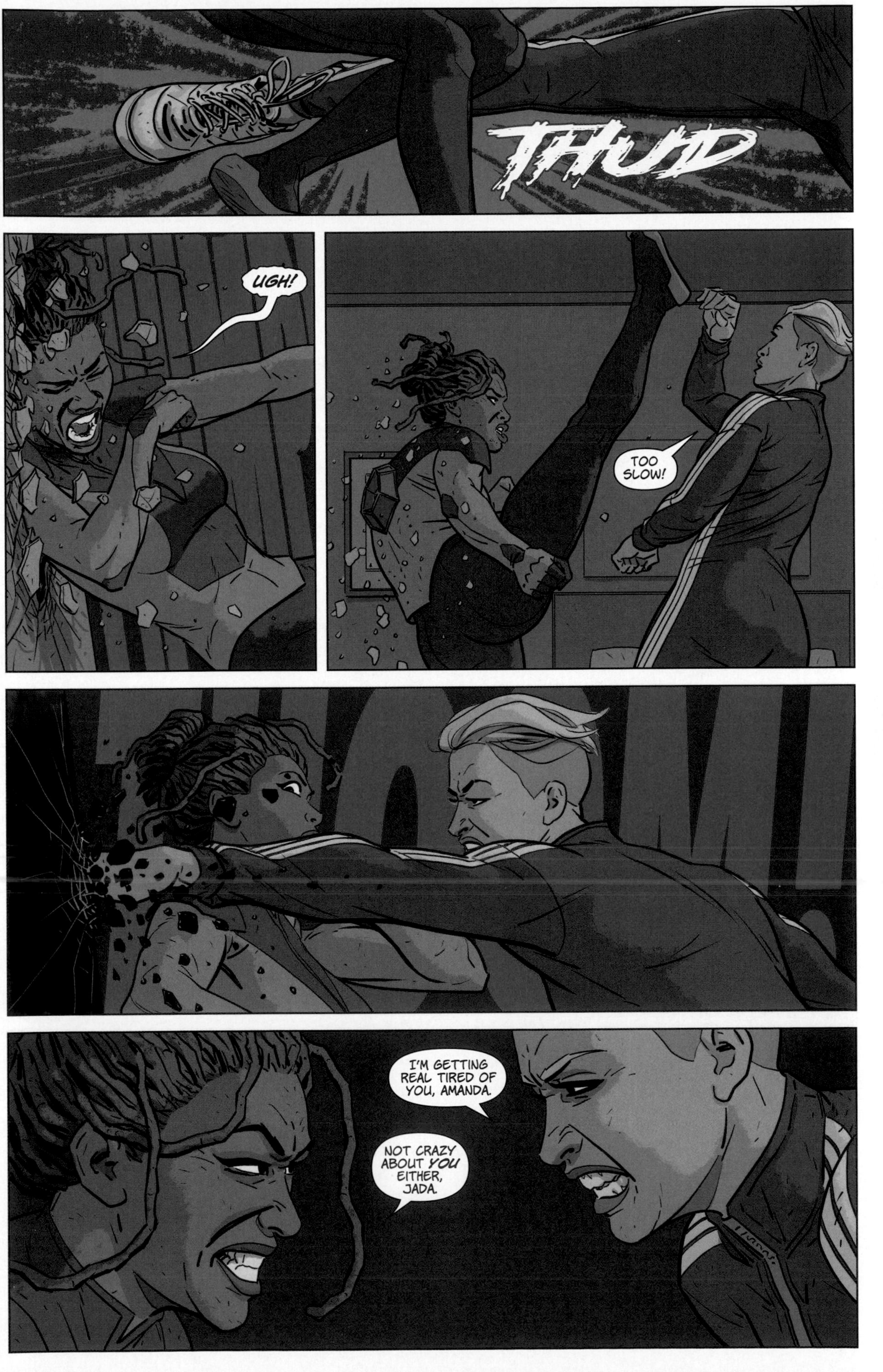
THUD
UGH!
TOO SLOW!
I'M GETTING REAL TIRED OF YOU, AMANDA.
NOT CRAZY ABOUT YOU EITHER, JADA.

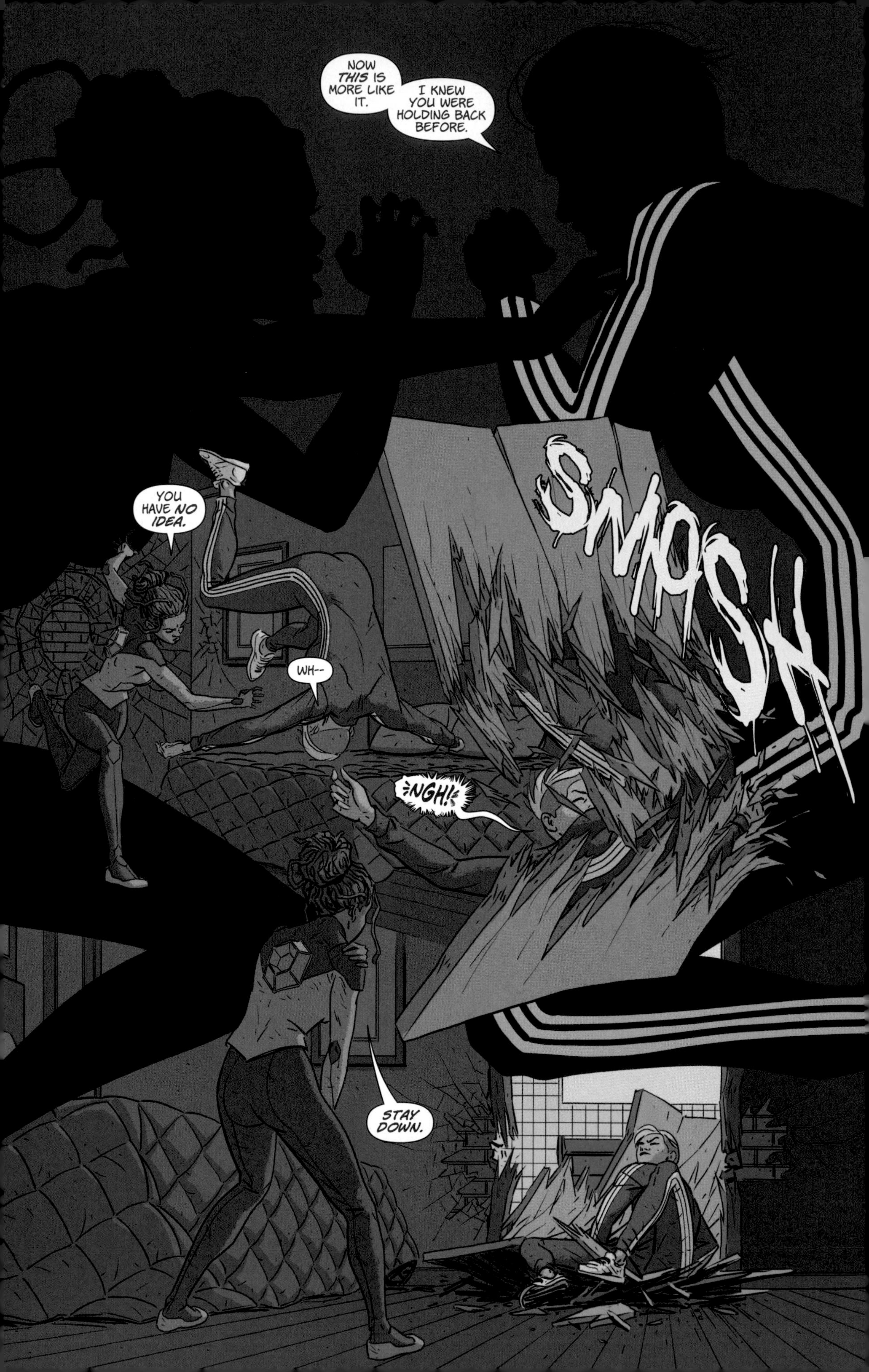

NOW *THIS* IS MORE LIKE IT.
I KNEW YOU WERE HOLDING BACK BEFORE.
YOU HAVE *NO IDEA.*
SMASH
WH--
NGH!
STAY DOWN.

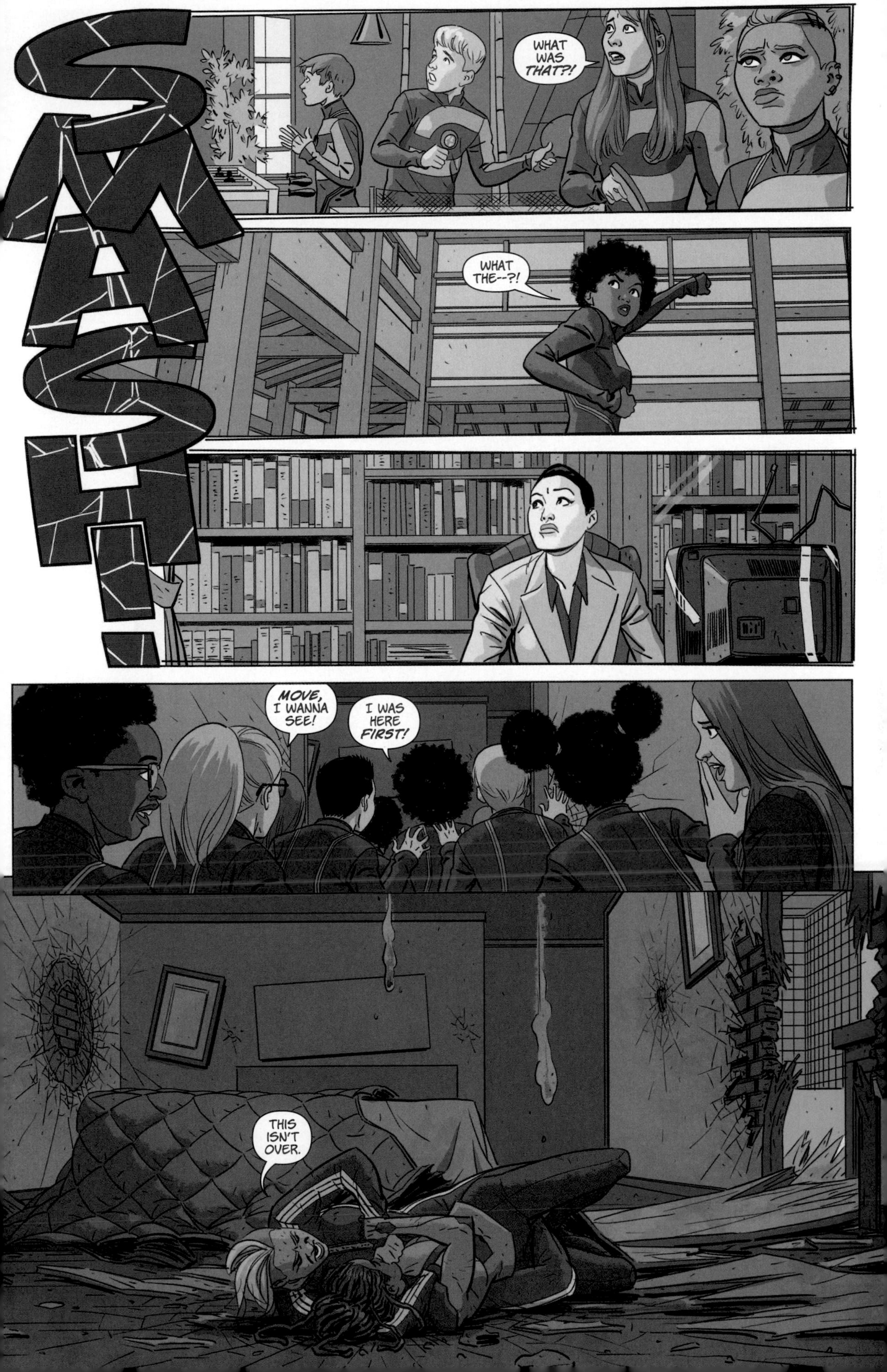
SMASH!!
WHAT WAS THAT?!
WHAT THE--?!
MOVE, I WANNA SEE!
I WAS HERE FIRST!
THIS ISN'T OVER.

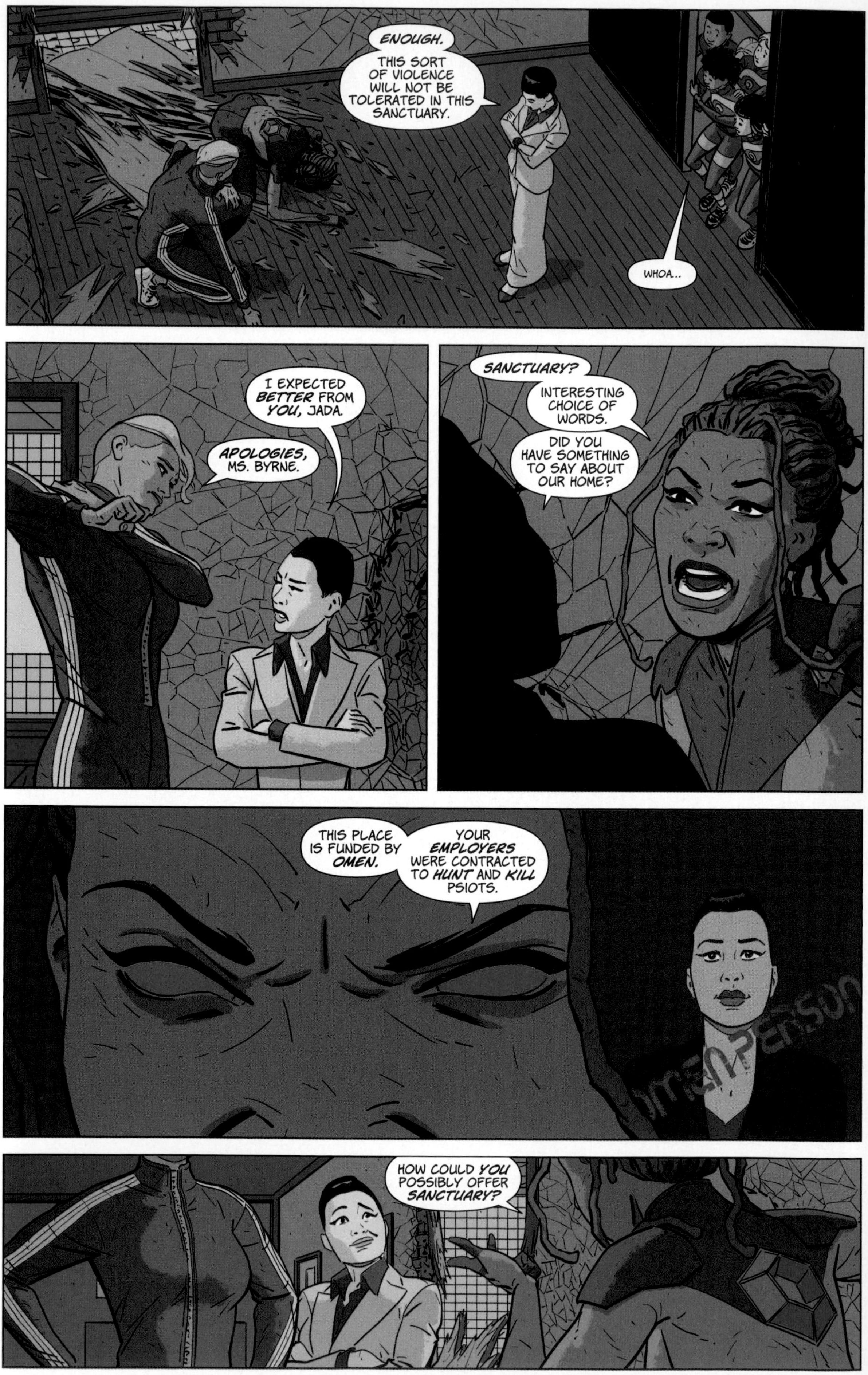
ENOUGH.
THIS SORT OF VIOLENCE WILL NOT BE TOLERATED IN THIS SANCTUARY.
WHOA..
I EXPECTED BETTER FROM YOU, JADA.
APOLOGIES, MS. BYRNE.
SANCTUARY?
INTERESTING CHOICE OF WORDS.
DID YOU HAVE SOMETHING TO SAY ABOUT OUR HOME?
THIS PLACE IS FUNDED BY OMEN.
YOUR EMPLOYERS WERE CONTRACTED TO HUNT AND KILL PSIOTS.
HOW COULD YOU POSSIBLY OFFER SANCTUARY?

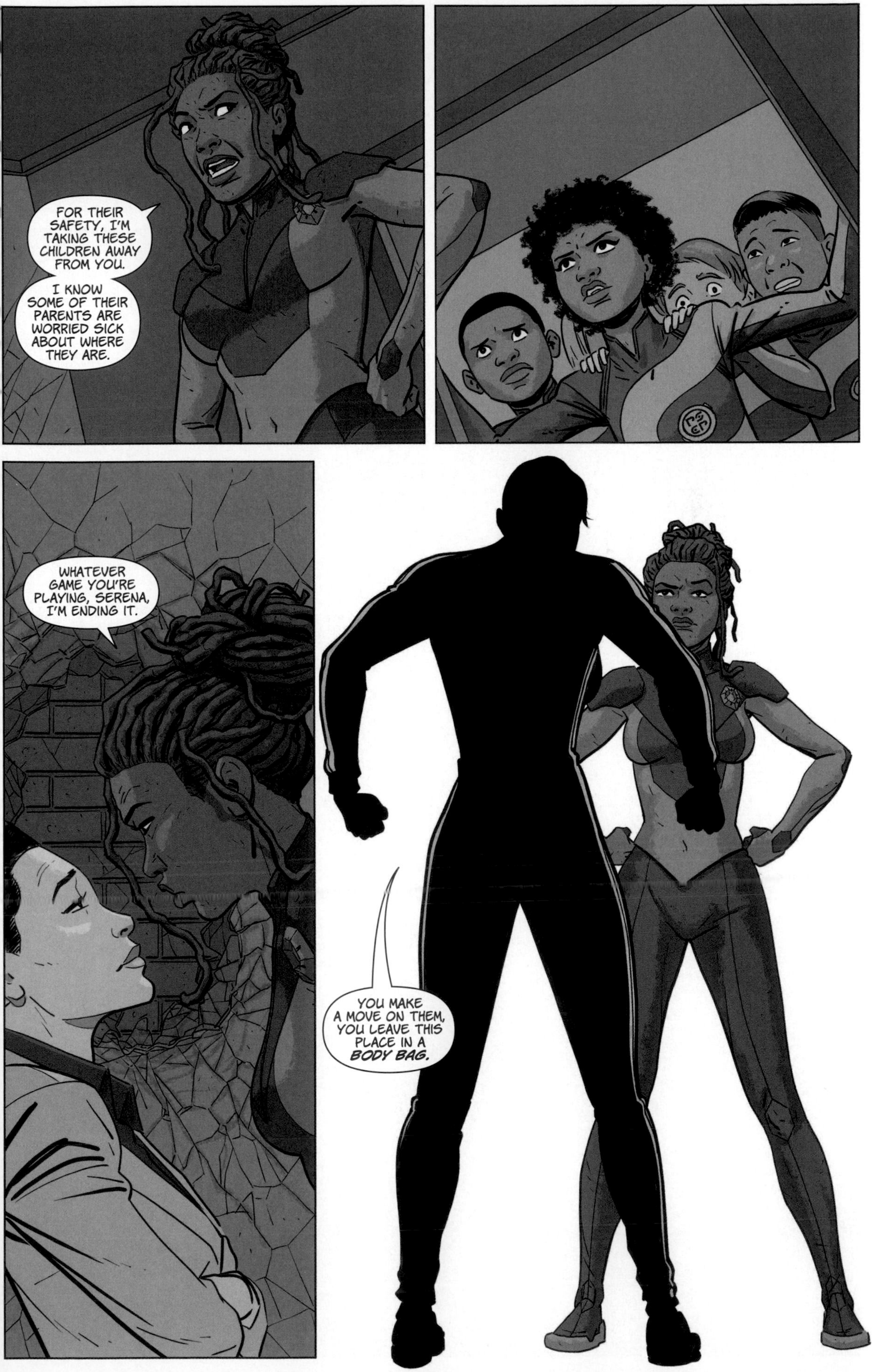
FOR THEIR SAFETY, I'M TAKING THESE CHILDREN AWAY FROM YOU.
I KNOW SOME OF THEIR PARENTS ARE WORRIED SICK ABOUT WHERE THEY ARE.
WHATEVER GAME YOU'RE PLAYING, SERENA, I'M ENDING IT.
YOU MAKE A MOVE ON THEM, YOU LEAVE THIS PLACE IN A *BODY BAG.*

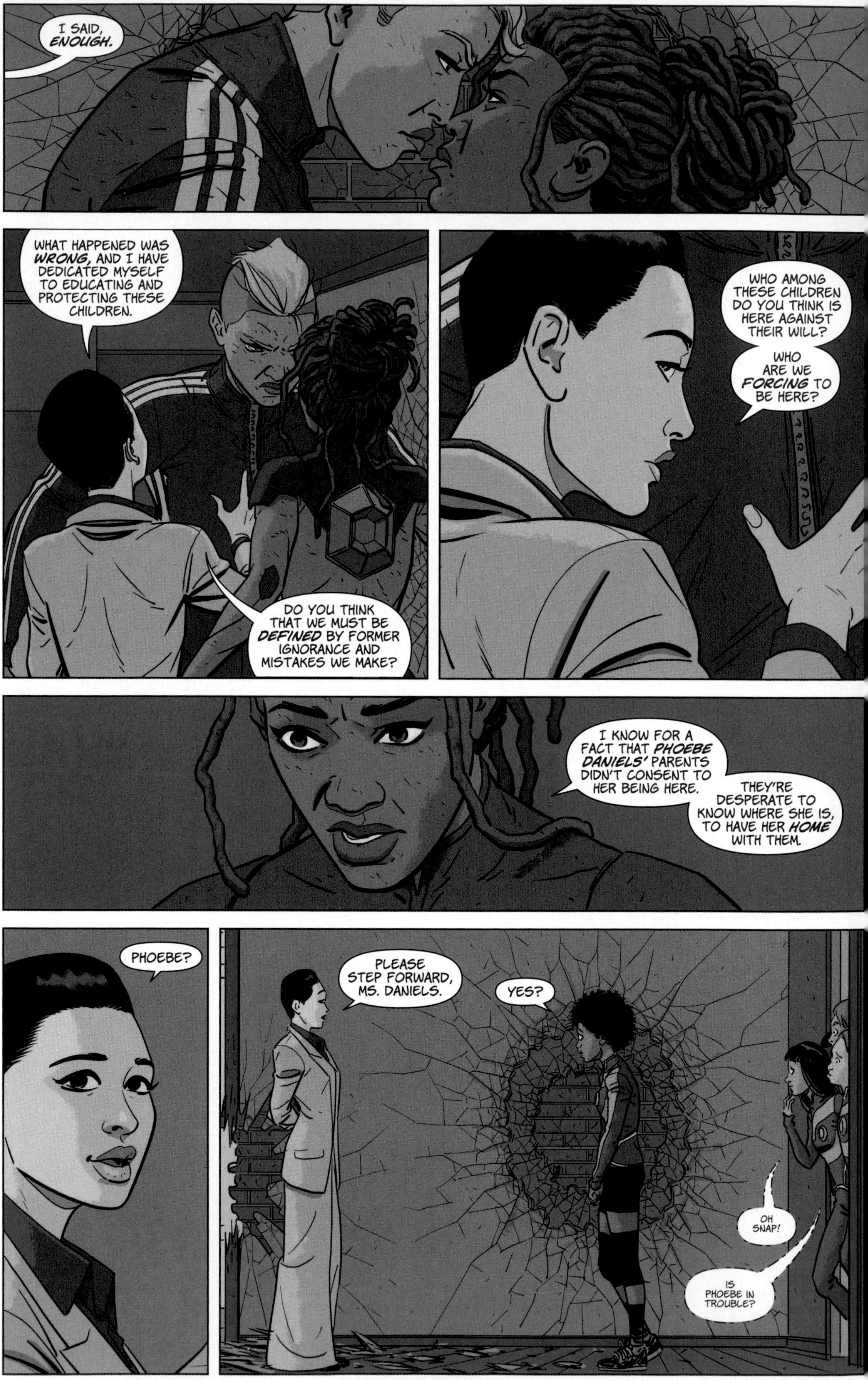
I SAID, ENOUGH.
WHAT HAPPENED WAS WRONG, AND I HAVE DEDICATED MYSELF TO EDUCATING AND PROTECTING THESE CHILDREN.
DO YOU THINK THAT WE MUST BE DEFINED BY FORMER IGNORANCE AND MISTAKES WE MAKE?
WHO AMONG THESE CHILDREN DO YOU THINK IS HERE AGAINST THEIR WILL?
WHO ARE WE FORCING TO BE HERE?
I KNOW FOR A FACT THAT PHOEBE DANIELS' PARENTS DIDN'T CONSENT TO HER BEING HERE.
THEY'RE DESPERATE TO KNOW WHERE SHE IS, TO HAVE HER HOME WITH THEM.
PHOEBE?
PLEASE STEP FORWARD, MS. DANIELS.
YES?
OH SNAP!
IS PHOEBE IN TROUBLE?

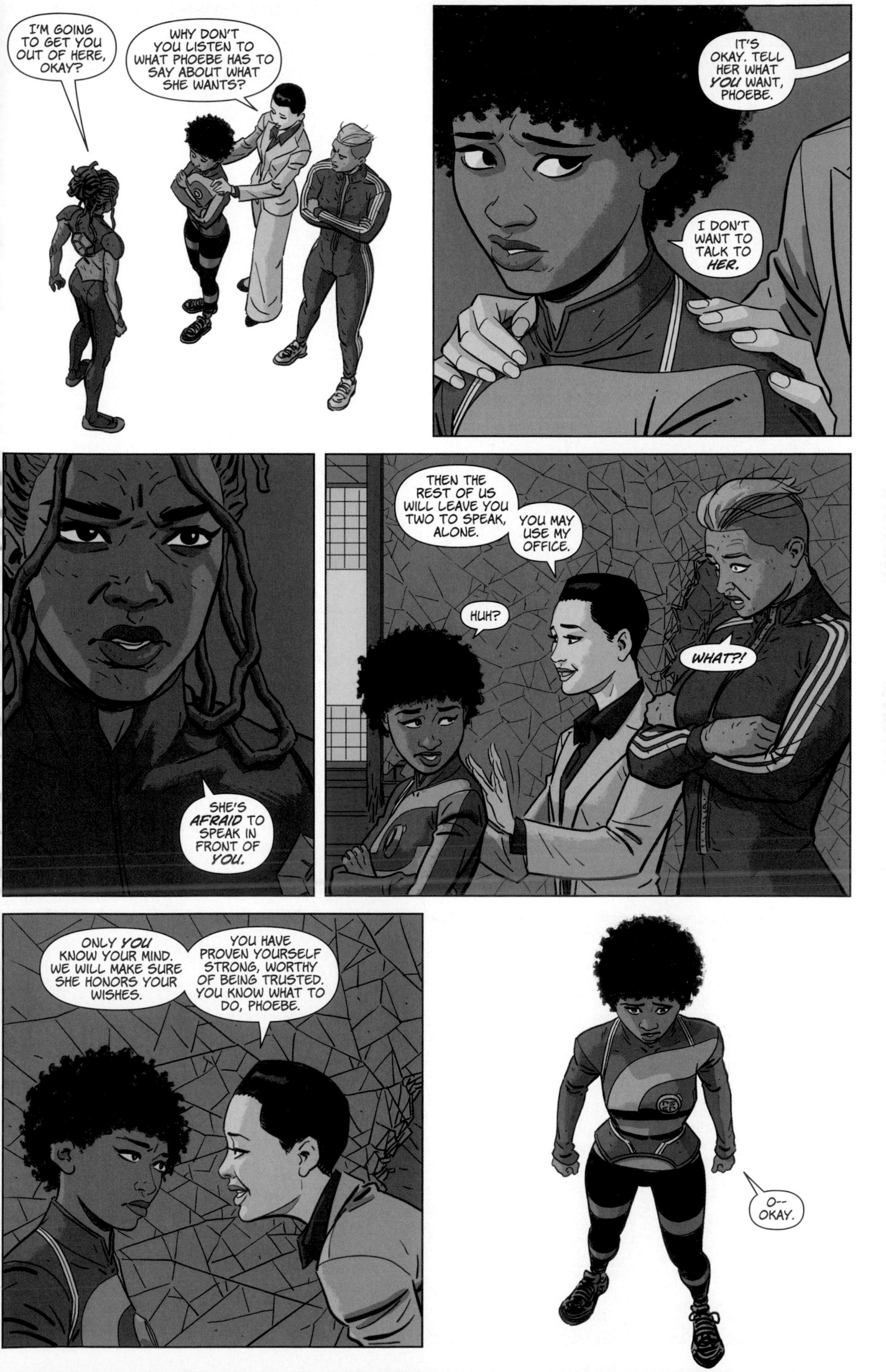
I'M GOING TO GET YOU OUT OF HERE, OKAY?
WHY DON'T YOU LISTEN TO WHAT PHOEBE HAS TO SAY ABOUT WHAT SHE WANTS?
IT'S OKAY. TELL HER WHAT *YOU* WANT, PHOEBE.
I DON'T WANT TO TALK TO *HER.*
SHE'S *AFRAID* TO SPEAK IN FRONT OF *YOU.*
THEN THE REST OF US WILL LEAVE YOU TWO TO SPEAK, ALONE.
YOU MAY USE MY OFFICE.
HUH?
WHAT?!
ONLY *YOU* KNOW YOUR MIND. WE WILL MAKE SURE SHE HONORS YOUR WISHES.
YOU HAVE PROVEN YOURSELF STRONG, WORTHY OF BEING TRUSTED. YOU KNOW WHAT TO DO, PHOEBE.
O-- OKAY.

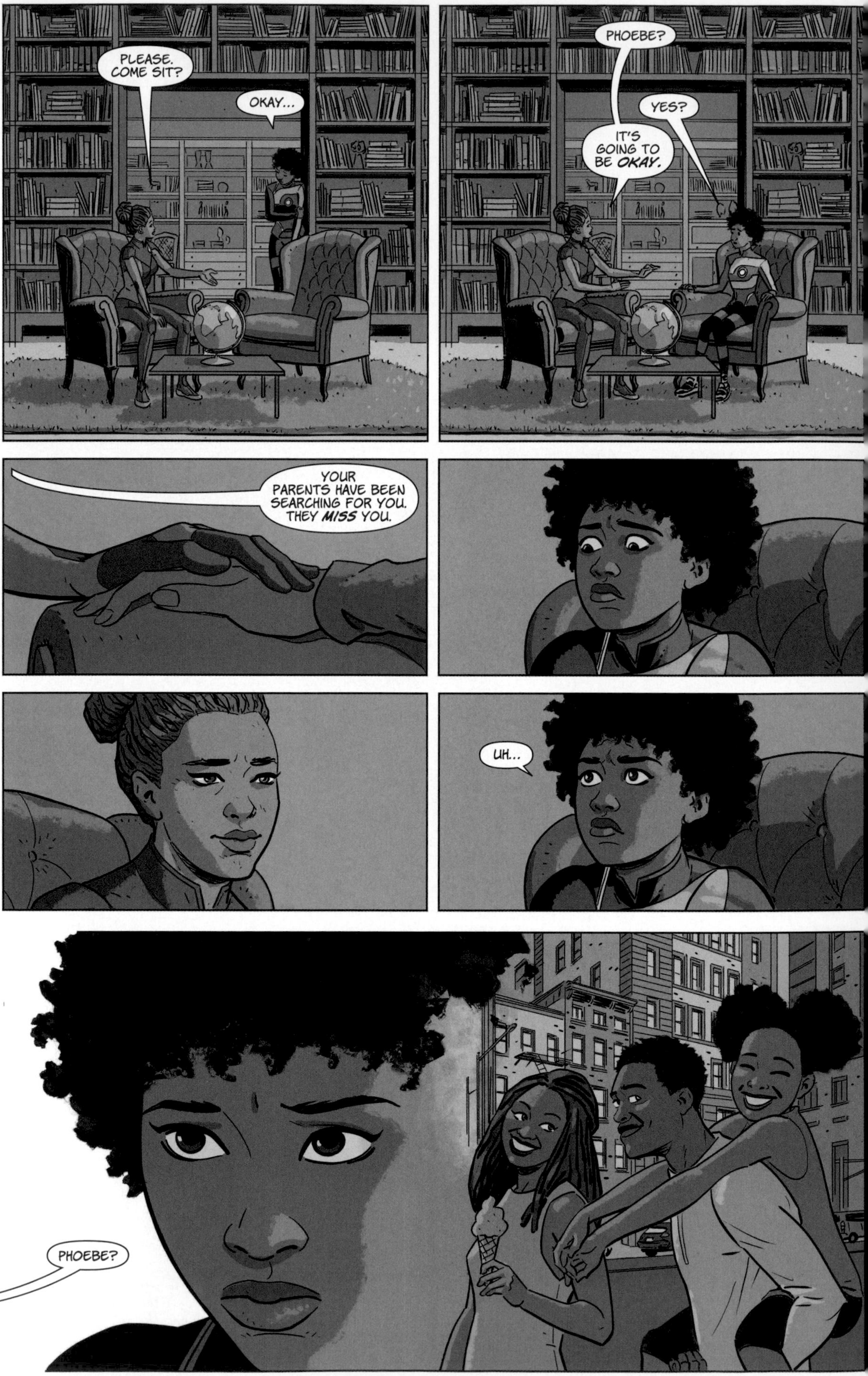
PLEASE. COME SIT?
OKAY...
PHOEBE?
YES?
IT'S GOING TO BE OKAY.
YOUR PARENTS HAVE BEEN SEARCHING FOR YOU. THEY MISS YOU.
UH...
PHOEBE?

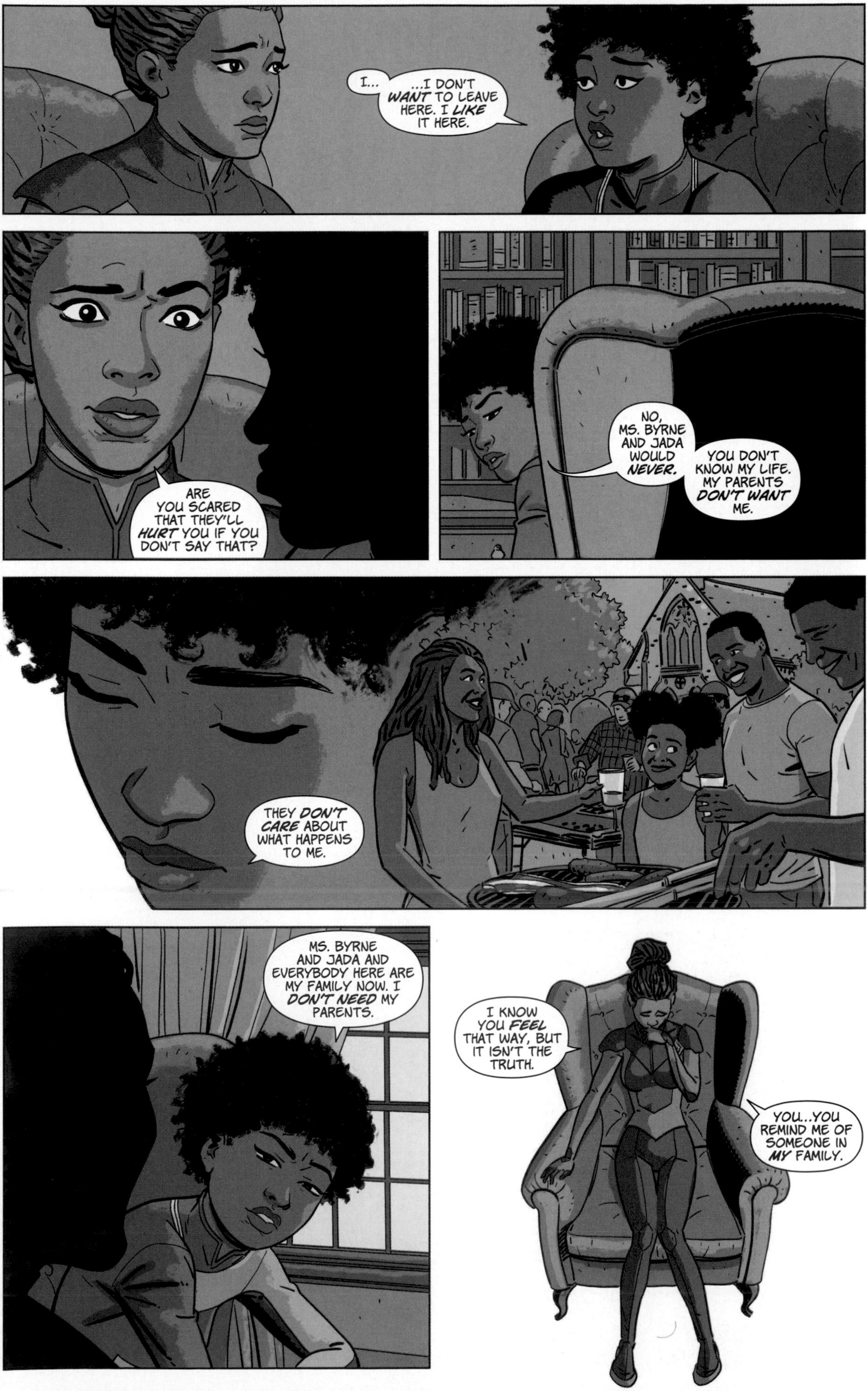
I...
...I DON'T WANT TO LEAVE HERE. I LIKE IT HERE.
ARE YOU SCARED THAT THEY'LL HURT YOU IF YOU DON'T SAY THAT?
NO, MS. BYRNE AND JADA WOULD NEVER.
YOU DON'T KNOW MY LIFE. MY PARENTS DON'T WANT ME.
THEY DON'T CARE ABOUT WHAT HAPPENS TO ME.
MS. BYRNE AND JADA AND EVERYBODY HERE ARE MY FAMILY NOW. I DON'T NEED MY PARENTS.
I KNOW YOU FEEL THAT WAY, BUT IT ISN'T THE TRUTH.
YOU...YOU REMIND ME OF SOMEONE IN MY FAMILY.

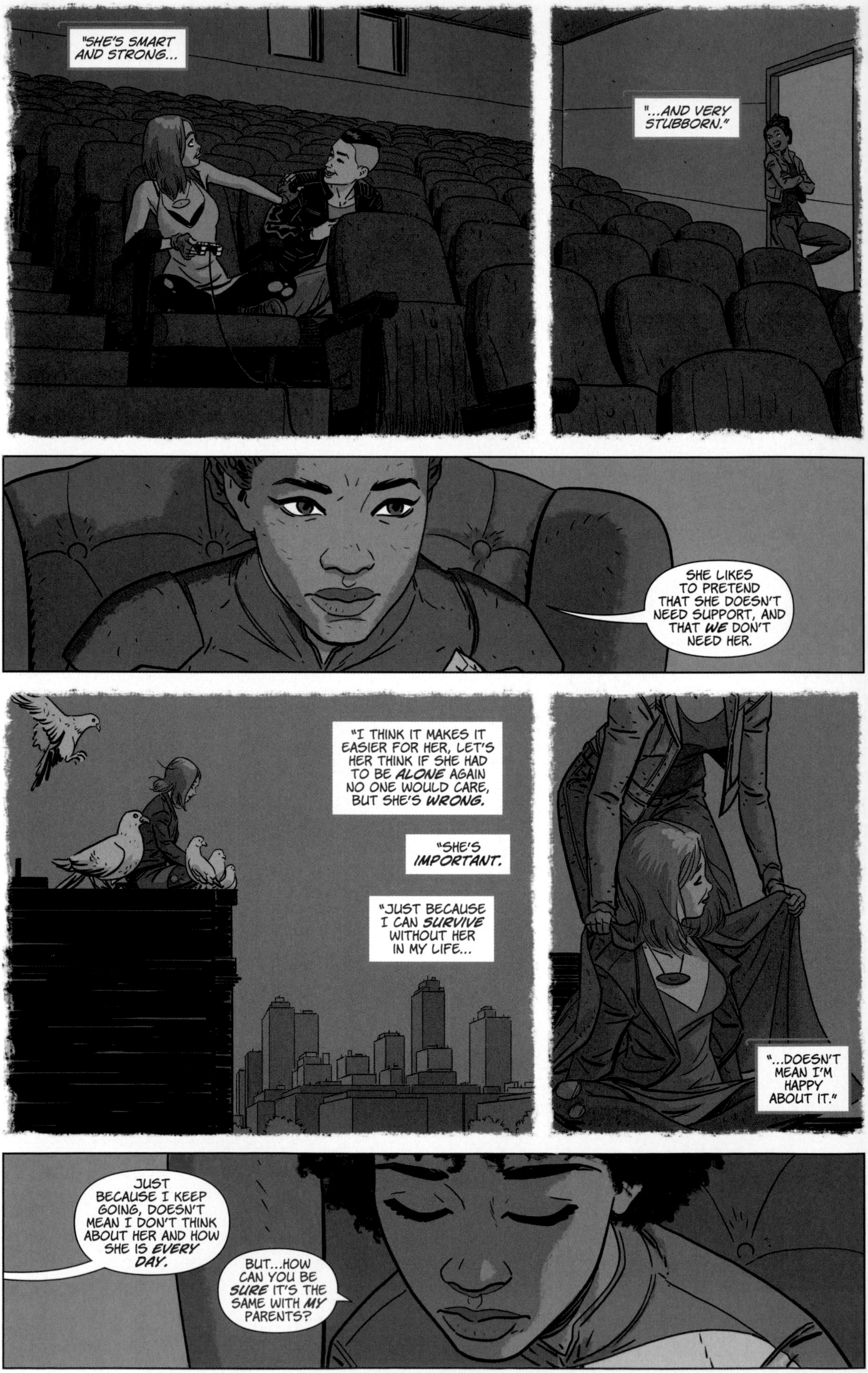
"SHE'S SMART AND STRONG...
"...AND VERY STUBBORN."
SHE LIKES TO PRETEND THAT SHE DOESN'T NEED SUPPORT, AND THAT WE DON'T NEED HER.
"I THINK IT MAKES IT EASIER FOR HER, LET'S HER THINK IF SHE HAD TO BE ALONE AGAIN NO ONE WOULD CARE, BUT SHE'S WRONG.
"SHE'S IMPORTANT.
"JUST BECAUSE I CAN SURVIVE WITHOUT HER IN MY LIFE...
"...DOESN'T MEAN I'M HAPPY ABOUT IT."
JUST BECAUSE I KEEP GOING, DOESN'T MEAN I DON'T THINK ABOUT HER AND HOW SHE IS EVERY DAY.
BUT...HOW CAN YOU BE SURE IT'S THE SAME WITH MY PARENTS?

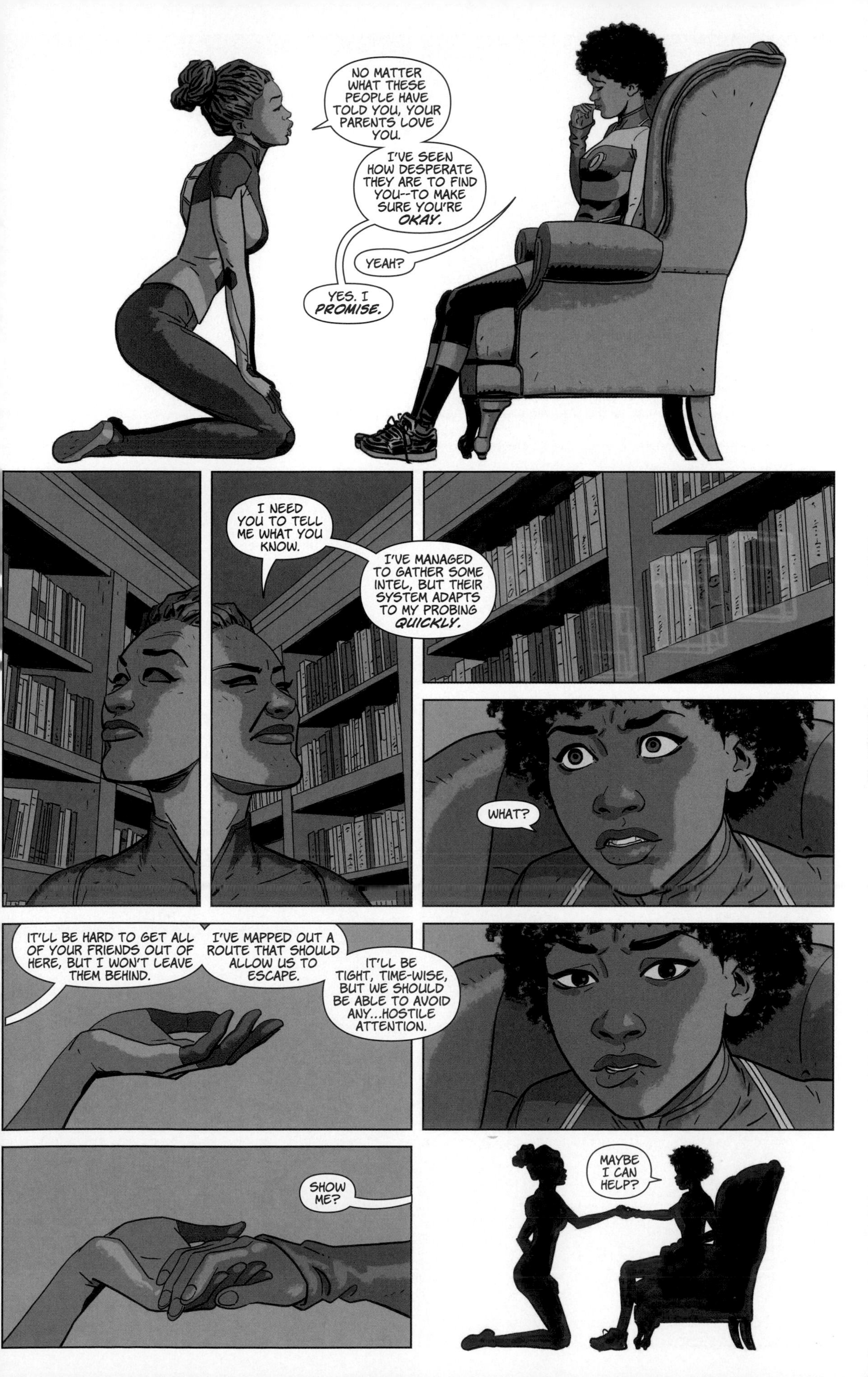
NO MATTER WHAT THESE PEOPLE HAVE TOLD YOU, YOUR PARENTS LOVE YOU.
I'VE SEEN HOW DESPERATE THEY ARE TO FIND YOU--TO MAKE SURE YOU'RE OKAY.
YEAH?
YES. I PROMISE.
I NEED YOU TO TELL ME WHAT YOU KNOW.
I'VE MANAGED TO GATHER SOME INTEL, BUT THEIR SYSTEM ADAPTS TO MY PROBING QUICKLY.
WHAT?
IT'LL BE HARD TO GET ALL OF YOUR FRIENDS OUT OF HERE, BUT I WON'T LEAVE THEM BEHIND.
I'VE MAPPED OUT A ROUTE THAT SHOULD ALLOW US TO ESCAPE.
IT'LL BE TIGHT, TIME-WISE, BUT WE SHOULD BE ABLE TO AVOID ANY...HOSTILE ATTENTION.
SHOW ME?
MAYBE I CAN HELP?

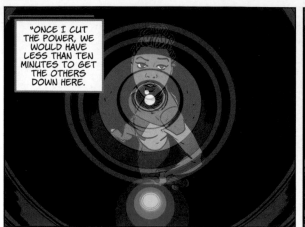

"ONCE I CUT THE POWER, WE WOULD HAVE LESS THAN TEN MINUTES TO GET THE OTHERS DOWN HERE.

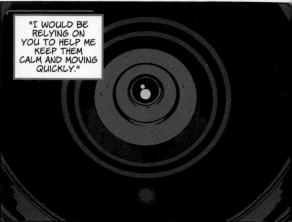

"I WOULD BE RELYING ON YOU TO HELP ME KEEP THEM CALM AND MOVING QUICKLY."

WHERE ARE WE?

THIS DOOR LEADS TO A MACHINE ROOM. THERE IS A LARGE ACCESS TUNNEL BACK THERE, ACCORDING TO THE BLUEPRINTS.

IT LEADS A HUNDRED YARDS OUT FROM THE BUILDING, TO THE UNDERGROUND POWER JUNCTURE.

ONCE WE'RE CLEAR, I HAVE A SAFE HOUSE WE CAN GO TO UNTIL I REUNITE YOU WITH YOUR PARENTS.

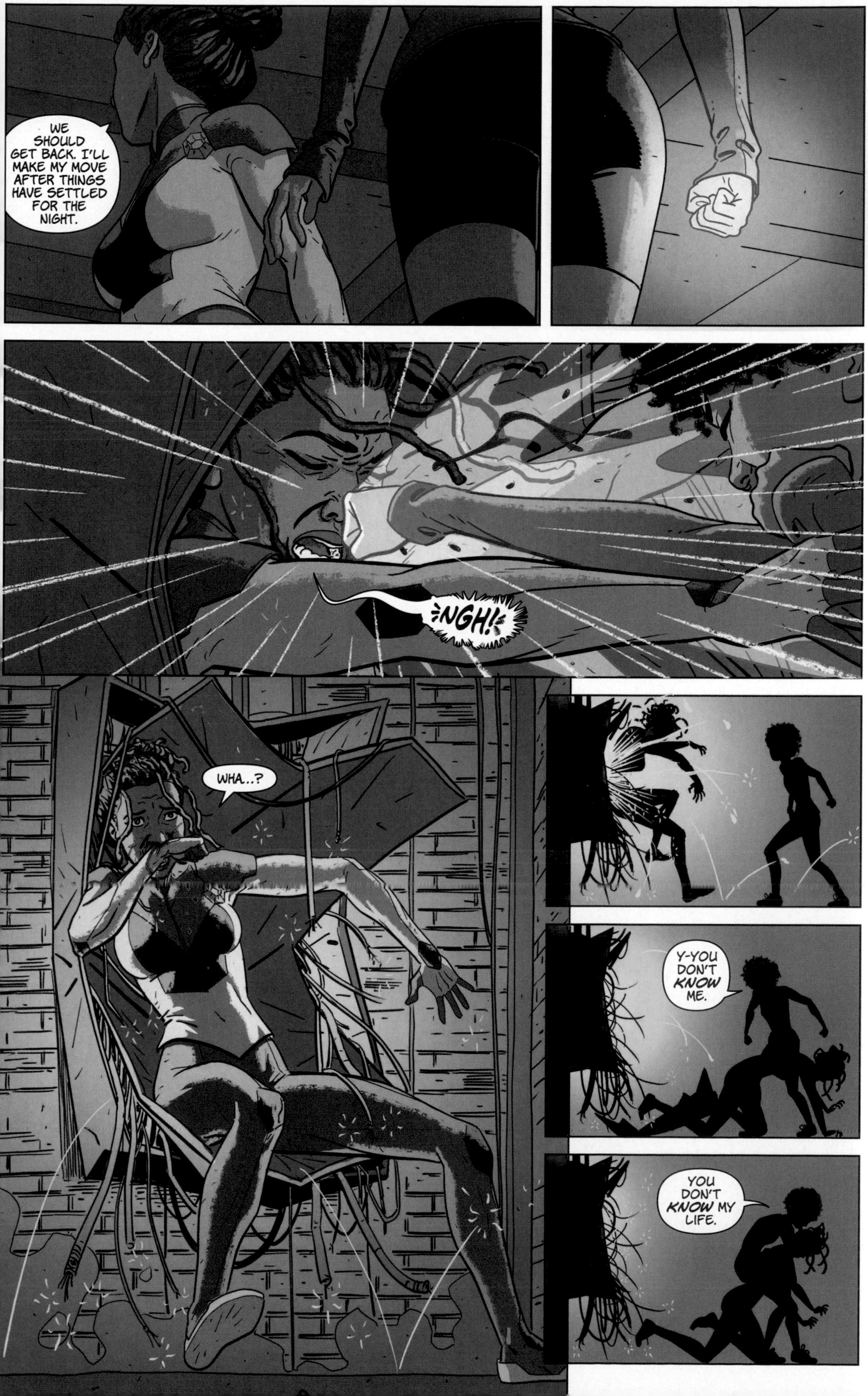
WE SHOULD GET BACK. I'LL MAKE MY MOVE AFTER THINGS HAVE SETTLED FOR THE NIGHT.
NGH!
WHA..?
Y-YOU DON'T KNOW ME.
YOU DON'T KNOW MY LIFE.

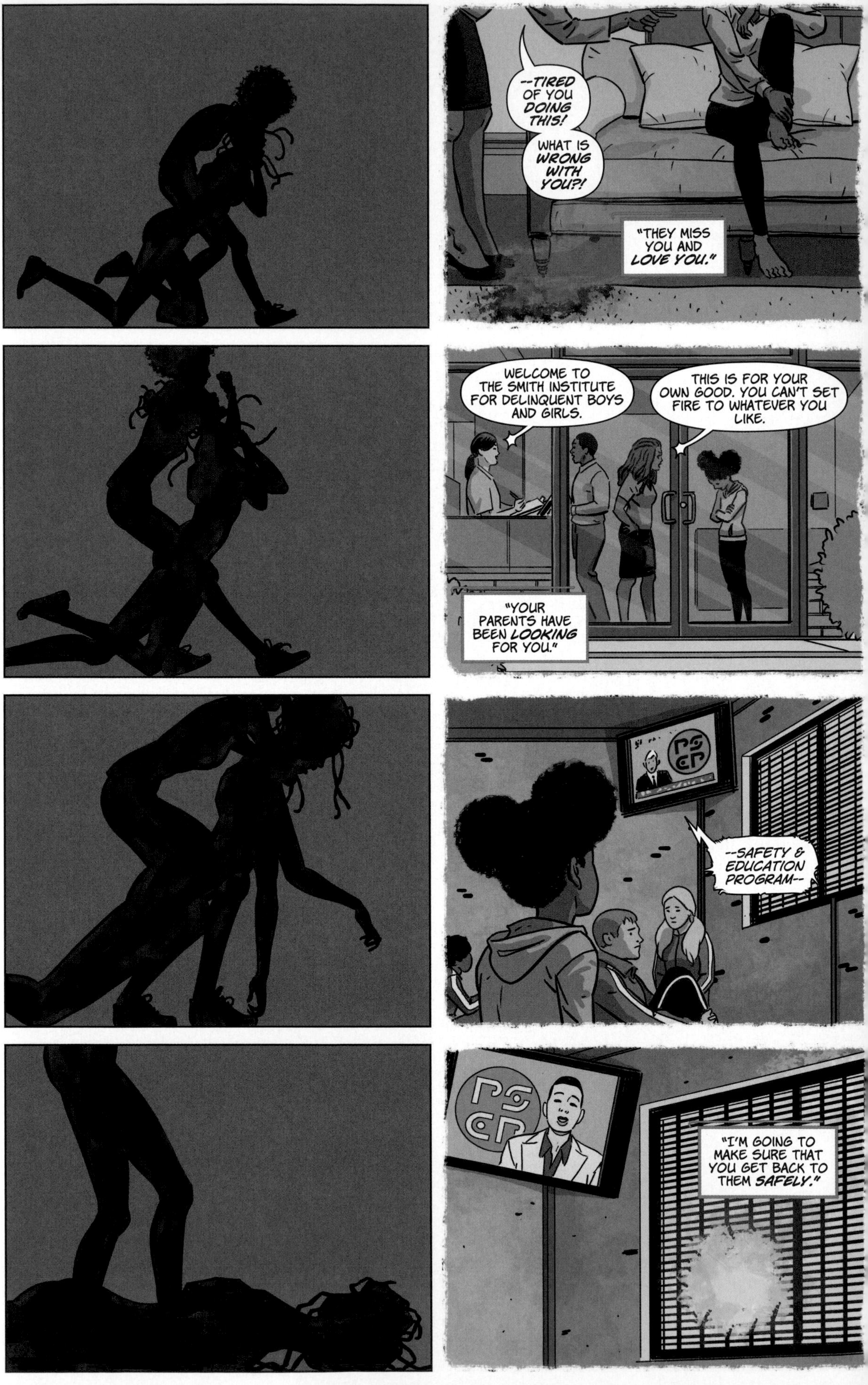
--*TIRED* OF YOU *DOING THIS!*
WHAT IS *WRONG WITH YOU?!*
"THEY MISS YOU AND *LOVE YOU.*"
WELCOME TO THE SMITH INSTITUTE FOR DELINQUENT BOYS AND GIRLS.
THIS IS FOR YOUR OWN GOOD. YOU CAN'T SET FIRE TO WHATEVER YOU LIKE.
"YOUR PARENTS HAVE BEEN *LOOKING* FOR YOU."
--*SAFETY & EDUCATION PROGRAM*--
"I'M GOING TO MAKE SURE THAT YOU GET BACK TO THEM *SAFELY.*"

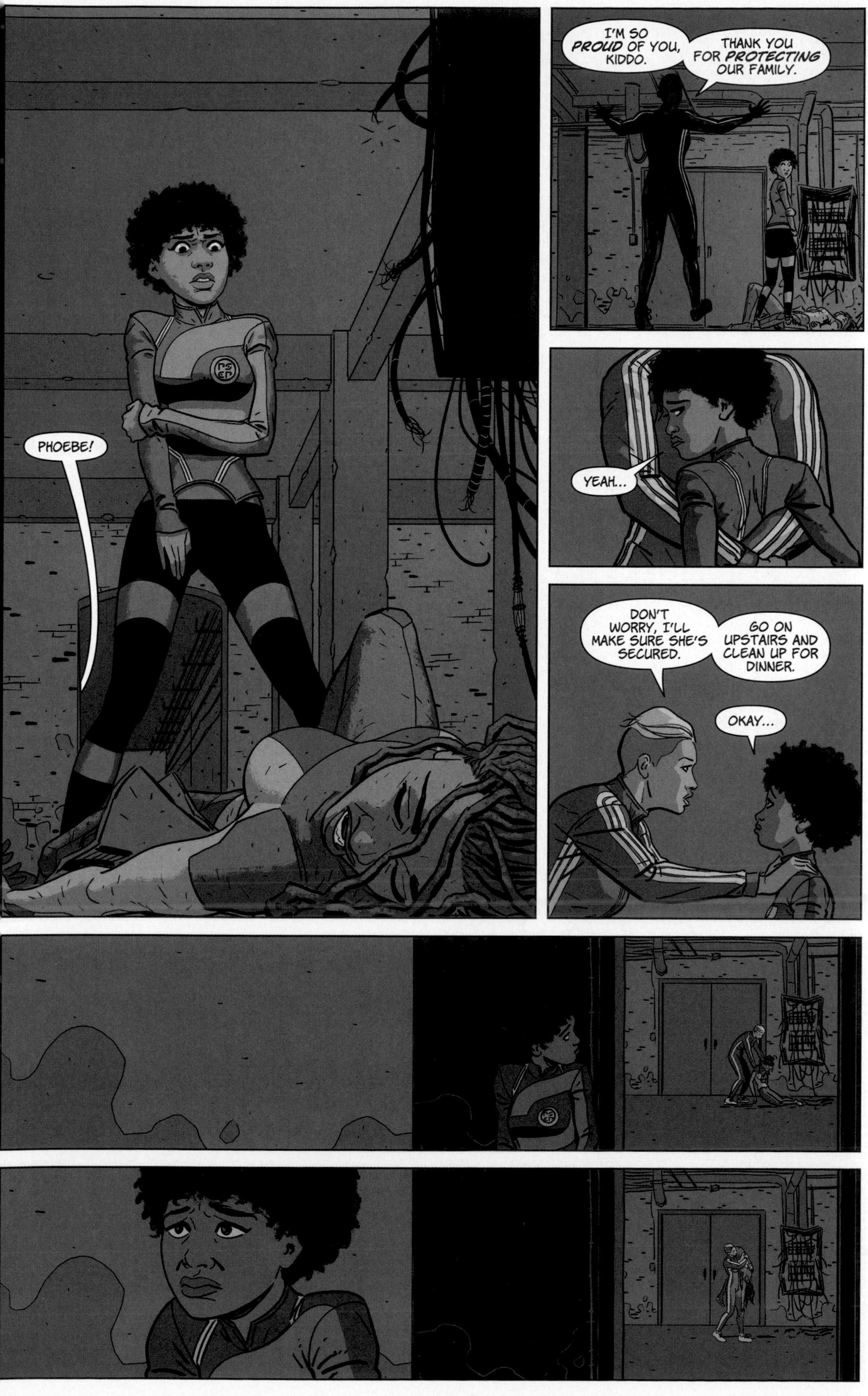
PHOEBE!
I'M SO PROUD OF YOU, KIDDO.
THANK YOU FOR PROTECTING OUR FAMILY.
YEAH...
DON'T WORRY, I'LL MAKE SURE SHE'S SECURED.
GO ON UPSTAIRS AND CLEAN UP FOR DINNER.
OKAY...

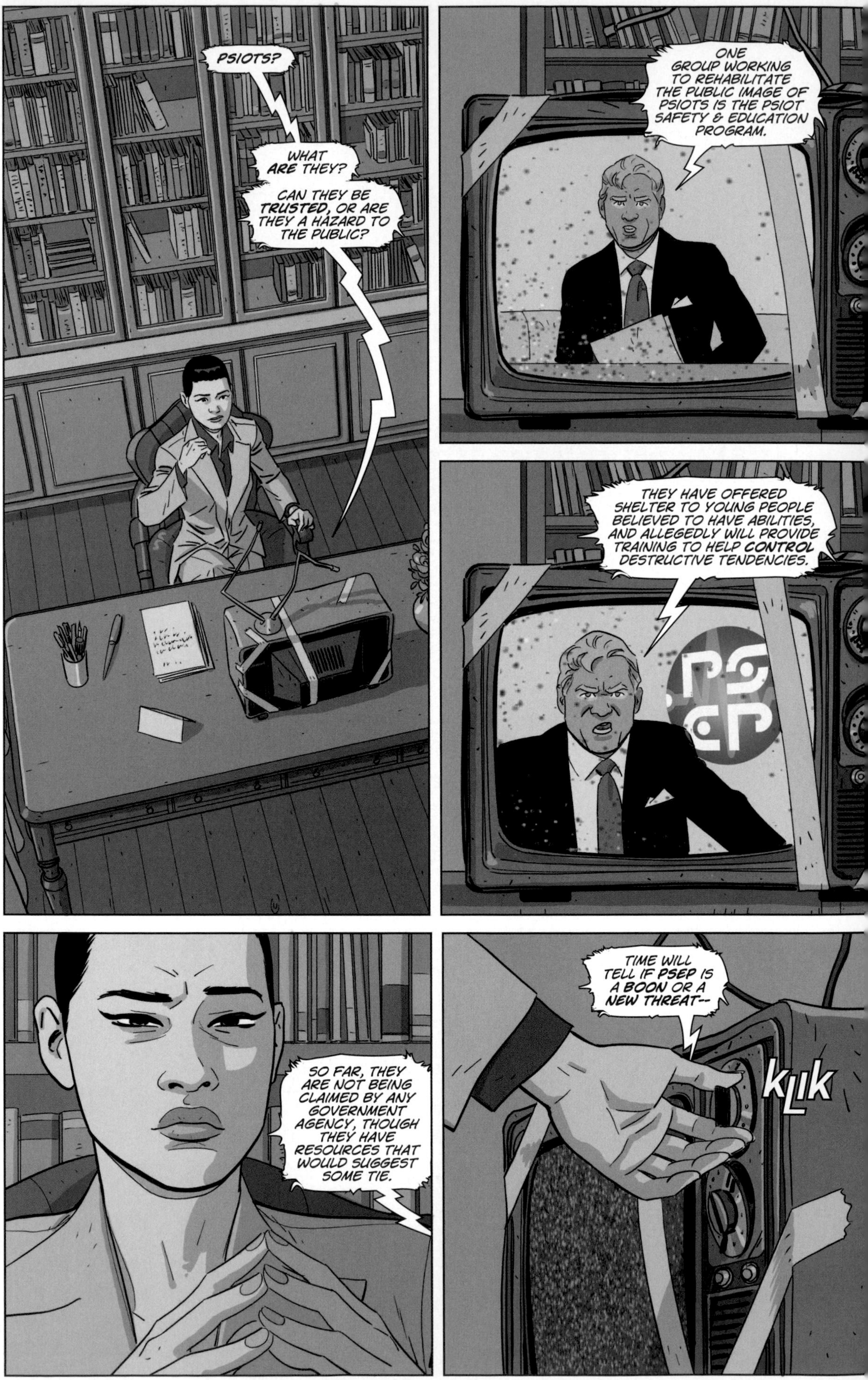
PSIOTS?
WHAT ARE THEY?
CAN THEY BE TRUSTED, OR ARE THEY A HAZARD TO THE PUBLIC?
ONE GROUP WORKING TO REHABILITATE THE PUBLIC IMAGE OF PSIOTS IS THE PSIOT SAFETY & EDUCATION PROGRAM.
THEY HAVE OFFERED SHELTER TO YOUNG PEOPLE BELIEVED TO HAVE ABILITIES, AND ALLEGEDLY WILL PROVIDE TRAINING TO HELP CONTROL DESTRUCTIVE TENDENCIES.
SO FAR, THEY ARE NOT BEING CLAIMED BY ANY GOVERNMENT AGENCY, THOUGH THEY HAVE RESOURCES THAT WOULD SUGGEST SOME TIE.
TIME WILL TELL IF PSEP IS A BOON OR A NEW THREAT--
KLIK

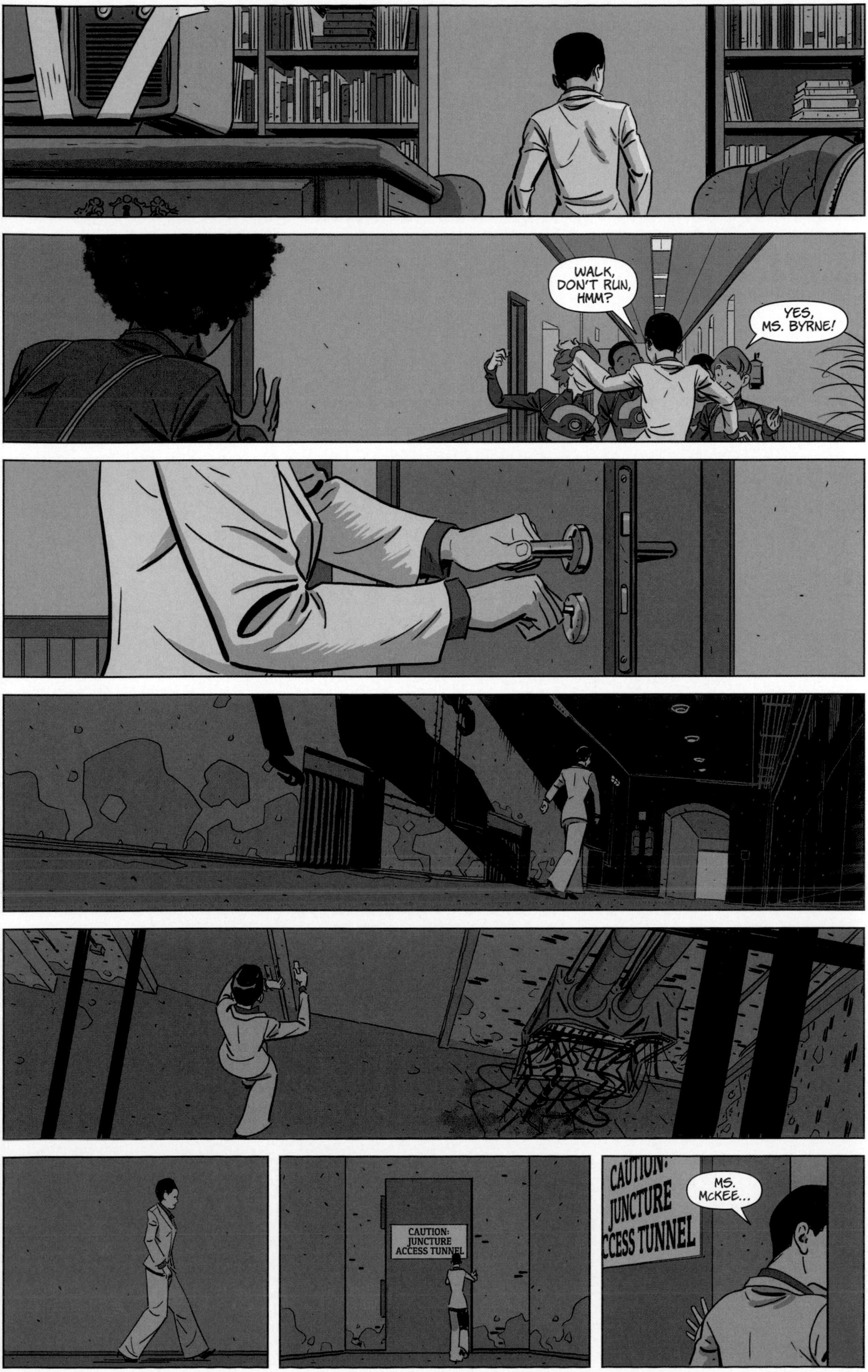
WALK, DON'T RUN, HMM?
YES, MS. BYRNE!
CAUTION: JUNCTURE ACCESS TUNNEL
CAUTION: JUNCTURE ACCESS TUNNEL
MS. McKEE...

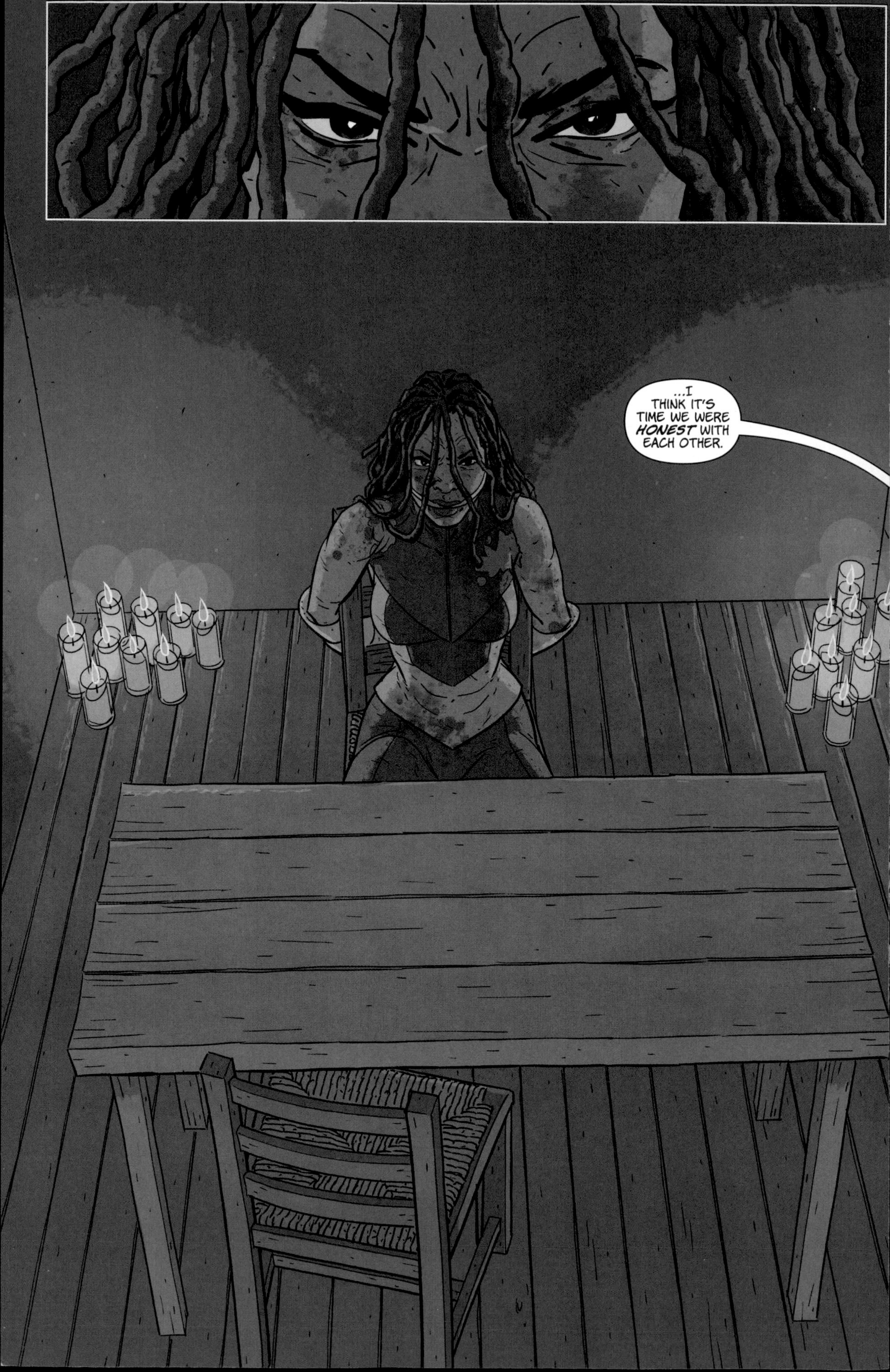
...I THINK IT'S TIME WE WERE *HONEST* WITH EACH OTHER.

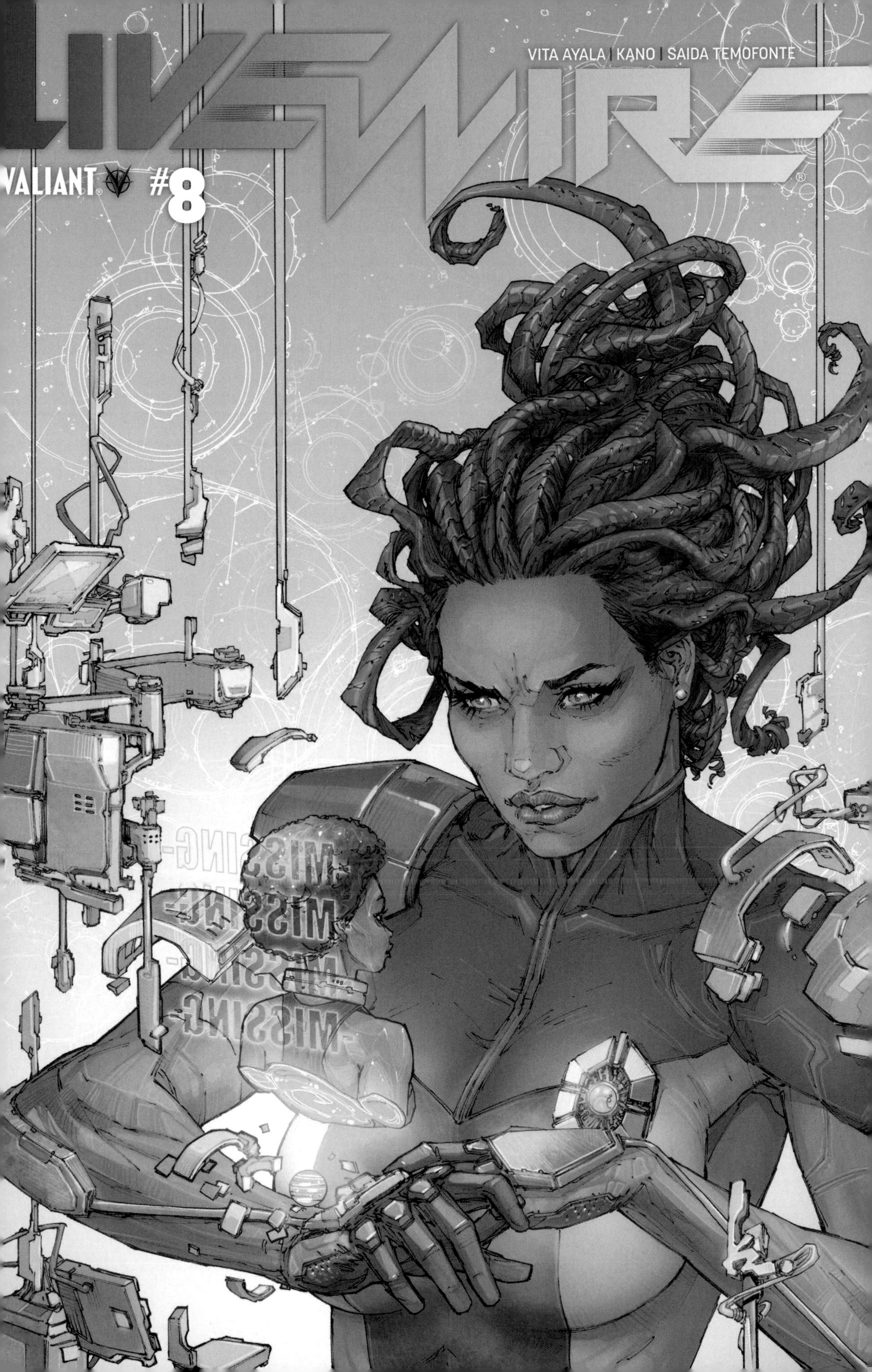
VITA AYALA | KANO | SAIDA TEMOFONTE
LIVEWIRE
VALIANT
#8
-MISSING-
-MISSING-
-MISSING-
-MISSING-

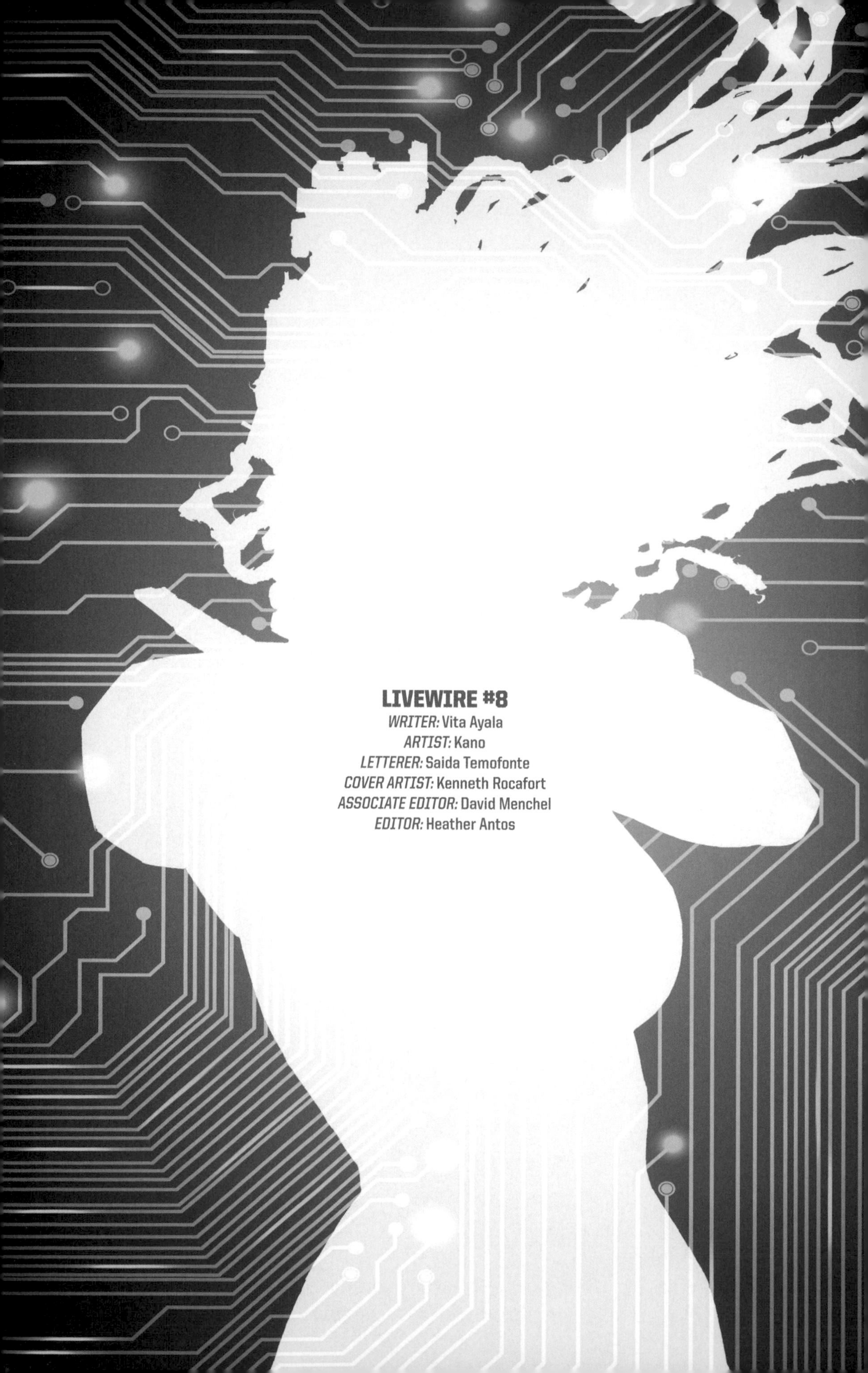

LIVEWIRE #8

WRITER: Vita Ayala
ARTIST: Kano
LETTERER: Saida Temofonte
COVER ARTIST: Kenneth Rocafort
ASSOCIATE EDITOR: David Menchel
EDITOR: Heather Antos

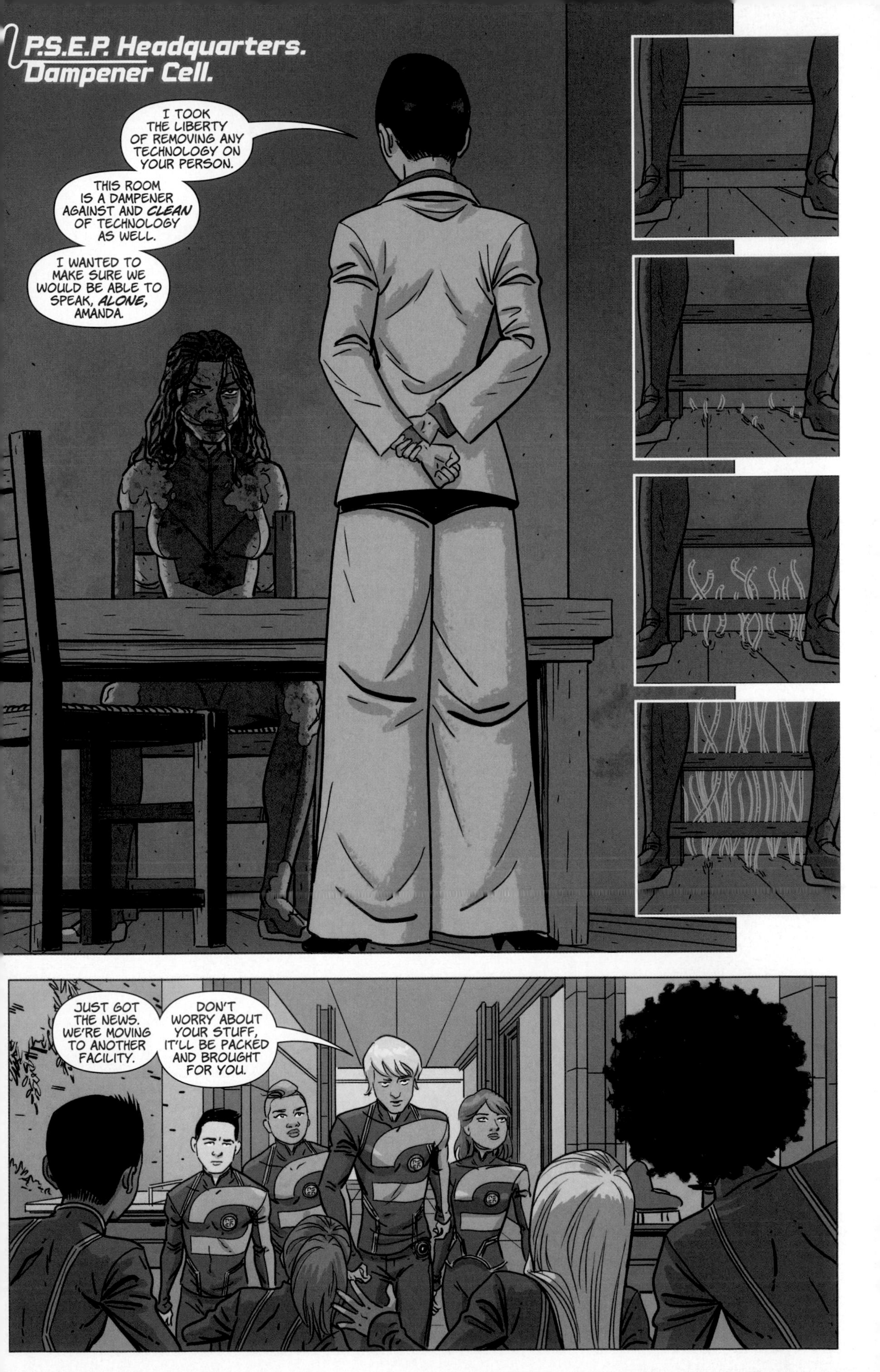
P.S.E.P. Headquarters.
Dampener Cell.
I TOOK THE LIBERTY OF REMOVING ANY TECHNOLOGY ON YOUR PERSON.
THIS ROOM IS A DAMPENER AGAINST AND CLEAN OF TECHNOLOGY AS WELL.
I WANTED TO MAKE SURE WE WOULD BE ABLE TO SPEAK, ALONE, AMANDA.
JUST GOT THE NEWS. WE'RE MOVING TO ANOTHER FACILITY.
DON'T WORRY ABOUT YOUR STUFF, IT'LL BE PACKED AND BROUGHT FOR YOU.

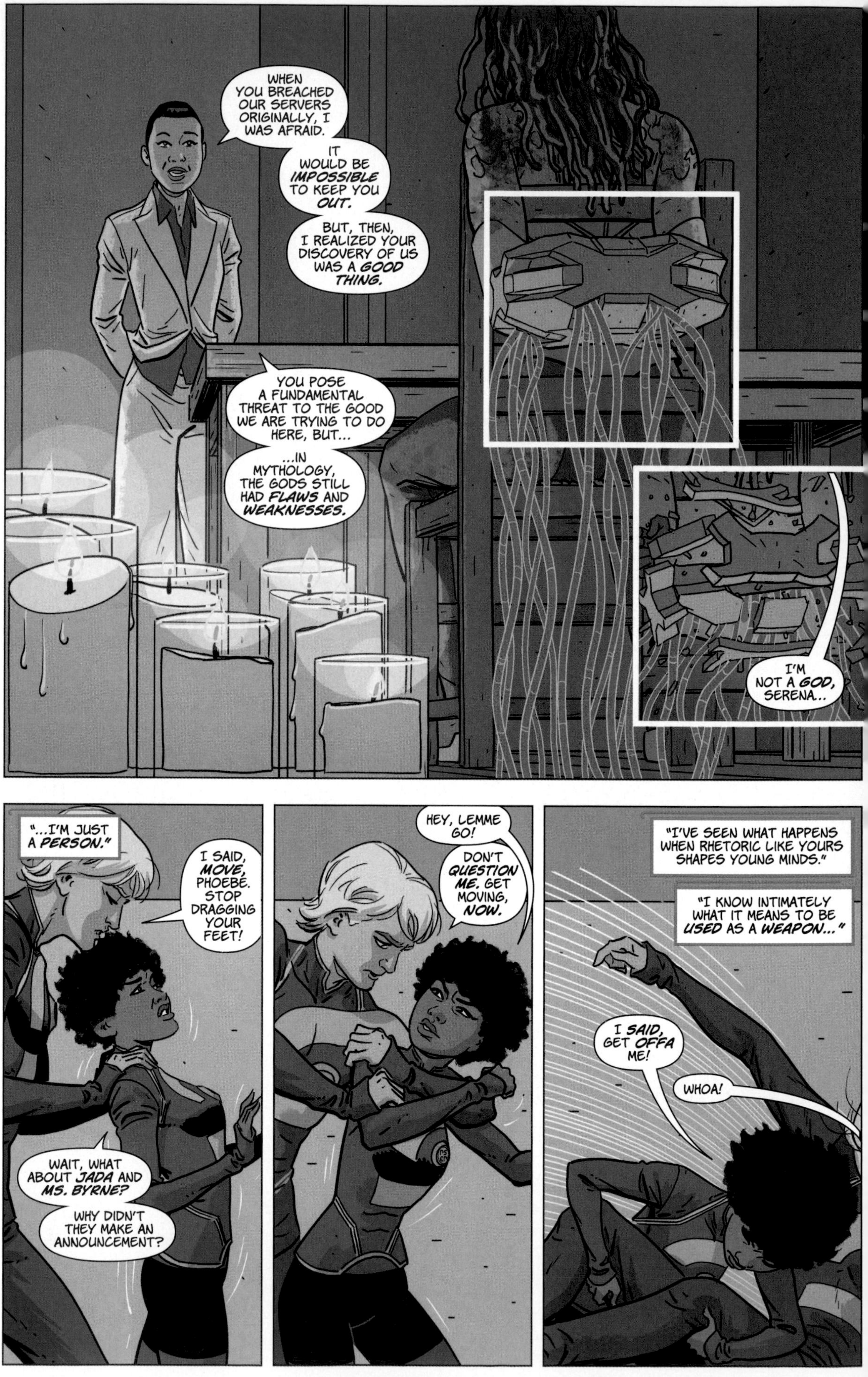
WHEN YOU BREACHED OUR SERVERS ORIGINALLY, I WAS AFRAID.
IT WOULD BE IMPOSSIBLE TO KEEP YOU OUT.
BUT, THEN, I REALIZED YOUR DISCOVERY OF US WAS A GOOD THING.
YOU POSE A FUNDAMENTAL THREAT TO THE GOOD WE ARE TRYING TO DO HERE, BUT...
...IN MYTHOLOGY, THE GODS STILL HAD FLAWS AND WEAKNESSES.
I'M NOT A GOD, SERENA...
"...I'M JUST A PERSON."
I SAID, MOVE, PHOEBE. STOP DRAGGING YOUR FEET!
WAIT, WHAT ABOUT JADA AND MS. BYRNE?
WHY DIDN'T THEY MAKE AN ANNOUNCEMENT?
HEY, LEMME GO!
DON'T QUESTION ME. GET MOVING, NOW.
"I'VE SEEN WHAT HAPPENS WHEN RHETORIC LIKE YOURS SHAPES YOUNG MINDS."
"I KNOW INTIMATELY WHAT IT MEANS TO BE USED AS A WEAPON..."
I SAID, GET OFFA ME!
WHOA!

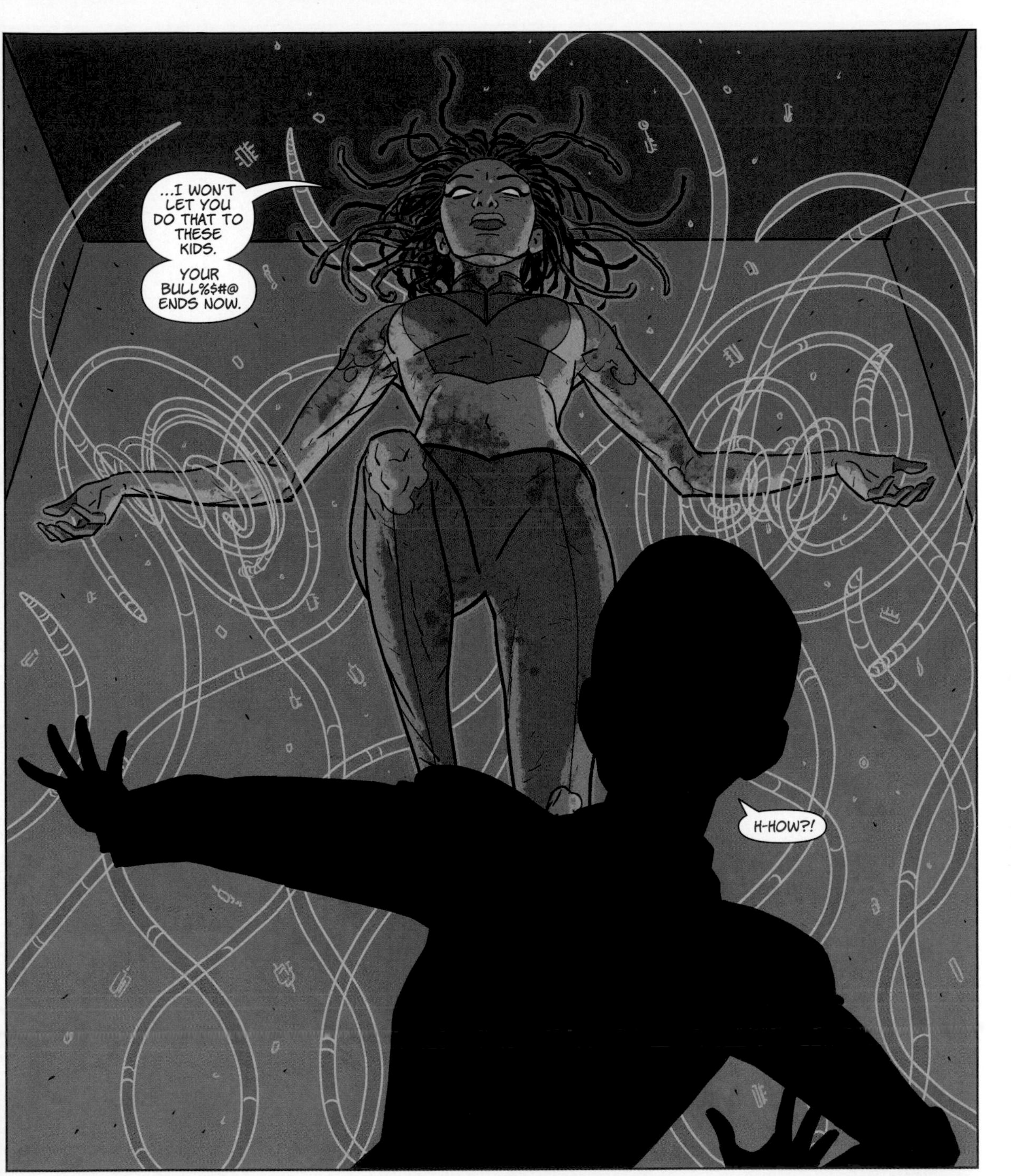
...I WON'T LET YOU DO THAT TO THESE KIDS.
YOUR BULL%$#@ ENDS NOW.
H-HOW?!

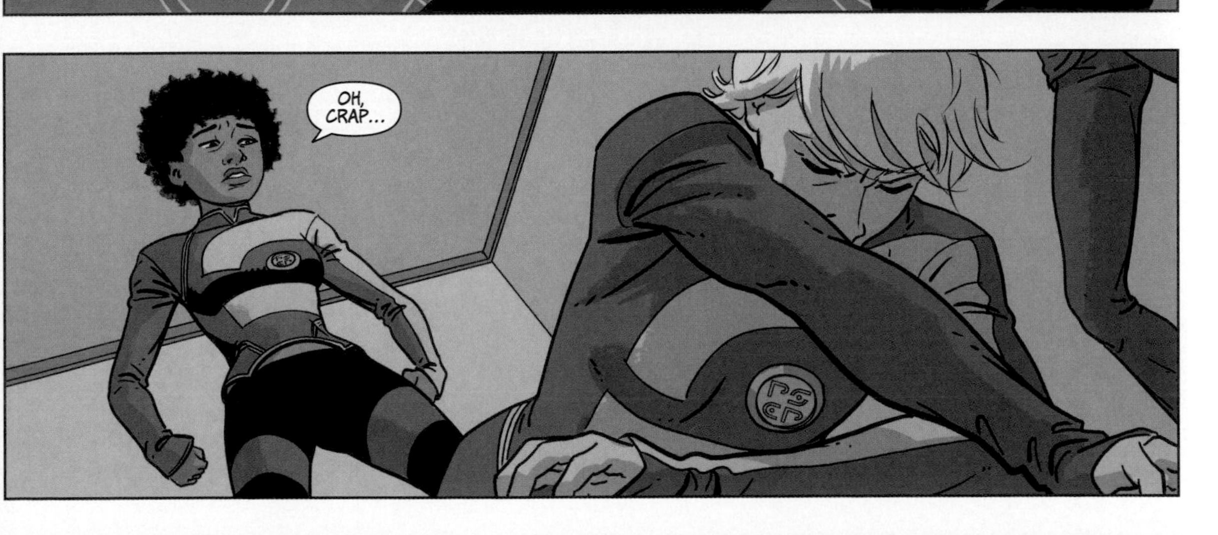
OH, CRAP...

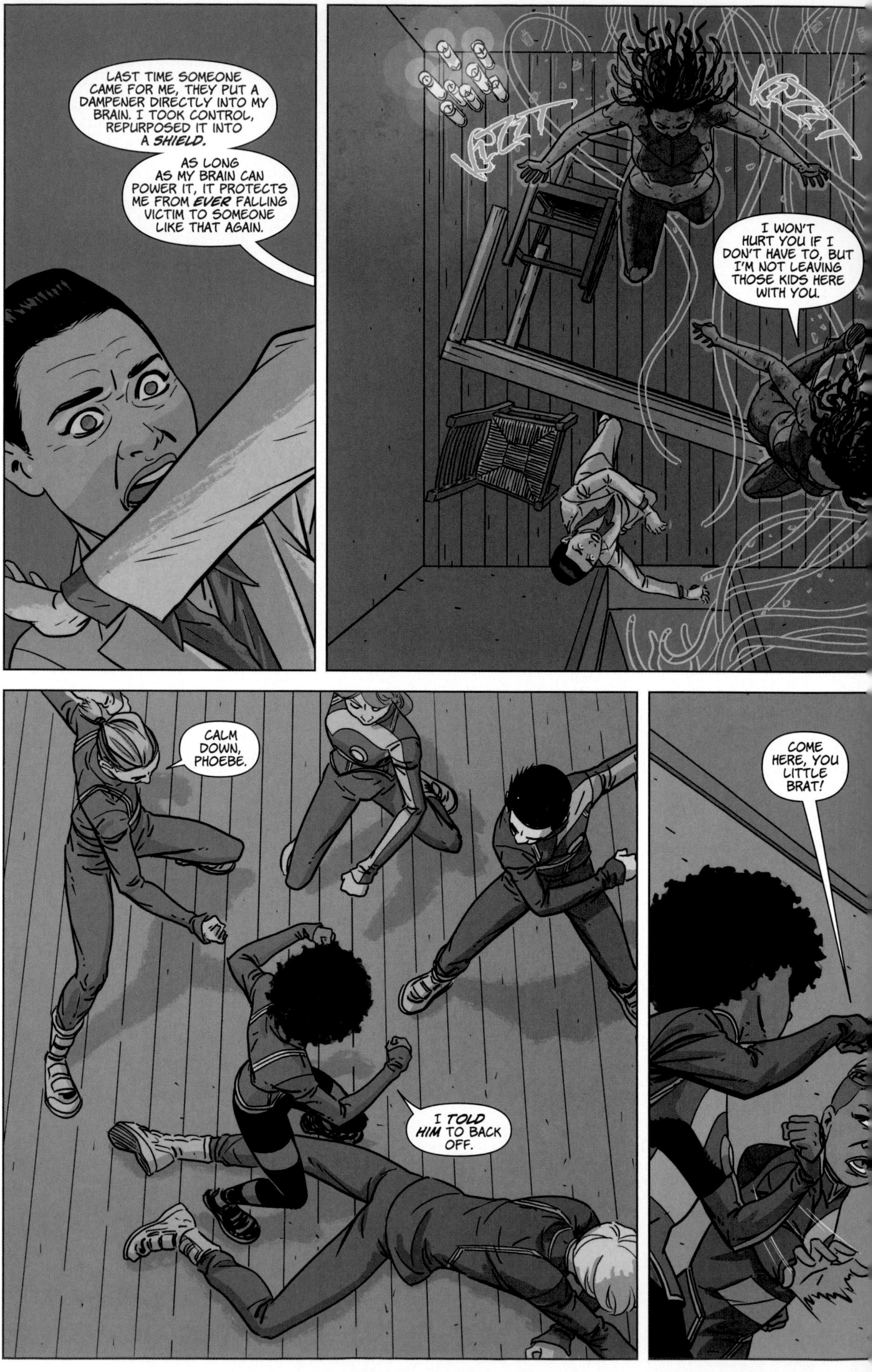
LAST TIME SOMEONE CAME FOR ME, THEY PUT A DAMPENER DIRECTLY INTO MY BRAIN. I TOOK CONTROL, REPURPOSED IT INTO A *SHIELD.*
AS LONG AS MY BRAIN CAN POWER IT, IT PROTECTS ME FROM *EVER* FALLING VICTIM TO SOMEONE LIKE THAT AGAIN.
KRZZT
KRZZT
I WON'T HURT YOU IF I DON'T HAVE TO, BUT I'M NOT LEAVING THOSE KIDS HERE WITH YOU.
CALM DOWN, PHOEBE.
I *TOLD HIM* TO BACK OFF.
COME HERE, YOU LITTLE BRAT!

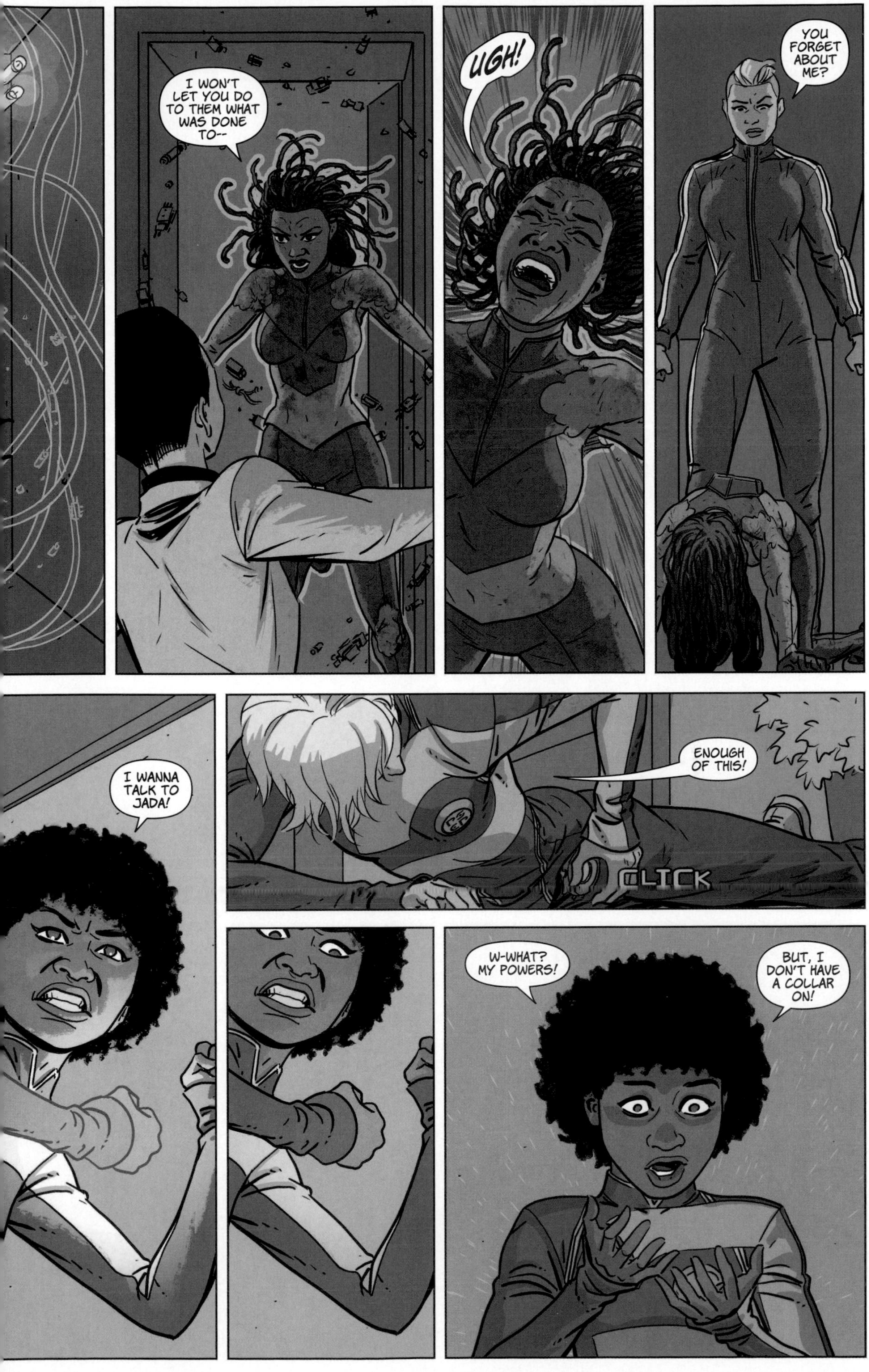
I WON'T LET YOU DO TO THEM WHAT WAS DONE TO--
UGH!
YOU FORGET ABOUT ME?
I WANNA TALK TO JADA!
ENOUGH OF THIS!
CLICK
W-WHAT? MY POWERS!
BUT, I DON'T HAVE A COLLAR ON!

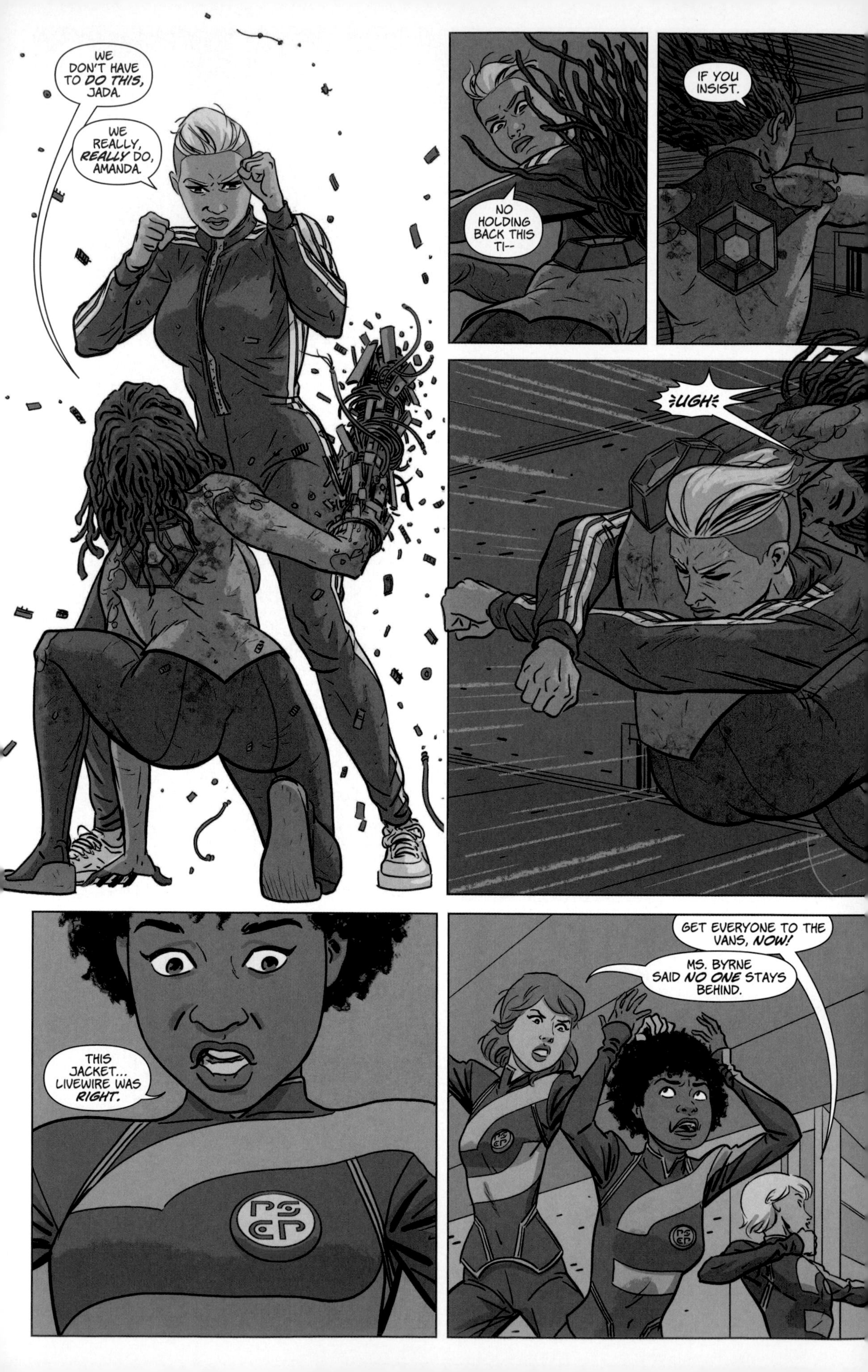
WE DON'T HAVE TO DO THIS, JADA.
WE REALLY, REALLY DO, AMANDA.
NO HOLDING BACK THIS TI--
IF YOU INSIST.
UGH
THIS JACKET... LIVEWIRE WAS RIGHT.
GET EVERYONE TO THE VANS, NOW!
MS. BYRNE SAID NO ONE STAYS BEHIND.

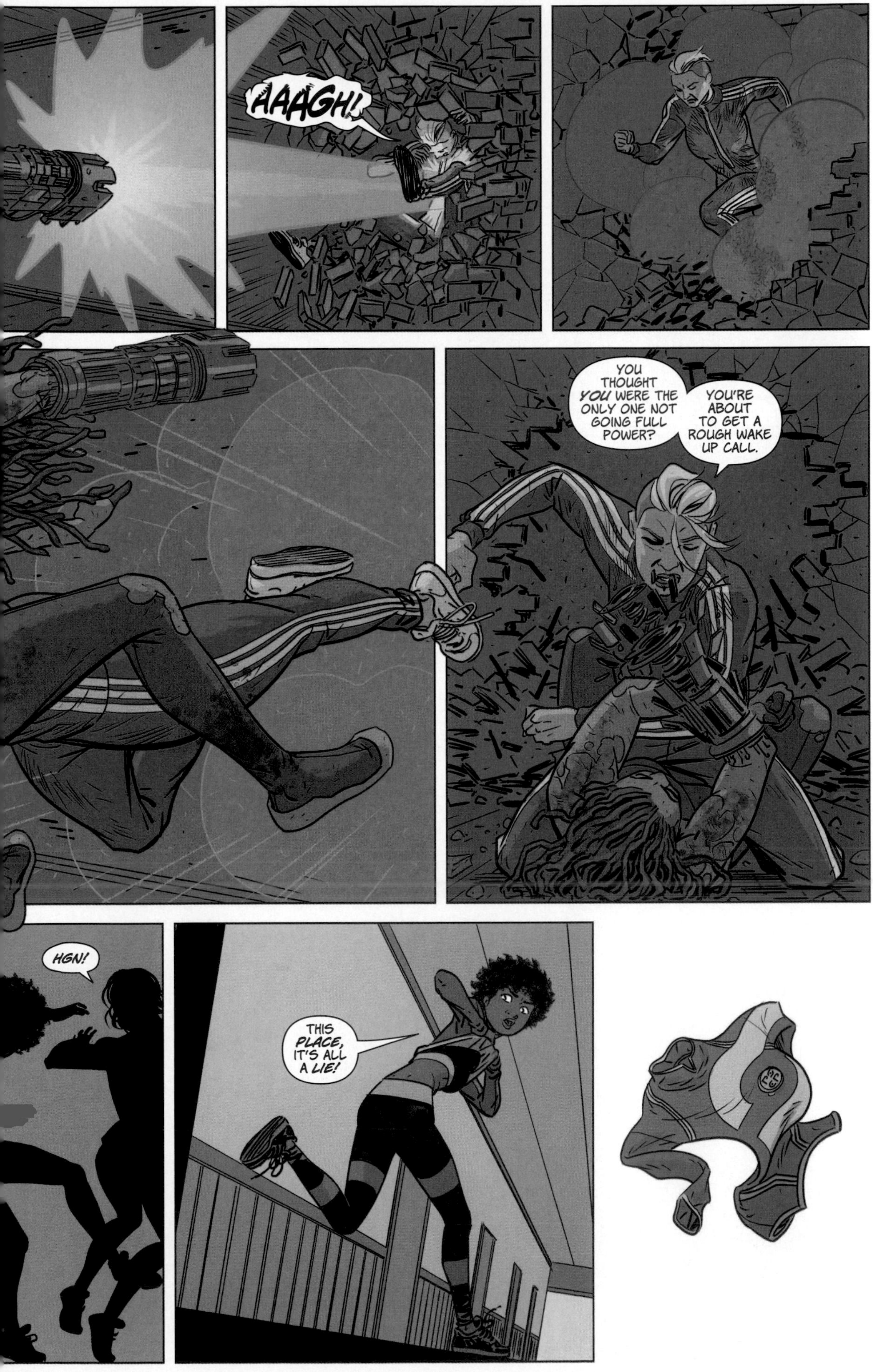
AAAGH!
YOU THOUGHT YOU WERE THE ONLY ONE NOT GOING FULL POWER?
YOU'RE ABOUT TO GET A ROUGH WAKE UP CALL.
HGN!
THIS PLACE, IT'S ALL A LIE!

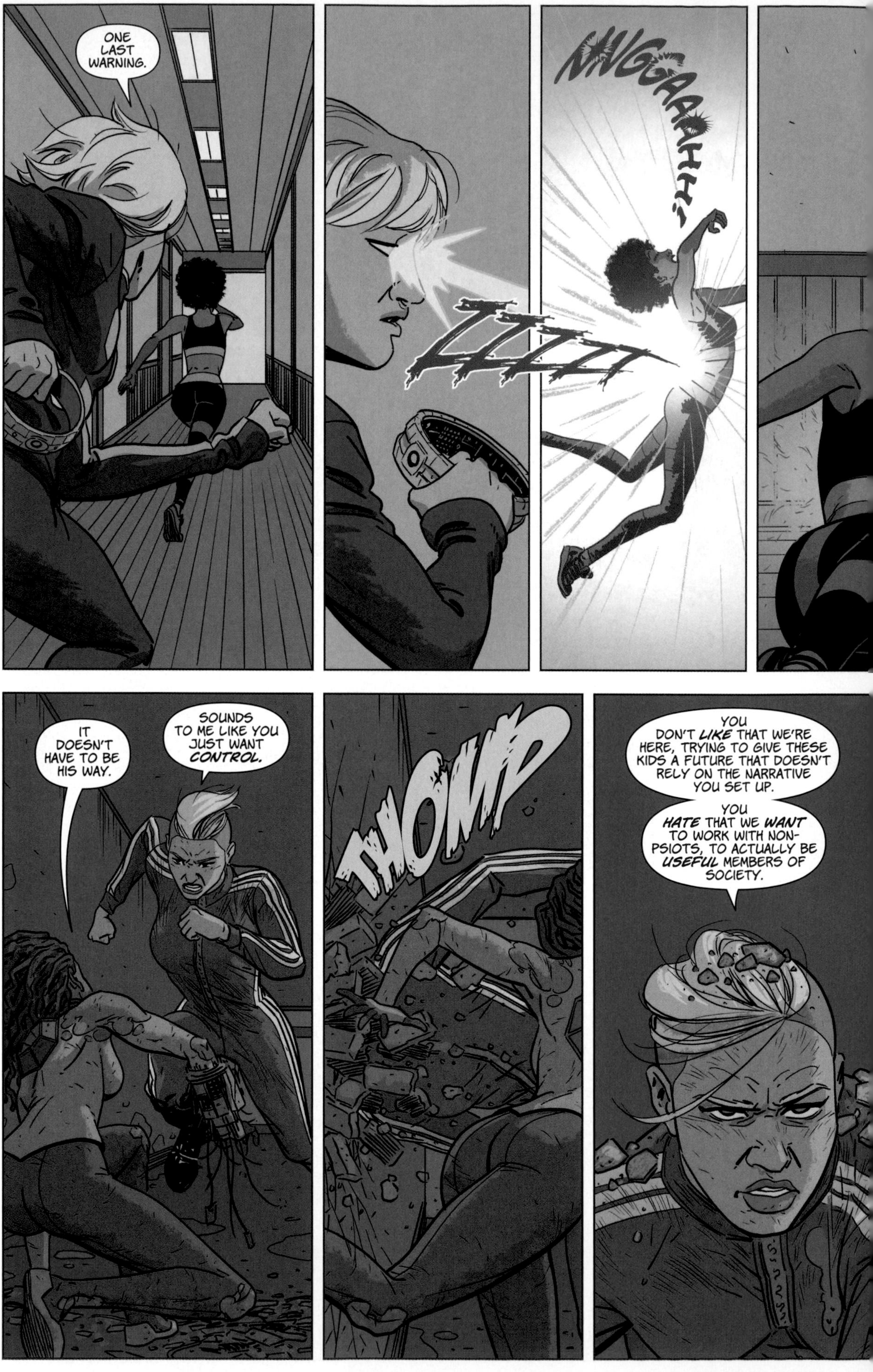
ONE LAST WARNING.
NNGGAAAHHH!!
ZZZZ
IT DOESN'T HAVE TO BE HIS WAY.
SOUNDS TO ME LIKE YOU JUST WANT *CONTROL.*
THOMP
YOU DON'T *LIKE* THAT WE'RE HERE, TRYING TO GIVE THESE KIDS A FUTURE THAT DOESN'T RELY ON THE NARRATIVE YOU SET UP.
YOU *HATE* THAT WE *WANT* TO WORK WITH NON-PSIOTS, TO ACTUALLY BE *USEFUL* MEMBERS OF SOCIETY.

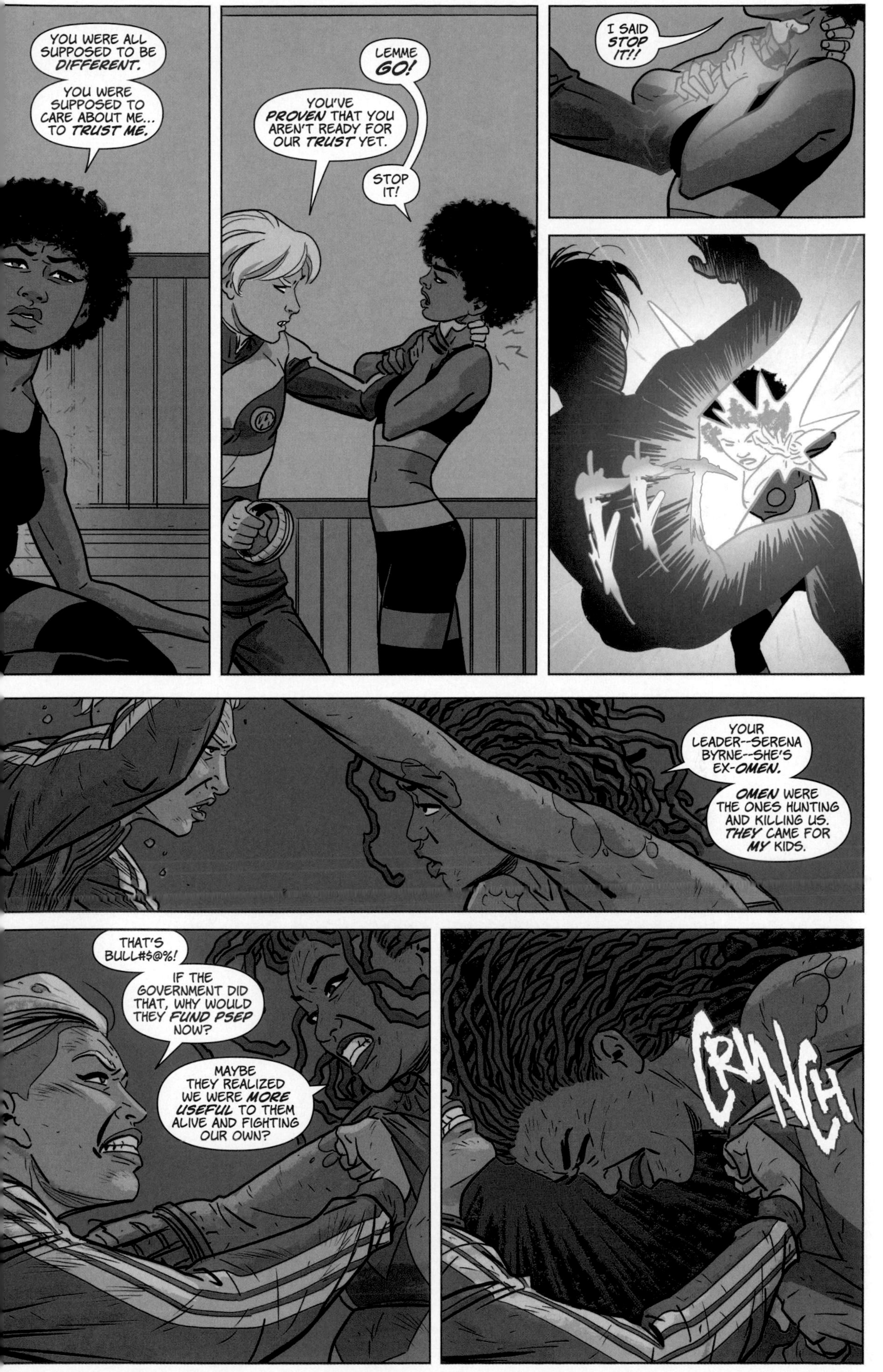
YOU WERE ALL SUPPOSED TO BE DIFFERENT.
YOU WERE SUPPOSED TO CARE ABOUT ME... TO TRUST ME.
LEMME GO!
YOU'VE PROVEN THAT YOU AREN'T READY FOR OUR TRUST YET.
STOP IT!
I SAID STOP IT!!
YOUR LEADER--SERENA BYRNE--SHE'S EX-OMEN.
OMEN WERE THE ONES HUNTING AND KILLING US. THEY CAME FOR MY KIDS.
THAT'S BULL#$@%!
IF THE GOVERNMENT DID THAT, WHY WOULD THEY FUND PSEP NOW?
MAYBE THEY REALIZED WE WERE MORE USEFUL TO THEM ALIVE AND FIGHTING OUR OWN?
CRUNCH

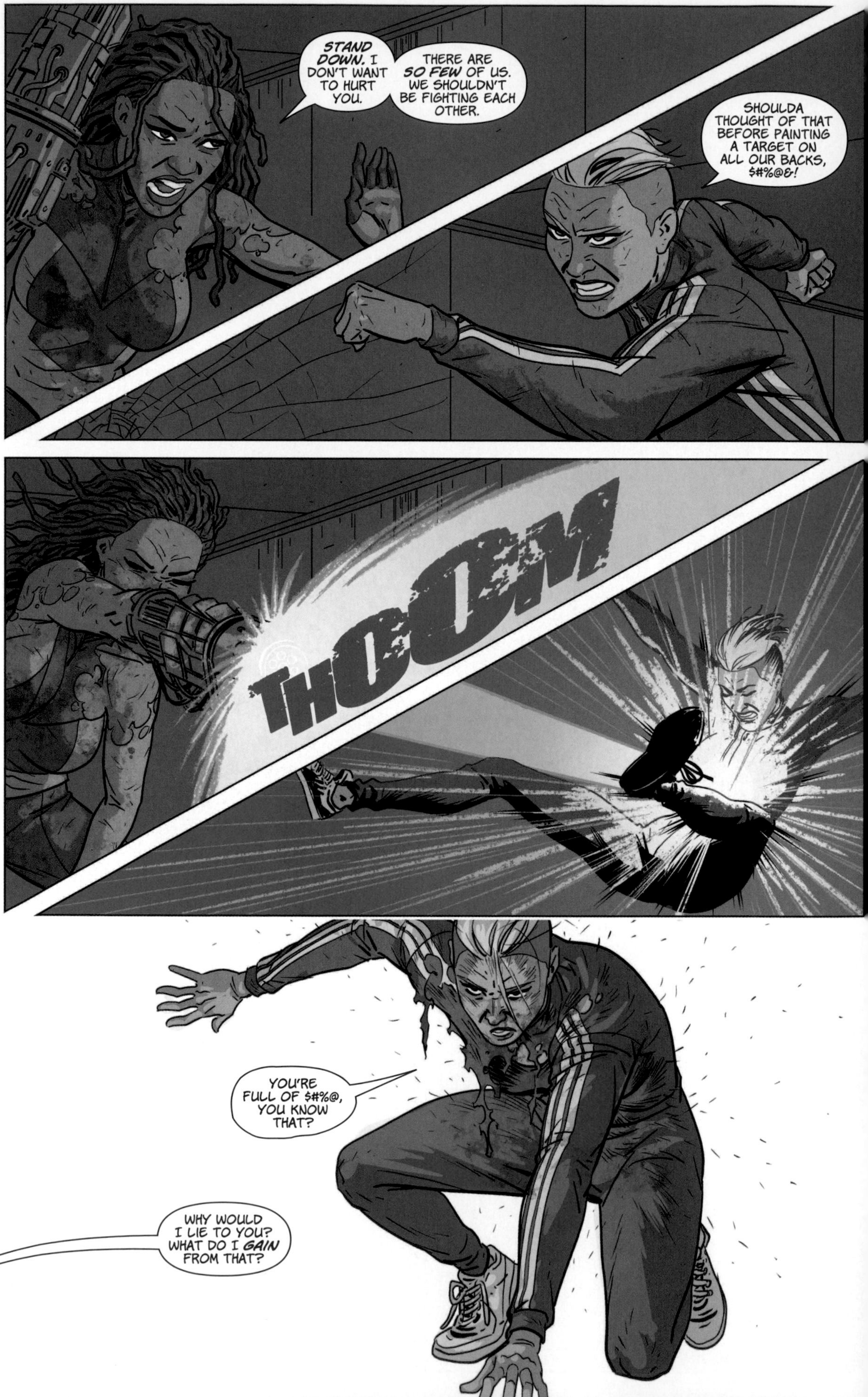
STAND DOWN. I DON'T WANT TO HURT YOU.
THERE ARE SO FEW OF US. WE SHOULDN'T BE FIGHTING EACH OTHER.
SHOULDA THOUGHT OF THAT BEFORE PAINTING A TARGET ON ALL OUR BACKS, $#%@&!
THOOM
YOU'RE FULL OF $#%@, YOU KNOW THAT?
WHY WOULD I LIE TO YOU? WHAT DO I GAIN FROM THAT?

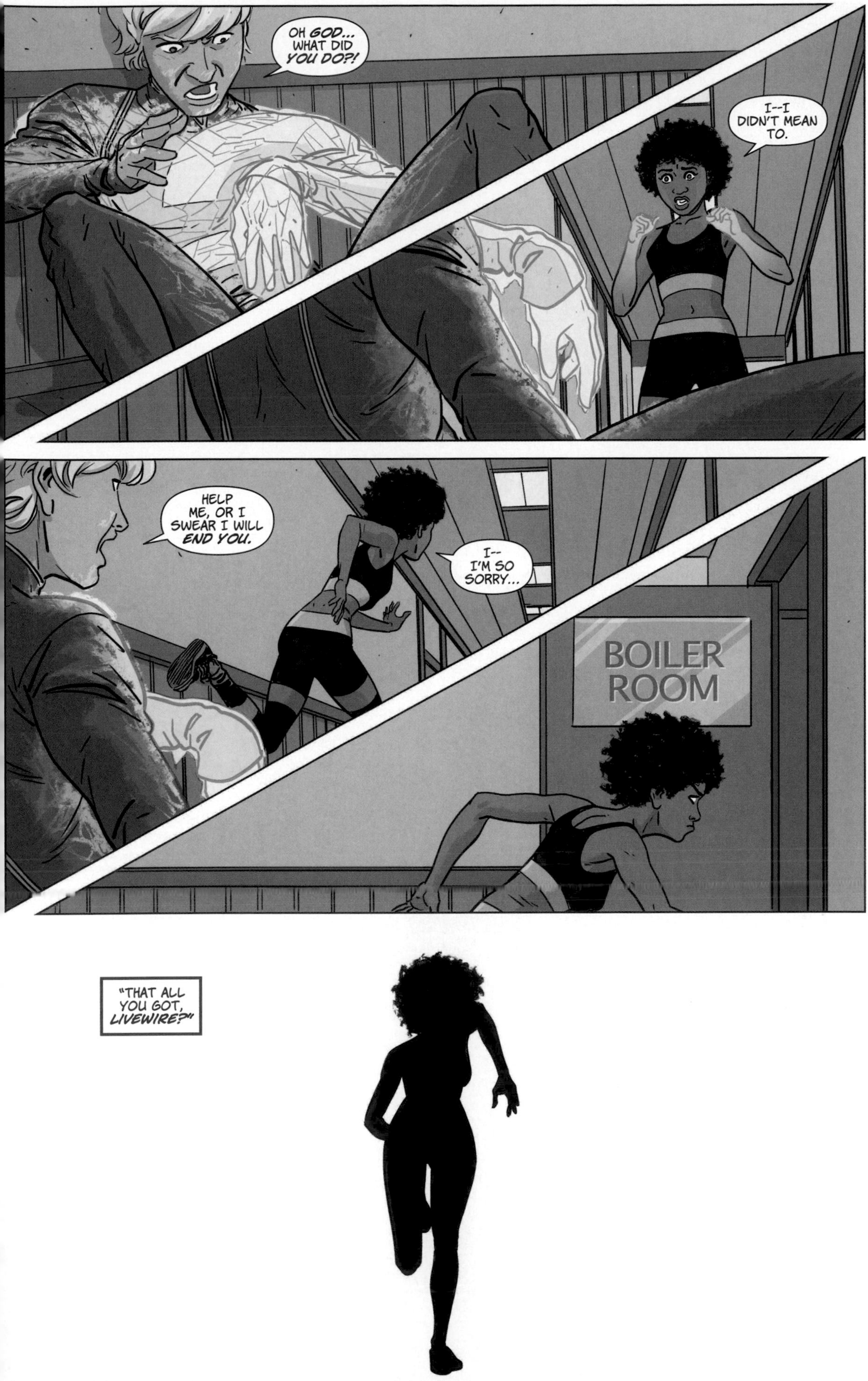

OH GOD... WHAT DID YOU DO?!
I--I DIDN'T MEAN TO.
HELP ME, OR I SWEAR I WILL END YOU.
I-- I'M SO SORRY...
BOILER ROOM
"THAT ALL YOU GOT, LIVEWIRE?"

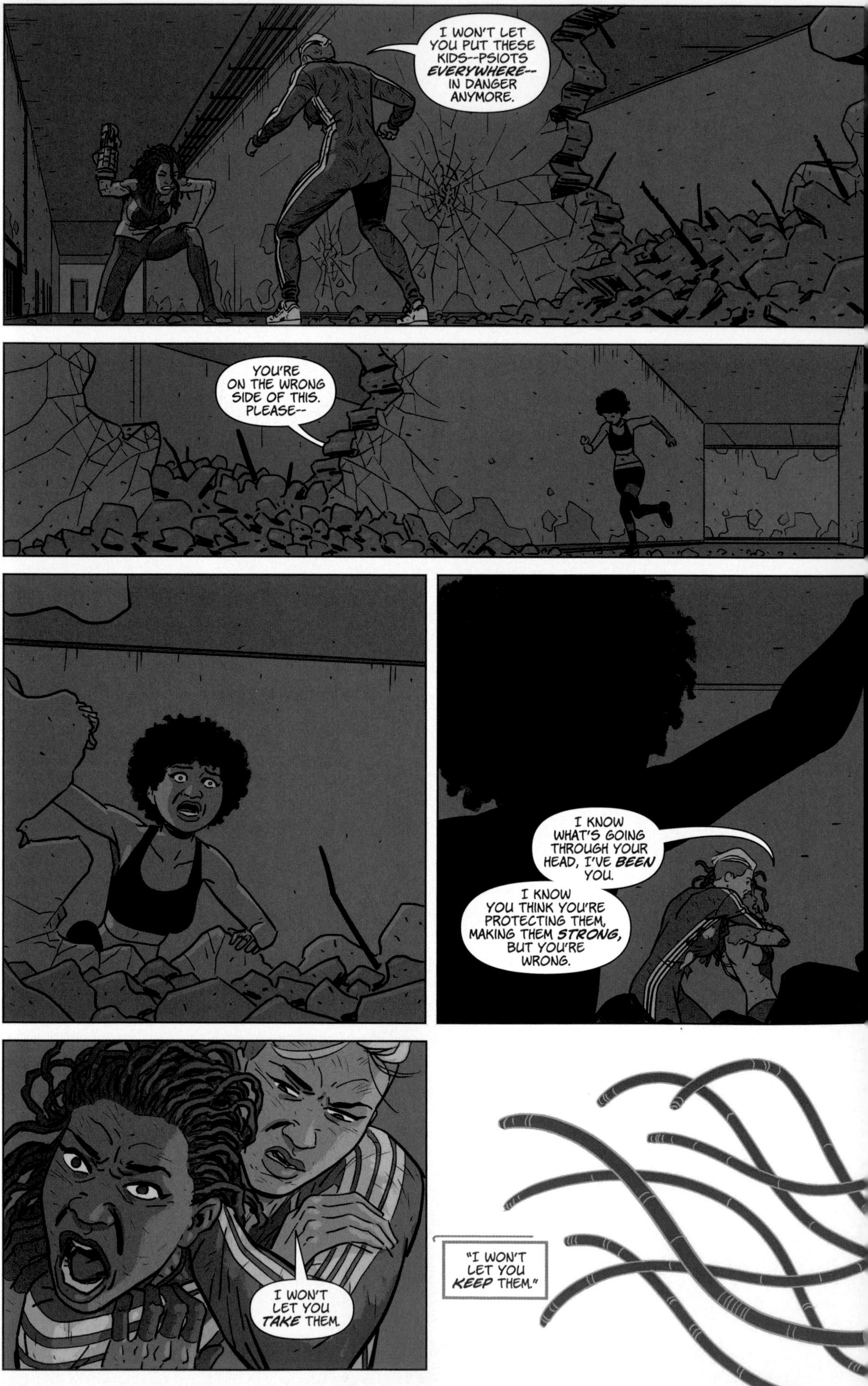
I WON'T LET YOU PUT THESE KIDS--PSIOTS EVERYWHERE--IN DANGER ANYMORE.
YOU'RE ON THE WRONG SIDE OF THIS. PLEASE--
I KNOW WHAT'S GOING THROUGH YOUR HEAD, I'VE BEEN YOU.
I KNOW YOU THINK YOU'RE PROTECTING THEM, MAKING THEM STRONG, BUT YOU'RE WRONG.
I WON'T LET YOU TAKE THEM.
"I WON'T LET YOU KEEP THEM."

THESE KIDS DESERVE TO NOT LIVE THEIR LIVES LOOKING OVER THEIR SHOULDERS.

THESE KIDS DESERVE THE CHANCE TO BE *CHILDREN.*

WE'RE GIVING THEM A *SECOND* CHANCE!

THUD!

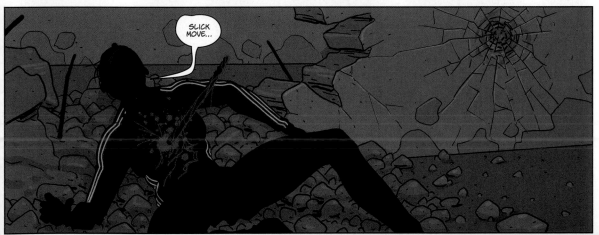

SLICK MOVE...

JADA? OH GOD...

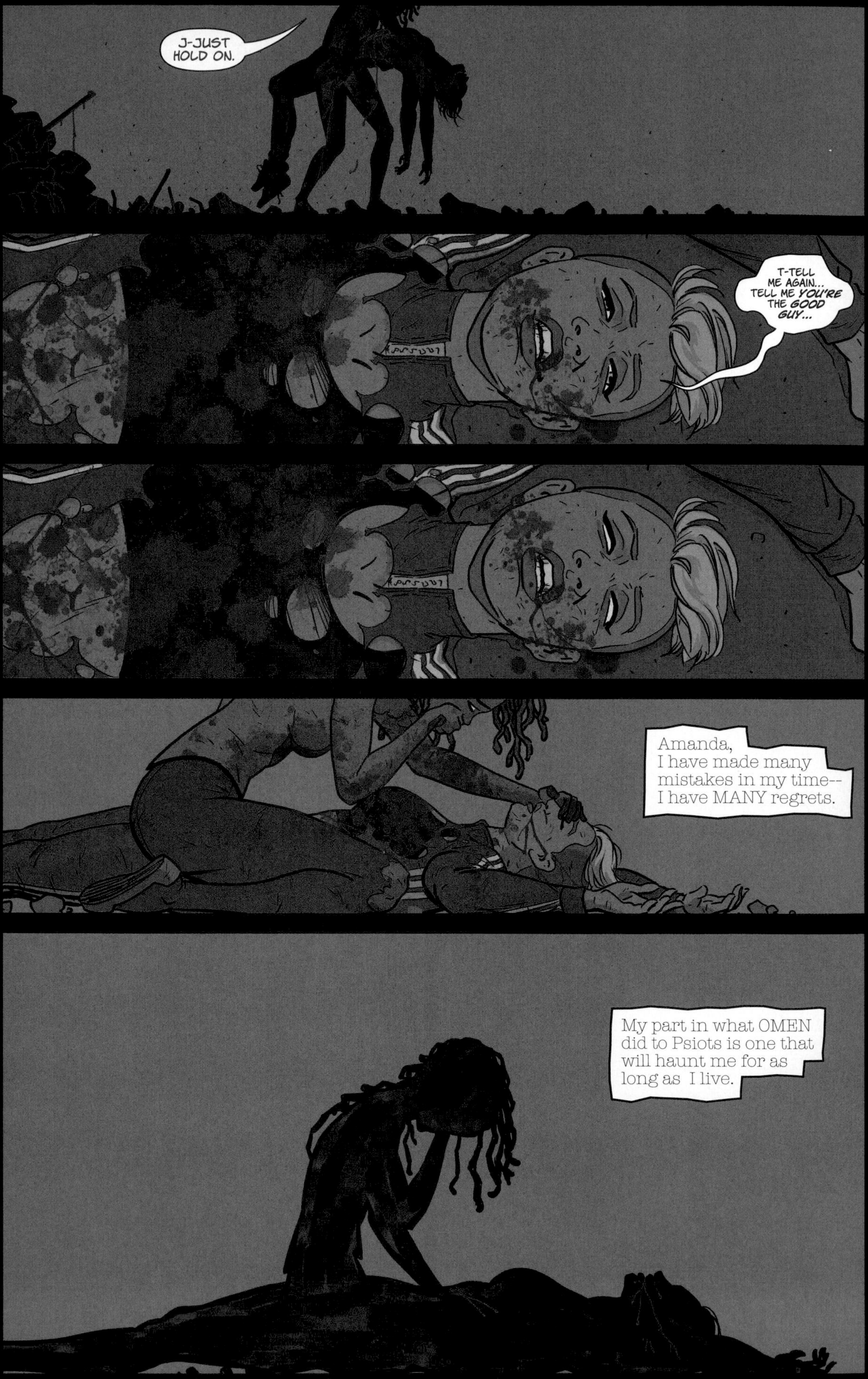
J-JUST HOLD ON.
T-TELL ME AGAIN... TELL ME YOU'RE THE GOOD GUY...
Amanda, I have made many mistakes in my time-- I have MANY regrets.
My part in what OMEN did to Psiots is one that will haunt me for as long as I live.

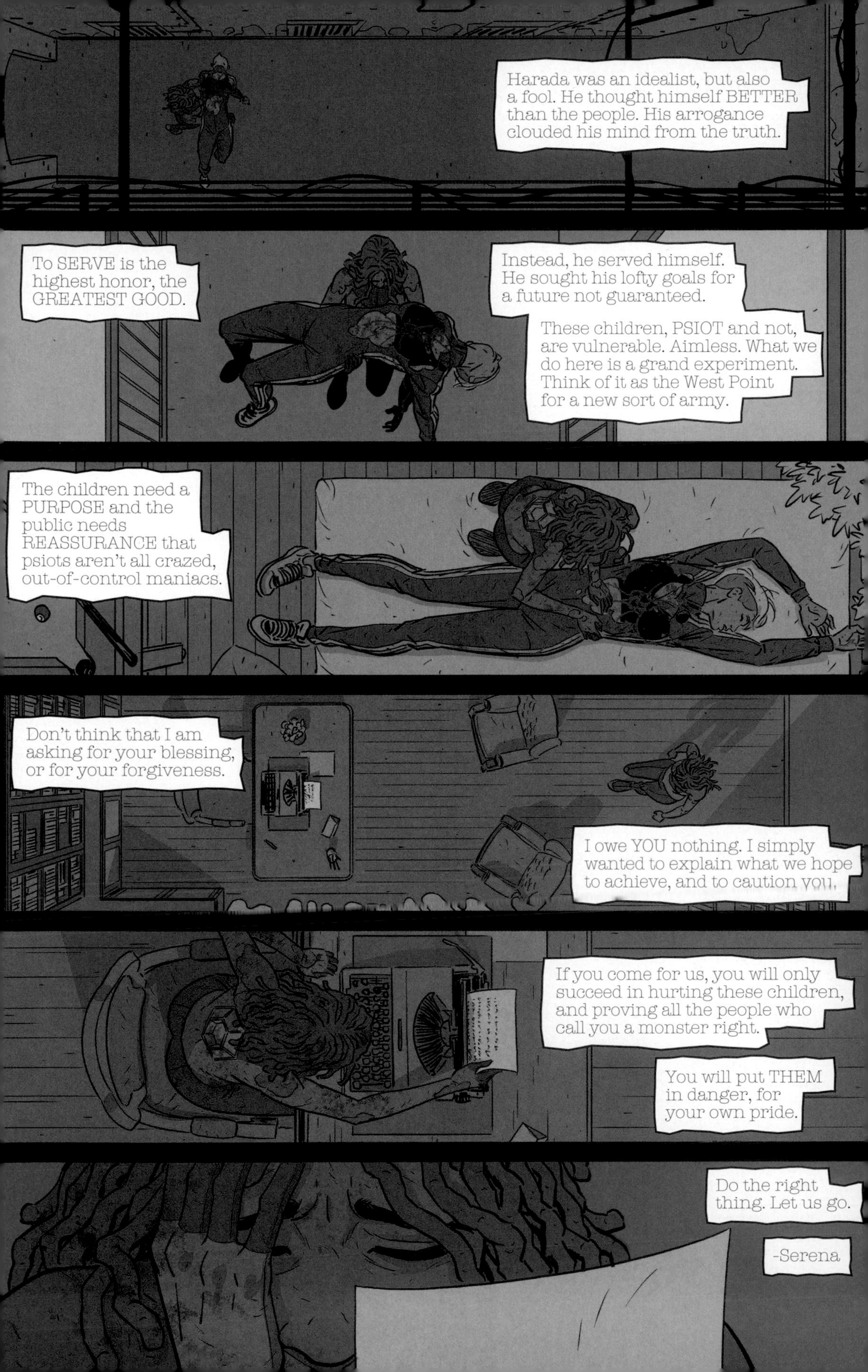

Harada was an idealist, but also a fool. He thought himself BETTER than the people. His arrogance clouded his mind from the truth.
To SERVE is the highest honor, the GREATEST GOOD.
Instead, he served himself. He sought his lofty goals for a future not guaranteed.
These children, PSIOT and not, are vulnerable. Aimless. What we do here is a grand experiment. Think of it as the West Point for a new sort of army.
The children need a PURPOSE and the public needs REASSURANCE that psiots aren't all crazed, out-of-control maniacs.
Don't think that I am asking for your blessing, or for your forgiveness.
I owe YOU nothing. I simply wanted to explain what we hope to achieve, and to caution you.
If you come for us, you will only succeed in hurting these children, and proving all the people who call you a monster right.
You will put THEM in danger, for your own pride.
Do the right thing. Let us go.
-Serena

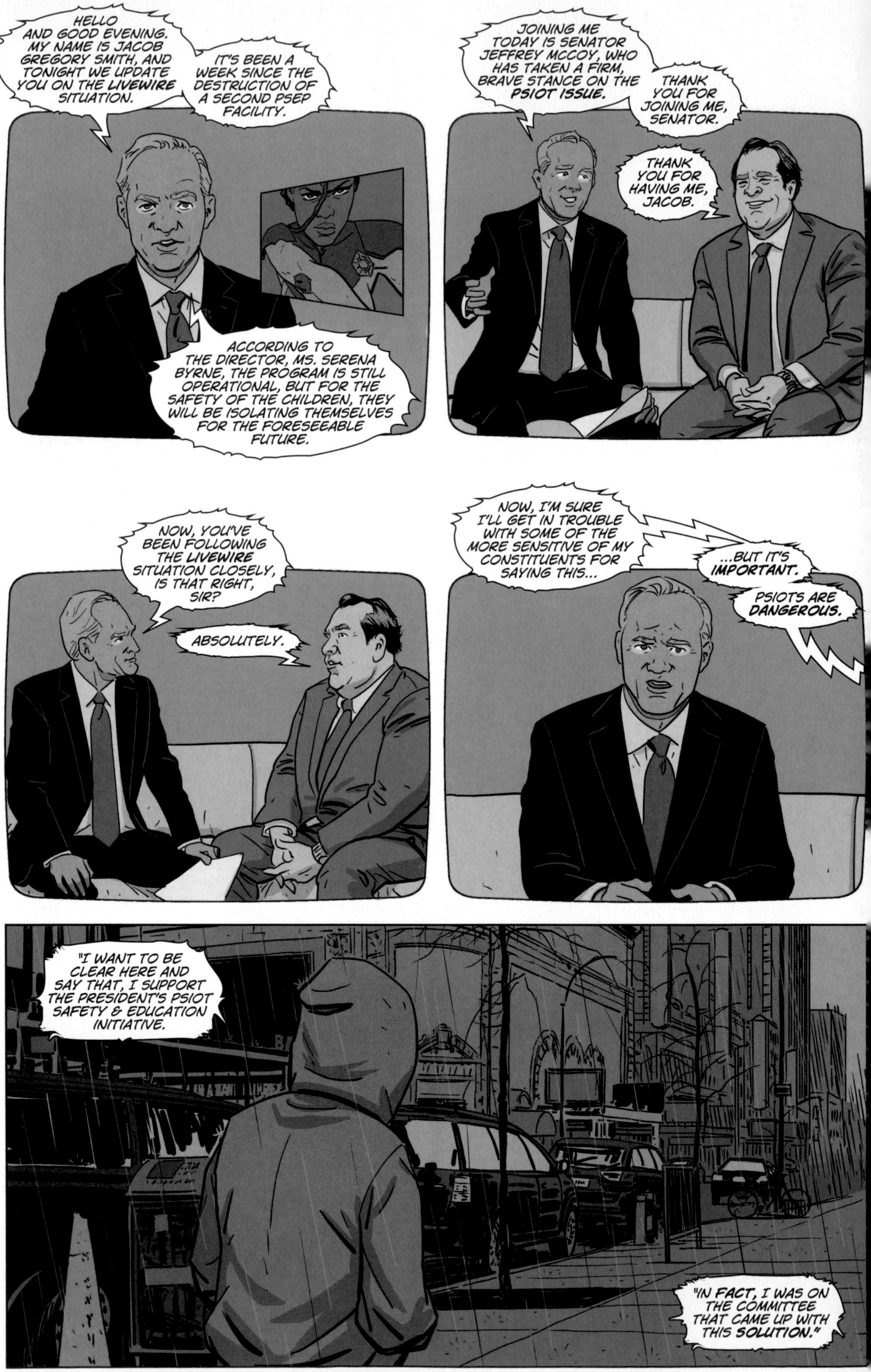
HELLO AND GOOD EVENING. MY NAME IS JACOB GREGORY SMITH, AND TONIGHT WE UPDATE YOU ON THE LIVEWIRE SITUATION.
IT'S BEEN A WEEK SINCE THE DESTRUCTION OF A SECOND PSEP FACILITY.
ACCORDING TO THE DIRECTOR, MS. SERENA BYRNE, THE PROGRAM IS STILL OPERATIONAL, BUT FOR THE SAFETY OF THE CHILDREN, THEY WILL BE ISOLATING THEMSELVES FOR THE FORESEEABLE FUTURE.
JOINING ME TODAY IS SENATOR JEFFREY MCCOY, WHO HAS TAKEN A FIRM, BRAVE STANCE ON THE PSIOT ISSUE.
THANK YOU FOR JOINING ME, SENATOR.
THANK YOU FOR HAVING ME, JACOB.
NOW, YOU'VE BEEN FOLLOWING THE LIVEWIRE SITUATION CLOSELY, IS THAT RIGHT, SIR?
ABSOLUTELY.
NOW, I'M SURE I'LL GET IN TROUBLE WITH SOME OF THE MORE SENSITIVE OF MY CONSTITUENTS FOR SAYING THIS...
...BUT IT'S IMPORTANT.
PSIOTS ARE DANGEROUS.
"I WANT TO BE CLEAR HERE AND SAY THAT, I SUPPORT THE PRESIDENT'S PSIOT SAFETY & EDUCATION INITIATIVE.
"IN FACT, I WAS ON THE COMMITTEE THAT CAME UP WITH THIS SOLUTION."

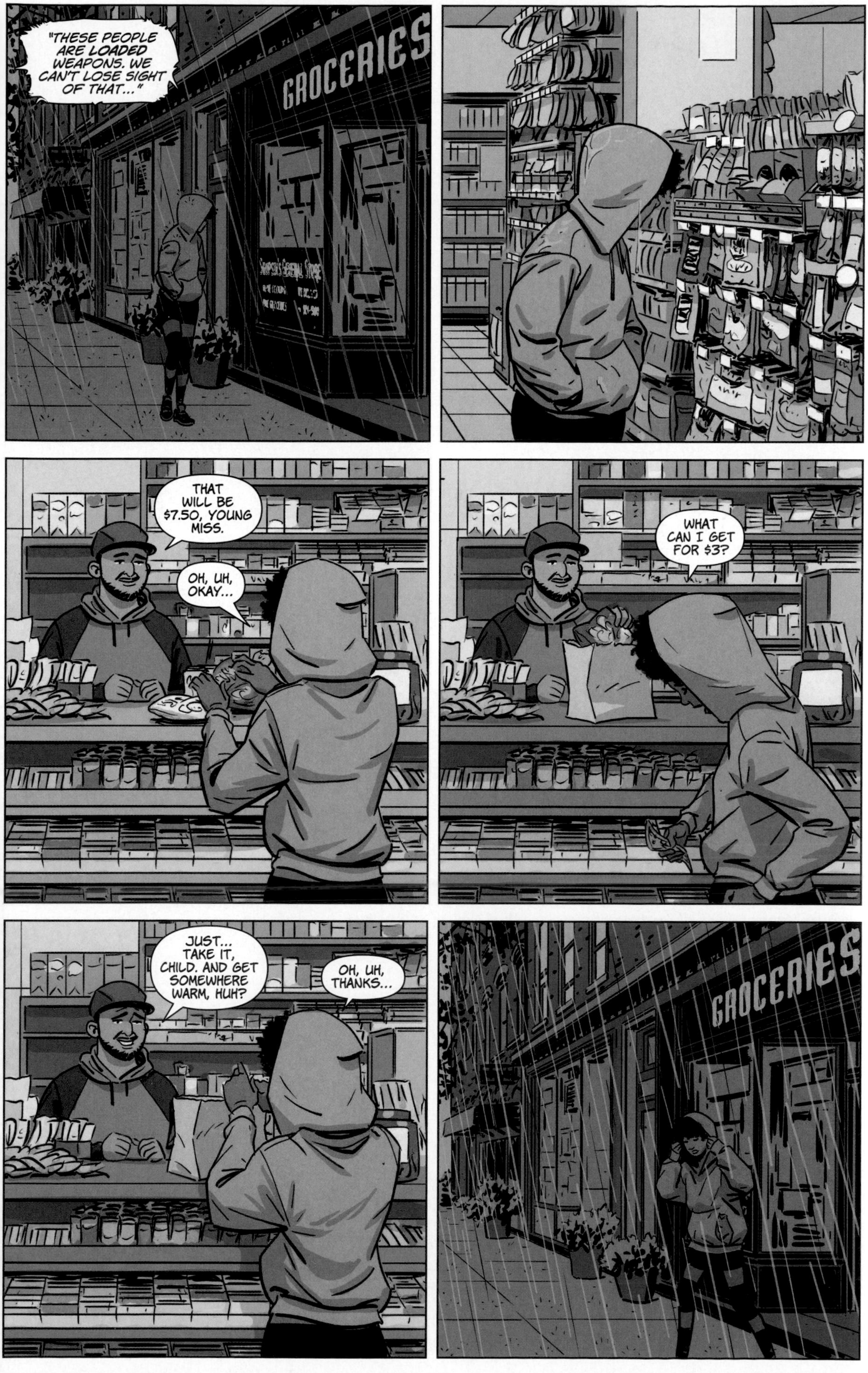
"THESE PEOPLE ARE LOADED WEAPONS. WE CAN'T LOSE SIGHT OF THAT..."
GROCERIES
THAT WILL BE $7.50, YOUNG MISS.
OH, UH, OKAY...
WHAT CAN I GET FOR $3?
JUST... TAKE IT, CHILD. AND GET SOMEWHERE WARM, HUH?
OH, UH, THANKS...
GROCERIES

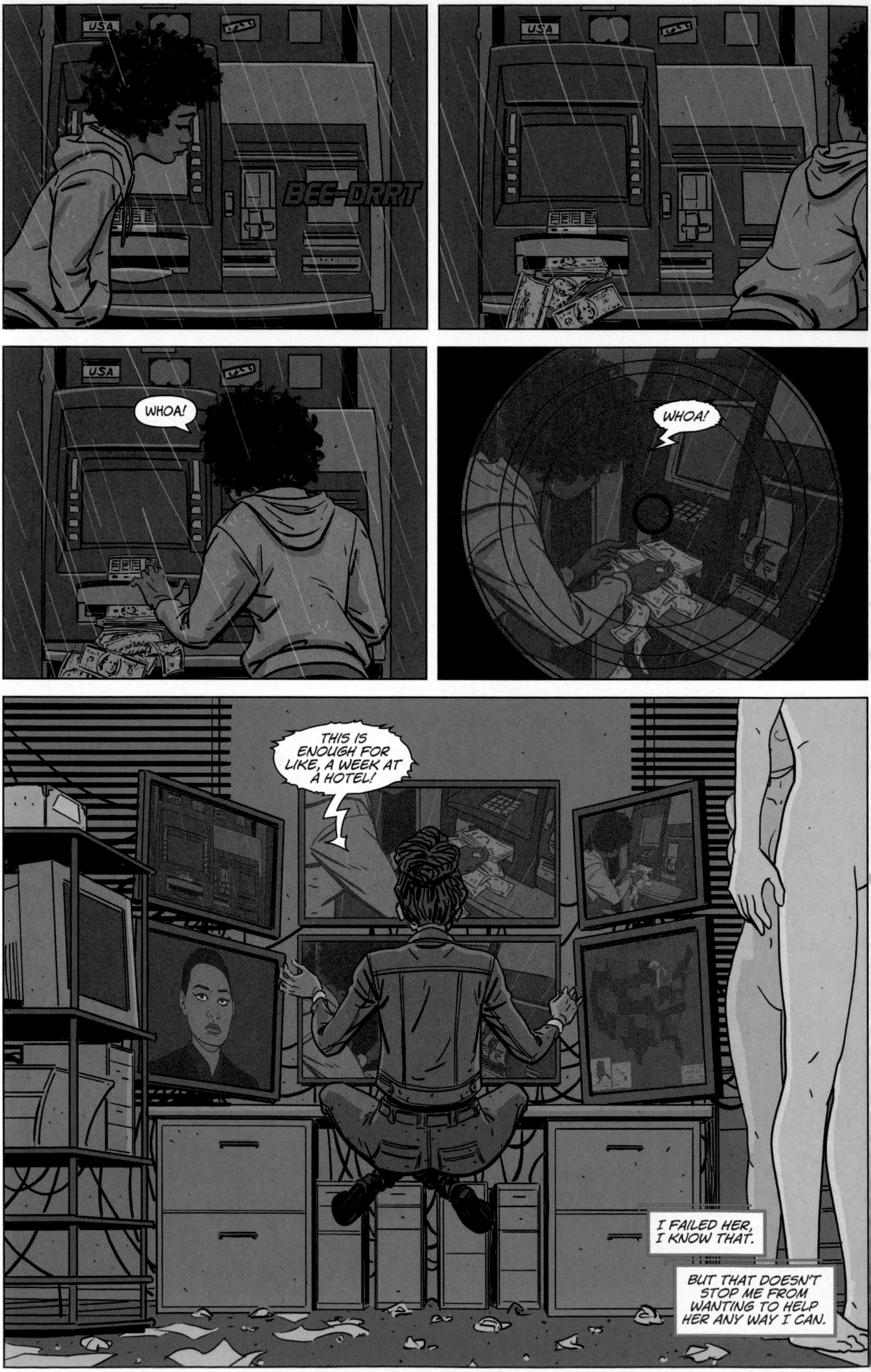
BEE-DRRT
WHOA!
WHOA!
THIS IS ENOUGH FOR LIKE, A WEEK AT A HOTEL!
I FAILED HER, I KNOW THAT.
BUT THAT DOESN'T STOP ME FROM WANTING TO HELP HER ANY WAY I CAN.

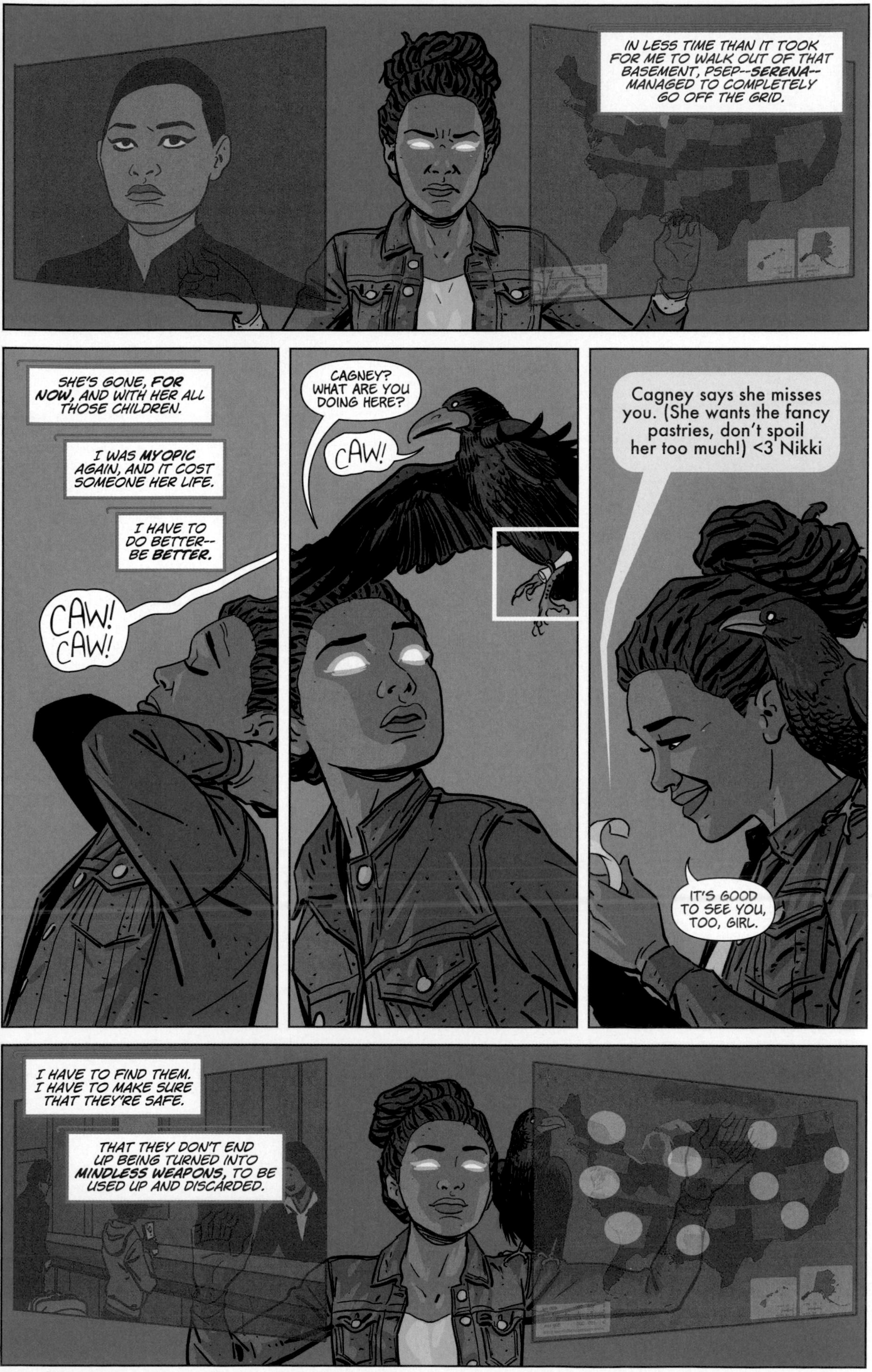
IN LESS TIME THAN IT TOOK FOR ME TO WALK OUT OF THAT BASEMENT, PSEP--SERENA--MANAGED TO COMPLETELY GO OFF THE GRID.
SHE'S GONE, FOR NOW, AND WITH HER ALL THOSE CHILDREN.
I WAS MYOPIC AGAIN, AND IT COST SOMEONE HER LIFE.
I HAVE TO DO BETTER-- BE BETTER.
CAW! CAW!
CAGNEY? WHAT ARE YOU DOING HERE?
CAW!
Cagney says she misses you. (She wants the fancy pastries, don't spoil her too much!) <3 Nikki
IT'S GOOD TO SEE YOU, TOO, GIRL.
I HAVE TO FIND THEM. I HAVE TO MAKE SURE THAT THEY'RE SAFE.
THAT THEY DON'T END UP BEING TURNED INTO MINDLESS WEAPONS, TO BE USED UP AND DISCARDED.

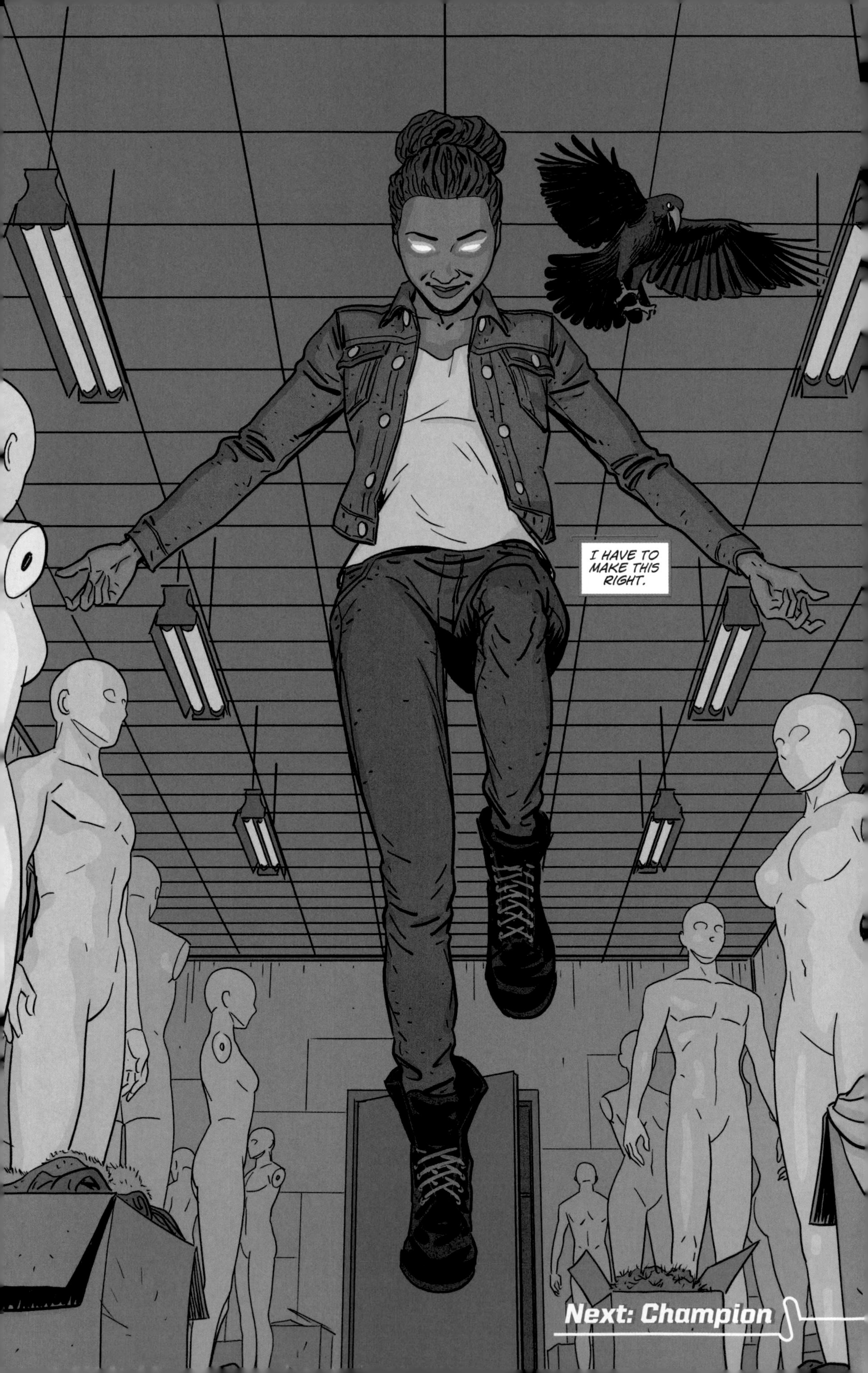
I HAVE TO MAKE THIS RIGHT.
Next: Champion

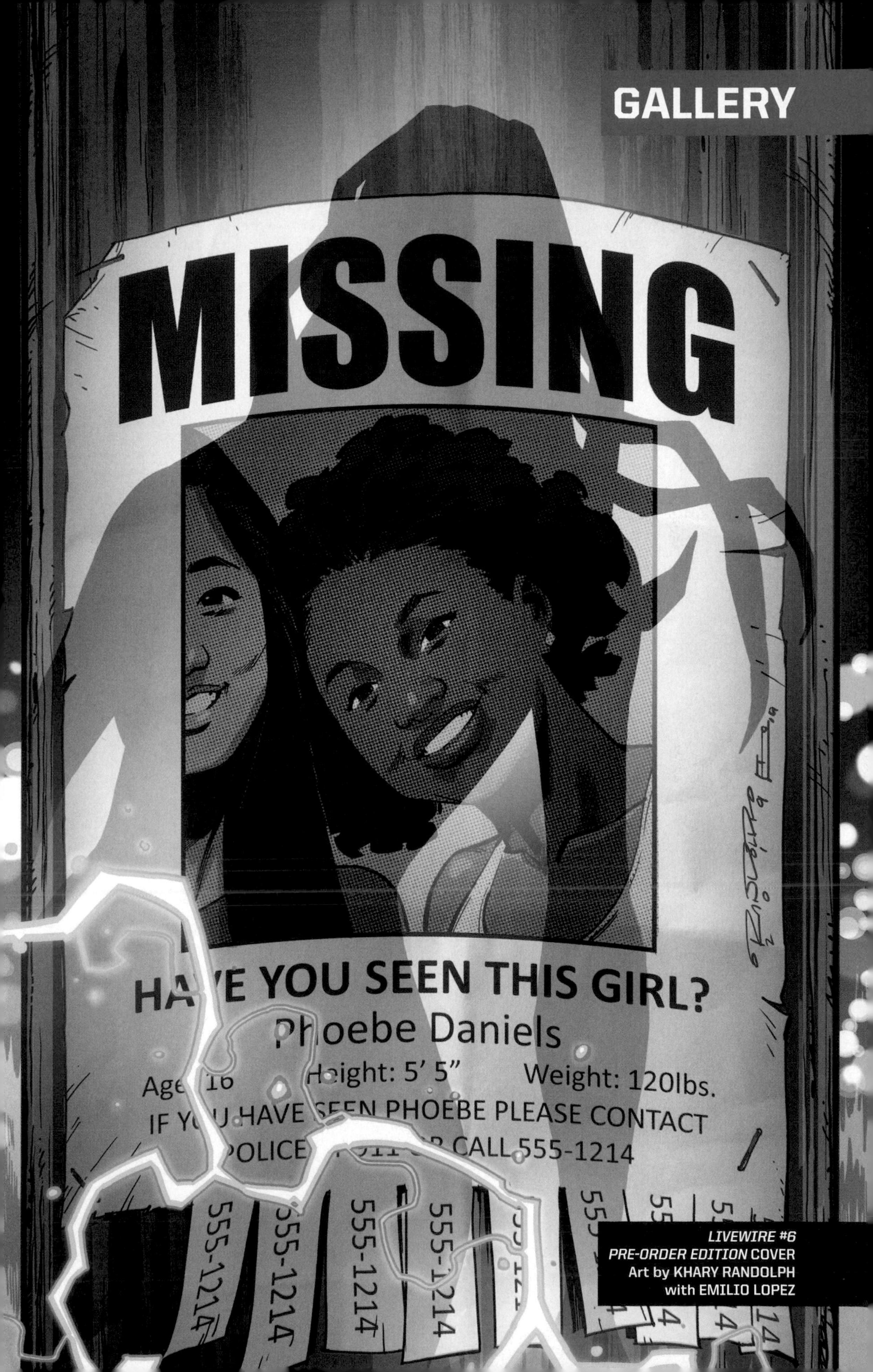
MISSING
YOU SEEN THIS GIRL?
Phoebe Daniels
Height: 5' 5"
Weight: 120lbs.
PHOEBE PLEASE CONTACT
CALL 555-1214
555-1214
555-1214
555-1214
555-1214

LIVEWIRE #6
PRE-ORDER EDITION COVER
Art by KHARY RANDOLPH
with EMILIO LOPEZ

THE PSIOT SAFETY AND EDUCATION PROGRAM
WITH SERIES WRITER **VITA AYALA**

This first page is going to start as an advertisement for PSEP, and then glitch out, and show us a flash of the truth beneath the sanitized public veneer.

PSEP is a public-facing arm of OMEN. They have (re) branded themselves to be a government sponsored public service. They claim that they can contain, control, and reform psiots into something safe.

I really want the first three panels to have this creepy, utopian vibe to them. Like cult propaganda from the 60s and 70s.

We open on SERENA BYRNE - face of the Psiot Safety & Education Program.

SERENA stands at a podium smiling gently, gesturing with one hand. She is flanked by JADA (who looks like the hired muscle). They are clearly giving a press conference - maybe we can see some of the press in the shot.

Behind her, on a large screen, the smiling faces of (psiot) children. The demographics of the kids (ethnicity, age, gender) is very mixed, a good cross section of people.

The PSEP logo is present, it is the initials of the program haloing around a shield. Inside the shield is a heart beat line.

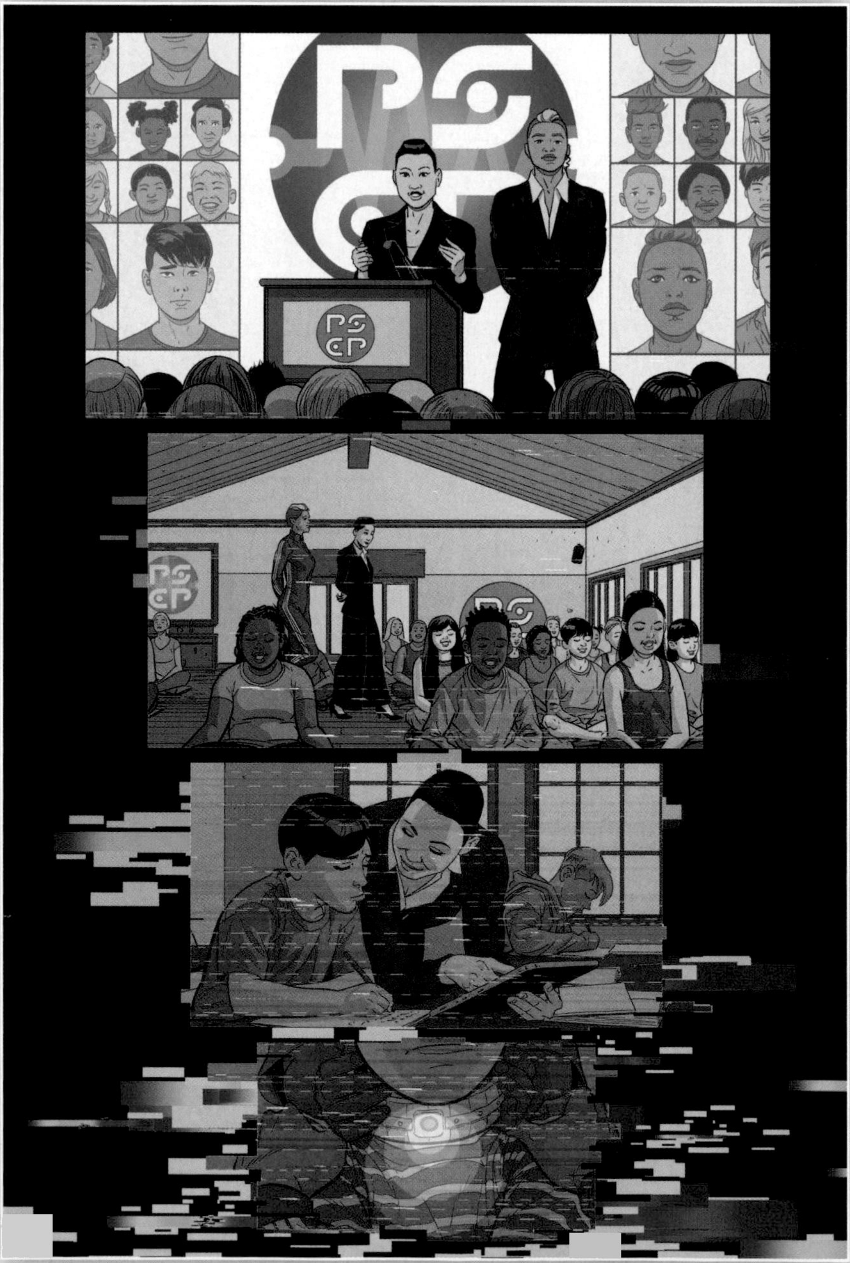

Originally published in *LIVEWIRE #5 PRE-ORDER EDITION.*

We have now entered cyberspace! Here we get to see a physical representation of Livewire rooting around in PSEP'S mainframe, and the gnarly security protocols that are there to keep people out.

I was thinking the security protocols could start off looking semi-normal/almost innocent things (maybe something sleek, something snake or fish-like?), and then when they are activated, they transform/morph into big, scary beasts. I am thinking the scene from Jurassic Park, where the Dilophosaurus goes from kinda cute into a freaky poison-spitting beast!

It is hard to envision an instantiation of cyberspace without thinking of Tron or Reboot. I would say err on the side of Tron – and even then, toward the aesthetic of the original movie and not the remake. I want to really differentiate the cyber world vibe from the real world.

I am thinking that this particular cyber-structure has the same layout as the PSEP facility that Amanda will visit later in this issue.

In this scene, we avoid the bird's eye view if we can – I want to differentiate the way she hacks into their system here, and that perspective will play a large role the next time she hacks.

I was also thinking it would be cool to have small versions of the Security Protocols in between the panels/in the borders, making their way from the top of the page to the bottom, kind of Pac-Man style. I want it to be charming at first, but when we get to Panel 5, we realize that, NOPE, these are things coming for Amanda!

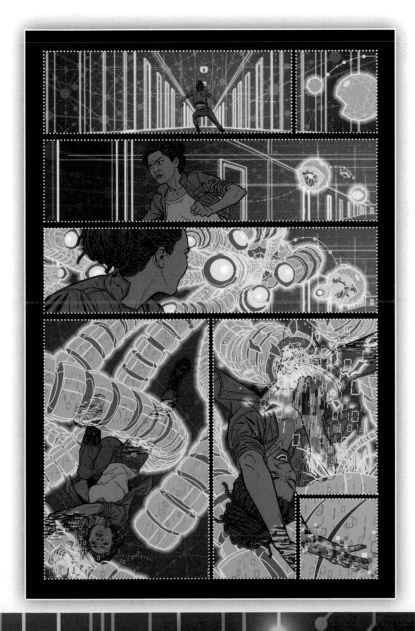

KEEPING AN EYE ON THE WORLD
WITH SERIES WRITER **VITA AYALA**

In this issue, the media angle we are pushing is the public opinion of psiots as a whole, and the comparison between the PSEP psiots and Livewire in particular.

It would be interesting to have some sort of CNN/MSNBC style "debate" by "experts" to really drive it home. The menace of Livewire, the potential threat of psiots in general, and the "well behaved" / "in control" / "useful" psiots of PSEP.

This issue is a much smaller amount of time, and we get to know Phoebe better through some flashbacks. It picks up immediately after the end of Issue 6, in Amanda's room as Jada is attacking her.

During the fight part of this scene, we can have that news coverage happening - stuff like tweets and click-batey headlines in the margins. I think it's a fun or interesting flavor to add, and it reminds us that even as X, Y, and Z are happening, Livewire is monitoring the rest of the world.

We use it to show how PSEP is spinning what happened as well.

Originally published in *LIVEWIRE #7 PRE-ORDER EDITION*.

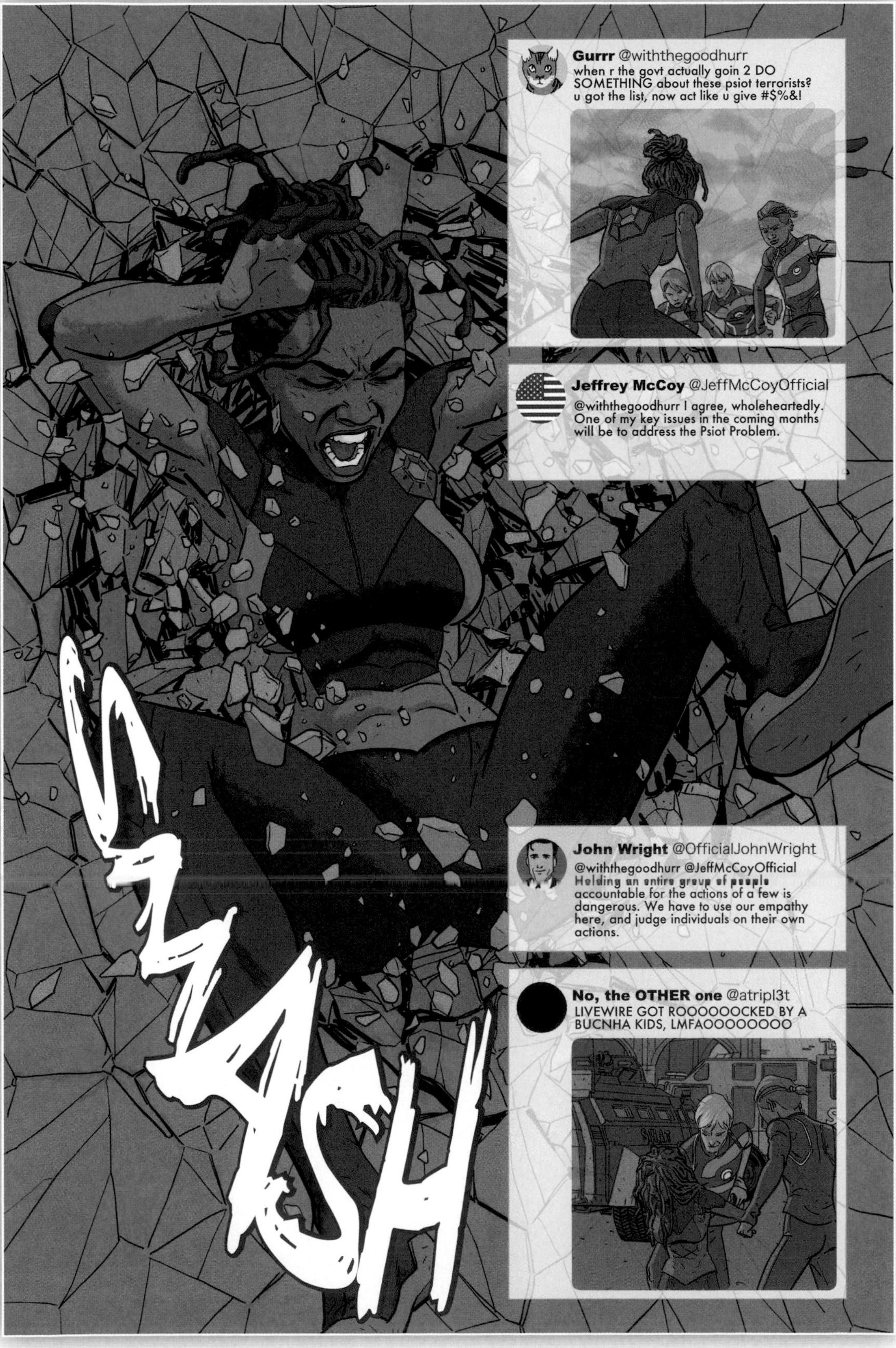
Gurrr @withthegoodhurr
when r the govt actually goin 2 DO SOMETHING about these psiot terrorists? u got the list, now act like u give #$%&!
Jeffrey McCoy @JeffMcCoyOfficial
@withthegoodhurr I agree, wholeheartedly. One of my key issues in the coming months will be to address the Psiot Problem.
John Wright @OfficialJohnWright
@withthegoodhurr @JeffMcCoyOfficial Holding an entire group of people accountable for the actions of a few is dangerous. We have to use our empathy here, and judge individuals on their own actions.
No, the OTHER one @atripl3t
LIVEWIRE GOT ROOOOOOCKED BY A BUCNHA KIDS, LMFAOOOOOOOO
SMASH

ART BY **KANO**

LIVEWIRE'S JOURNEY
WITH SERIES WRITER **VITA AYALA**

The core of this story was about self control. For Livewire, having to take responsibility of the consequences of shutting down the country and moving forward, this was an especially important journey. These ideas were also at the forefront of her mind as she navigated a world that viewed her as a terrorist, and the ultimate threat, while trying to be a hero.

The new character, PHOEBE DANIELS, was juxtaposed against Amanda, to help us explore a thread of "What If" and also underscore the core of the arc.

We weaved together a story told from Amanda and Phoebe's perspectives, partially to elevate Amanda's arc, but also partially to show real world consequences for other psiots after everything that happened with the release of the psiot master list, and Amanda's infamous blackout.

If this was the only Valiant book someone read, we wanted them to feel that it takes place in a rich context/ universe.

In this issue, the fight between Jada and Amanda will be live streamed. All of her actions will be twisted by PSEP/OMEN and used against her. She will be in worse standing with the public coming out of this, but also closer to understanding what her new direction must be as a hero.

Originally published in *LIVEWIRE #8 PRE-ORDER EDITION.*

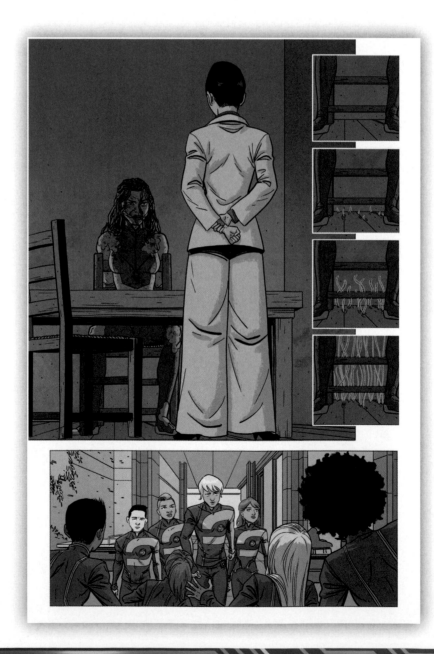

In the first arc, Amanda was implanted with a dampener directly into her brain. When it clicked off for that 5 second span, she took control of it, and re-purposed it into basically anti-dampening tech. She will never, as long as her brain has enough energy to power the chip, she will not be affected by the typical dampeners found in the Valiant universe.

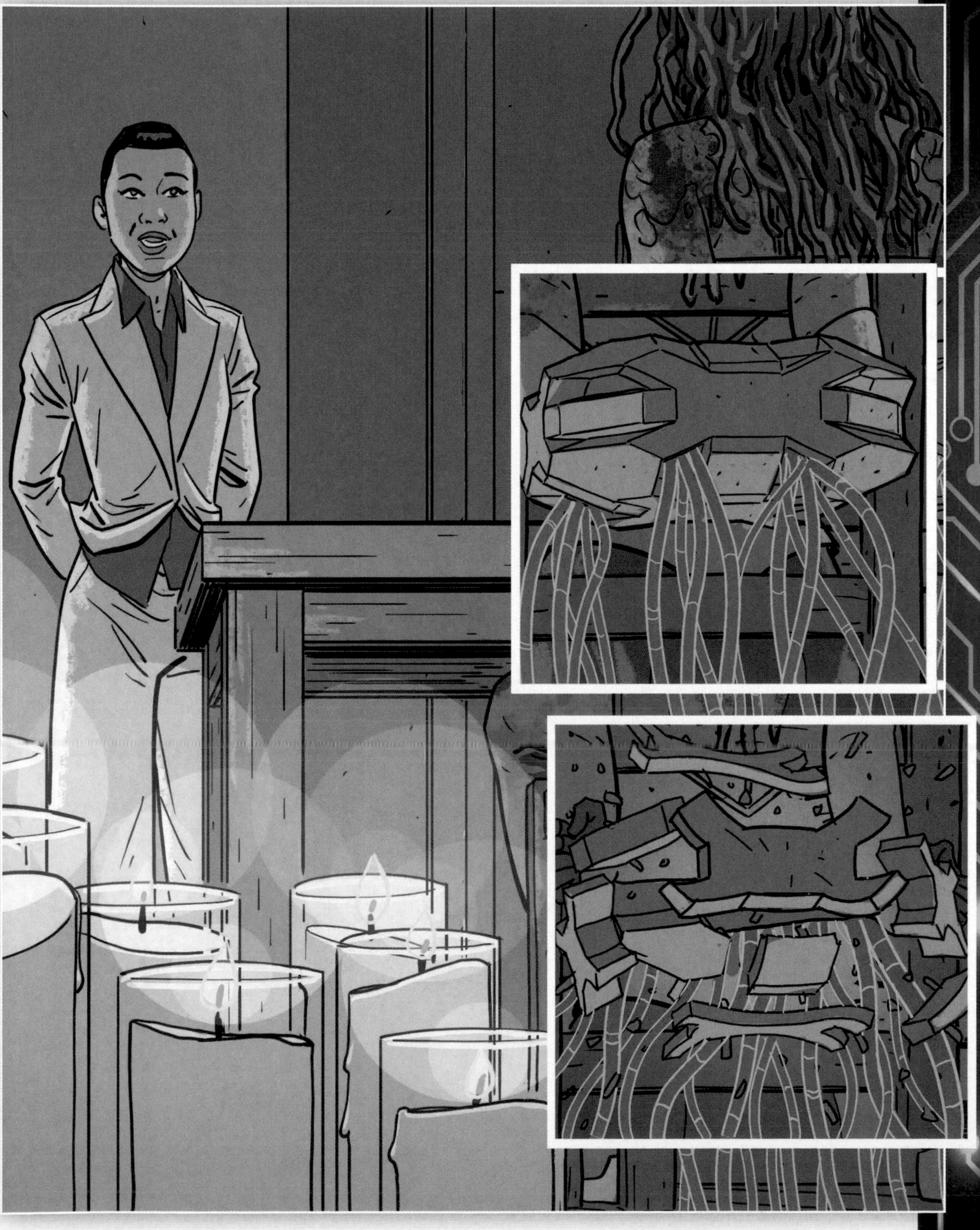

ART BY **KANO**

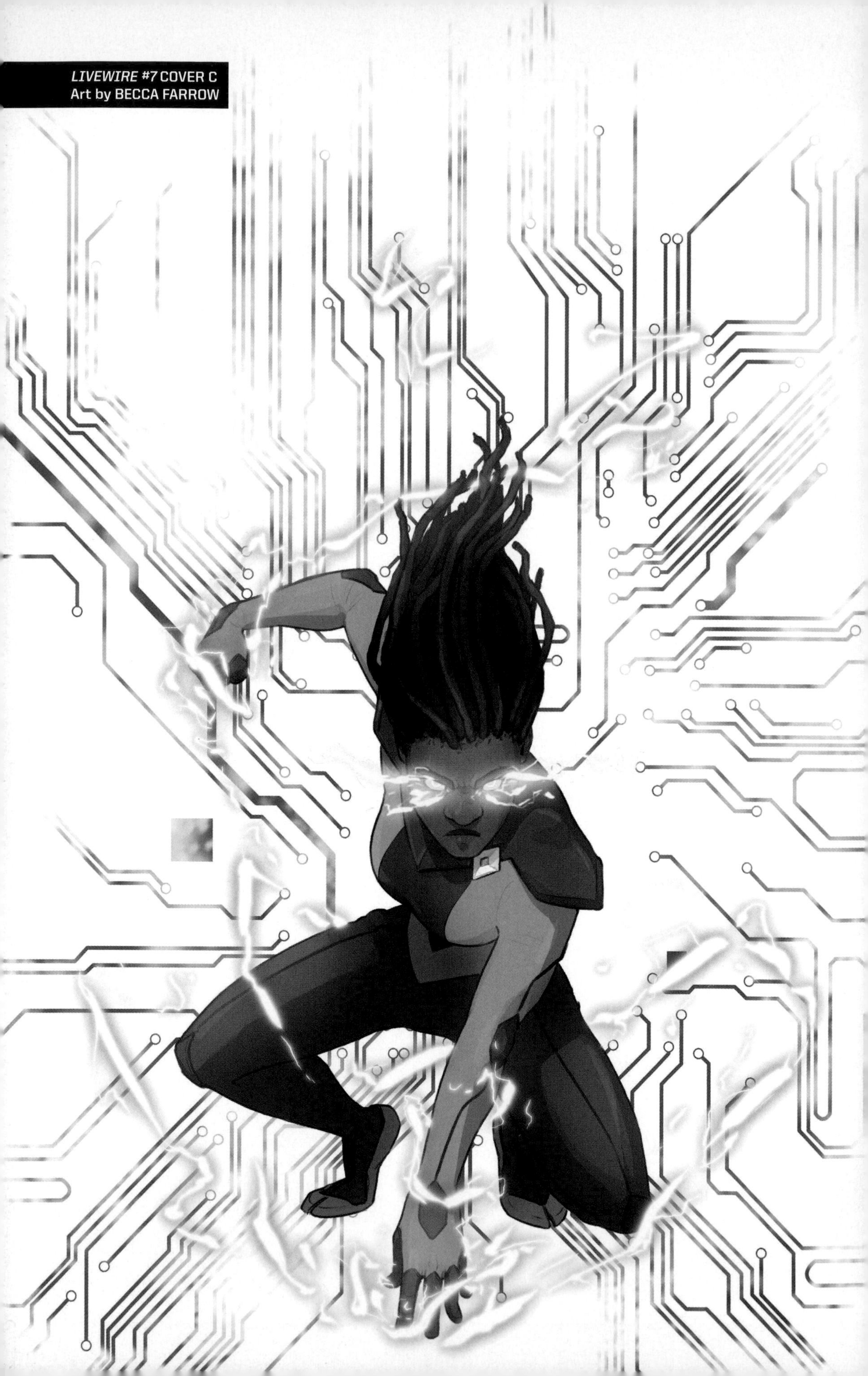

LIVEWIRE #7 COVER C
Art by BECCA FARROW

LIVEWIRE #5
PRE-ORDER EDITION COVER
Art by KHARI RANDOLPH
with EMILIO LOPEZ

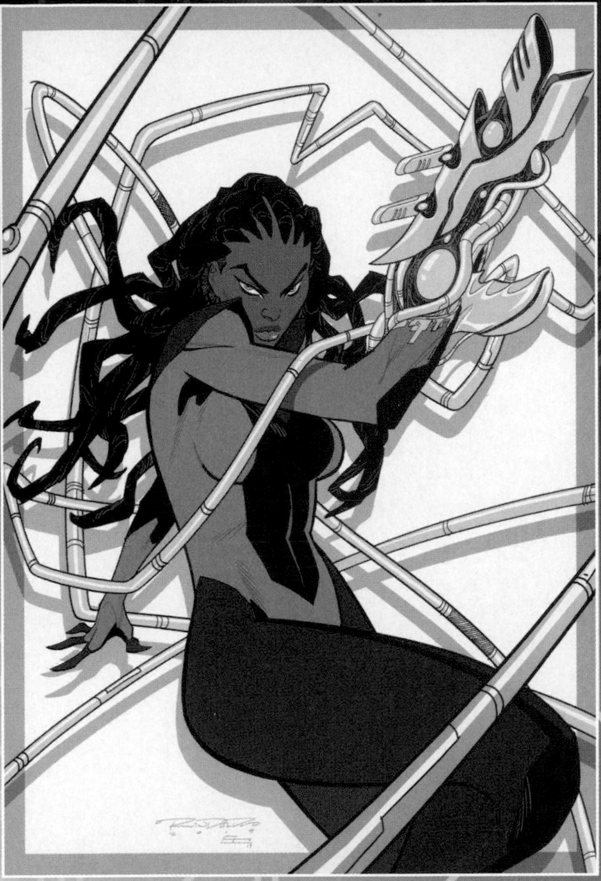

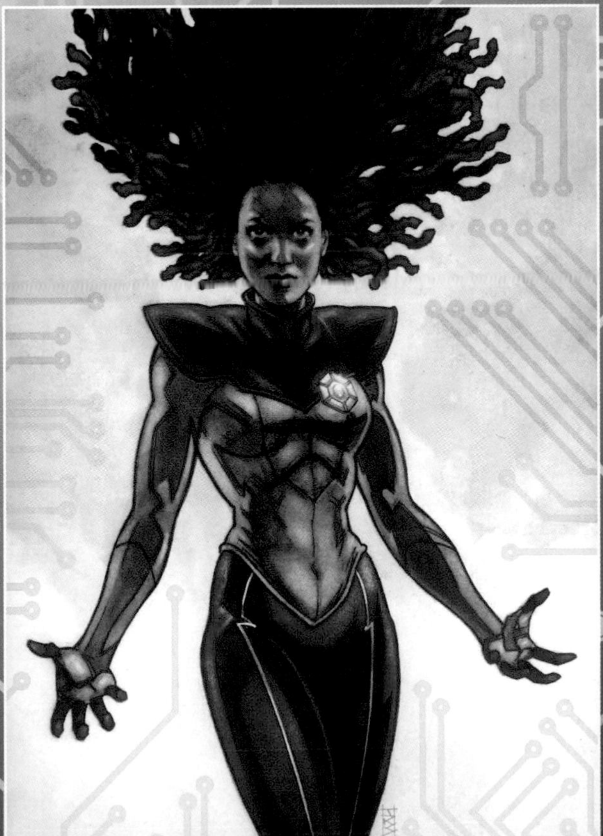

LIVEWIRE #6 COVER B
Art by JOHN K. SNYDER III
with JASON WRIGHT

LIVEWIRE #8 COVER B
Art by PAUL RENAUD

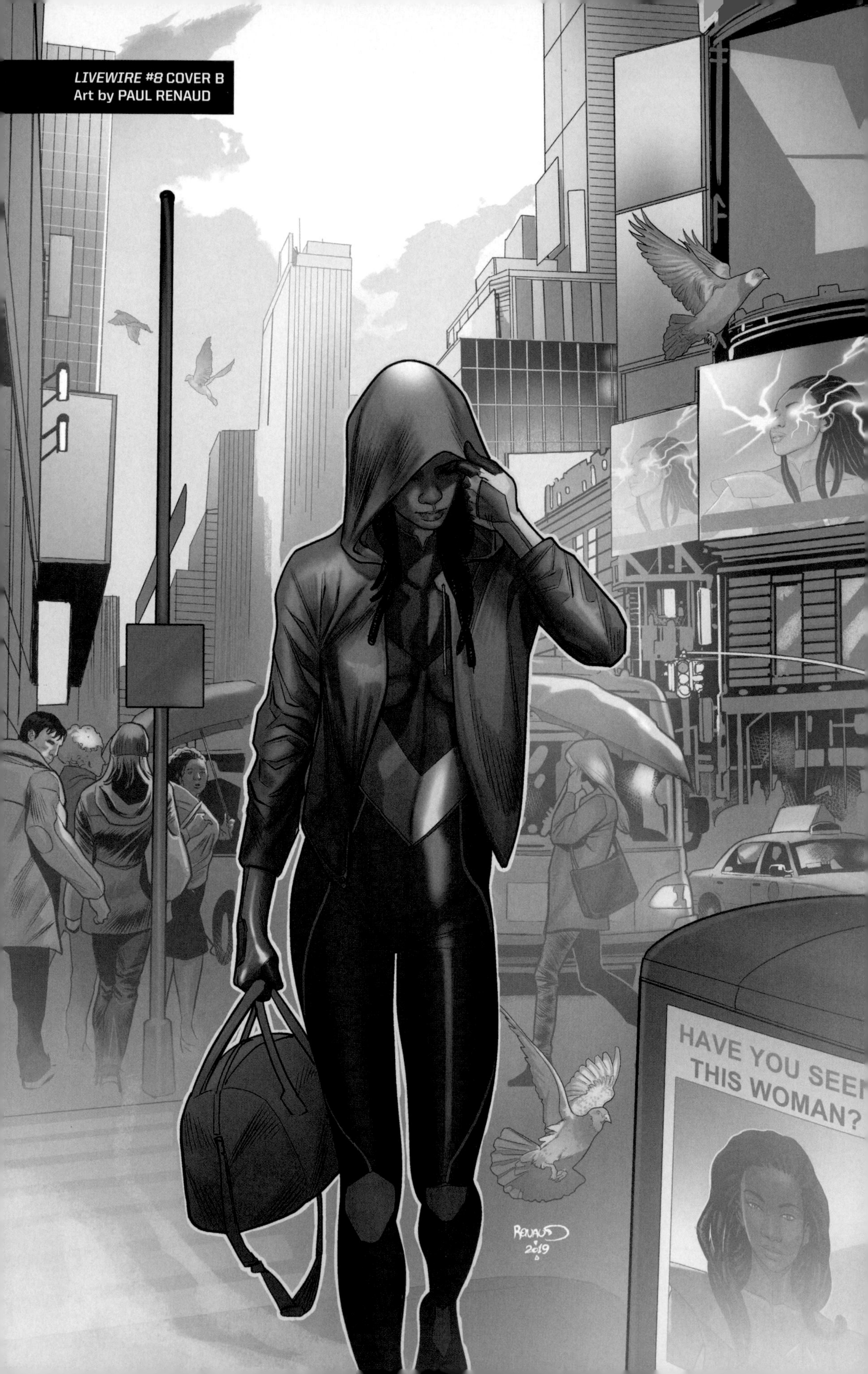
HAVE YOU SEE
THIS WOMAN?

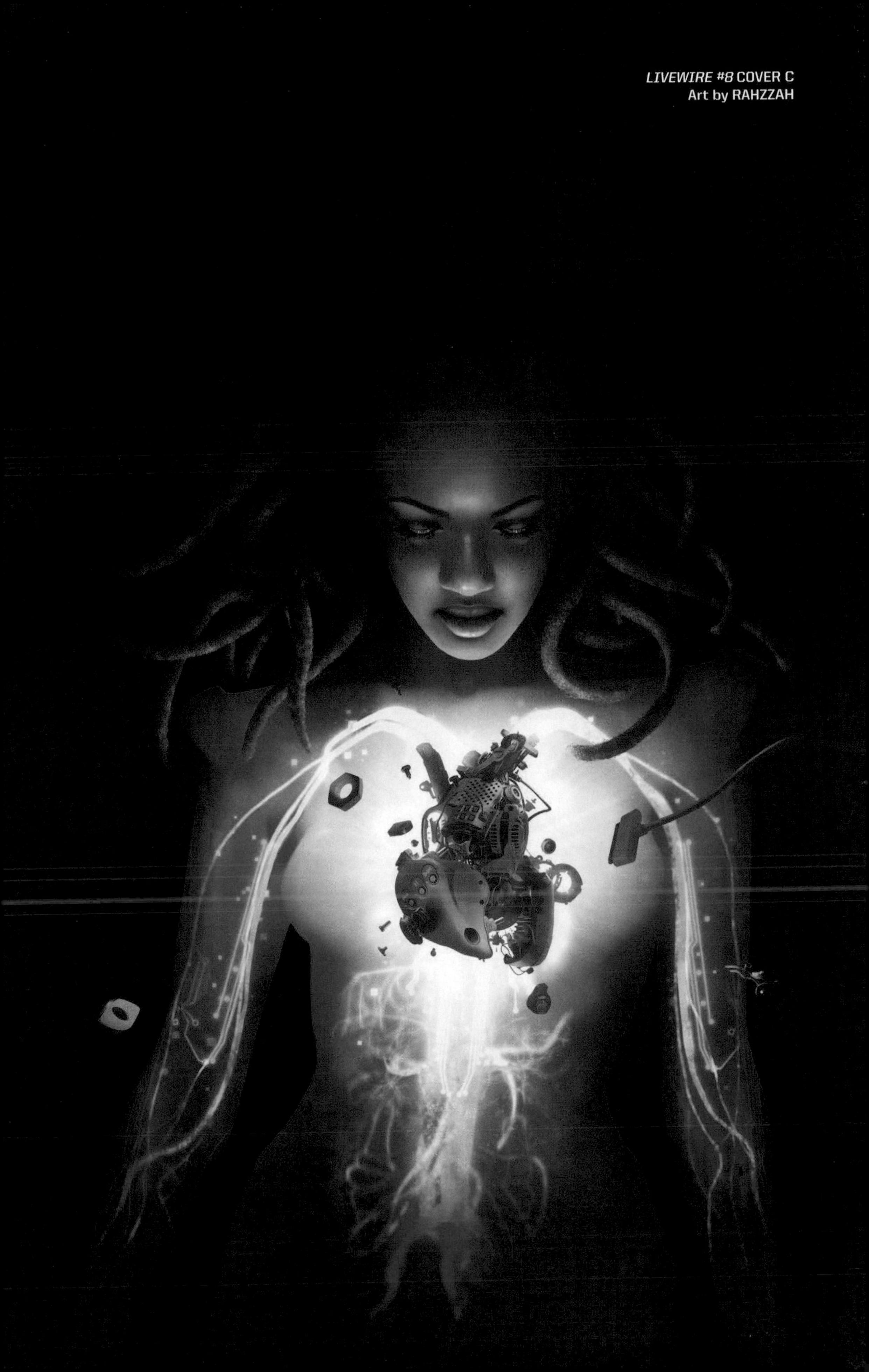

LIVEWIRE #8 COVER C
Art by RAHZZAH

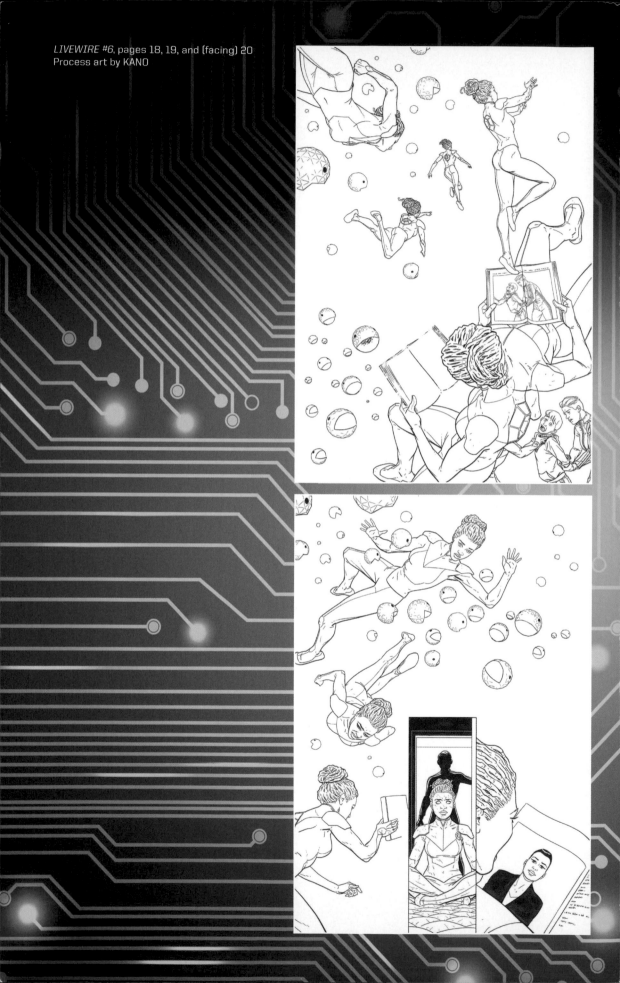

LIVEWIRE #6, pages 18, 19, and (facing) 20
Process art by KANO

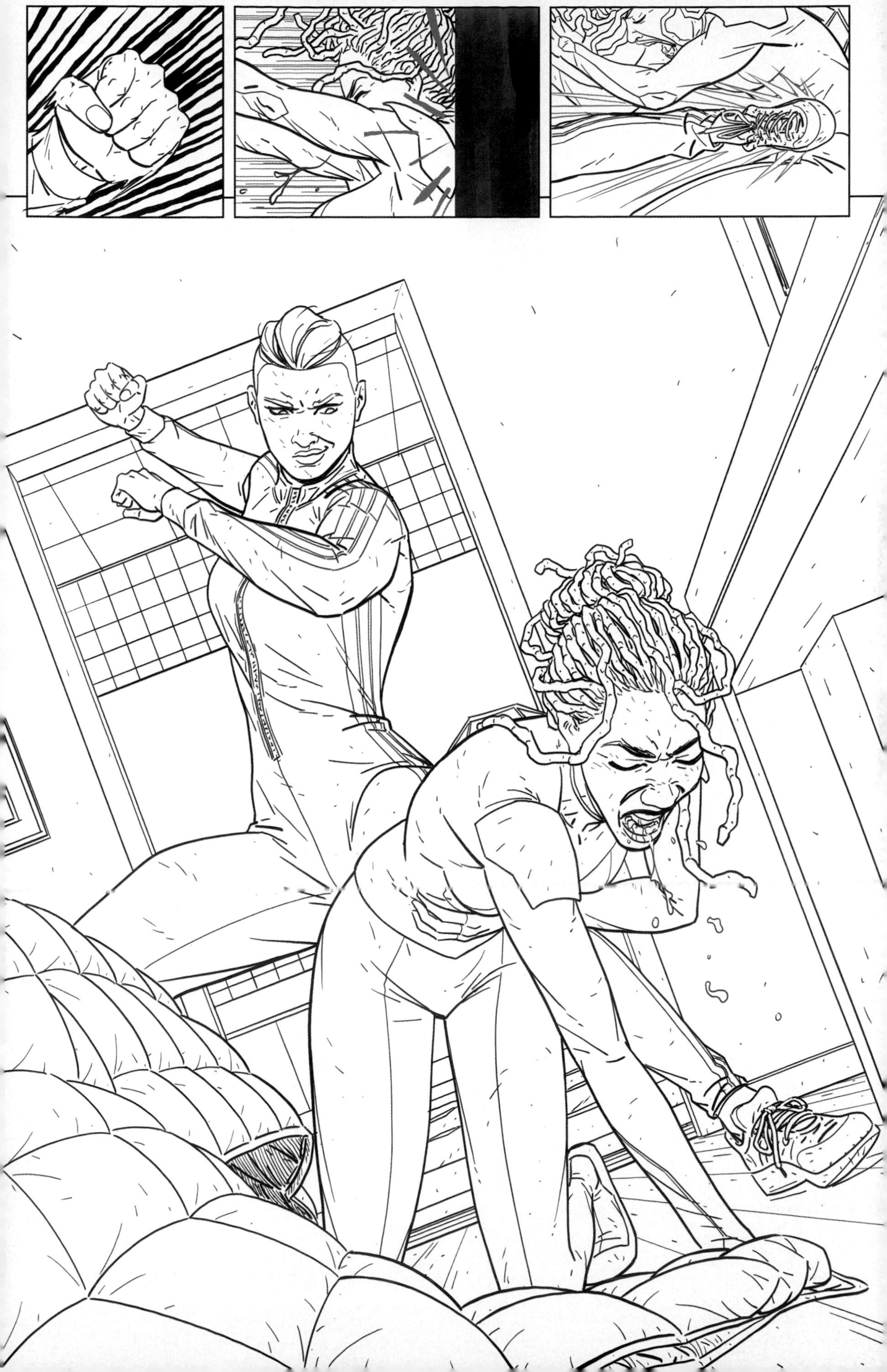

LIVEWIRE #7, pages 15, 16, and (facing) 20
Process art by KANO

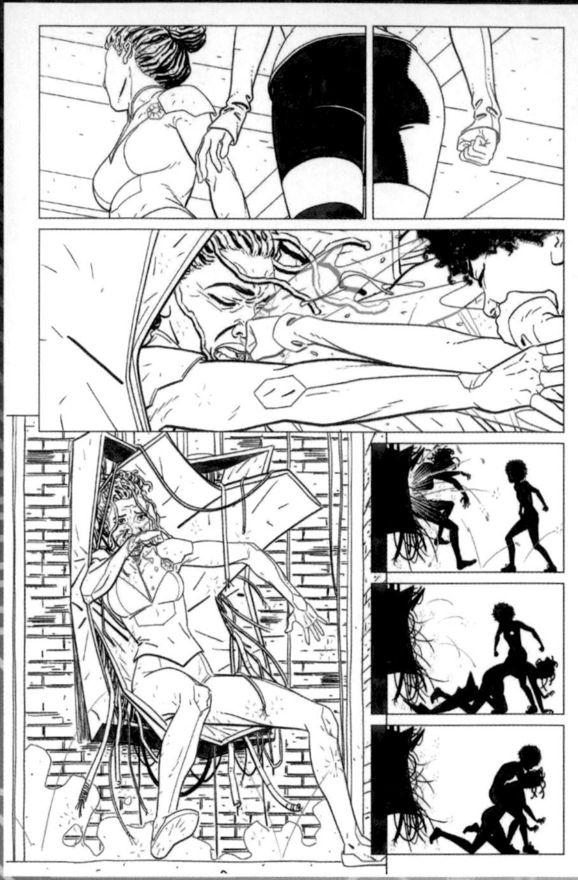

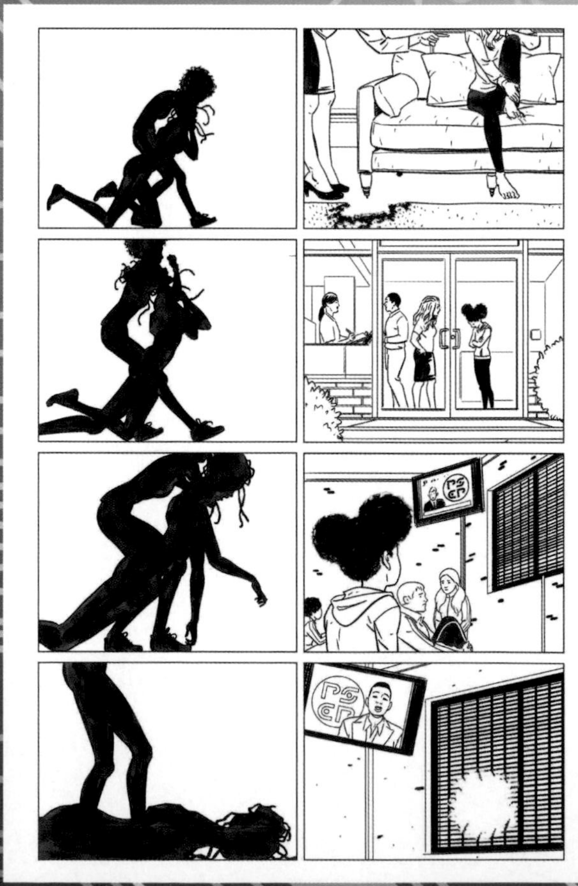

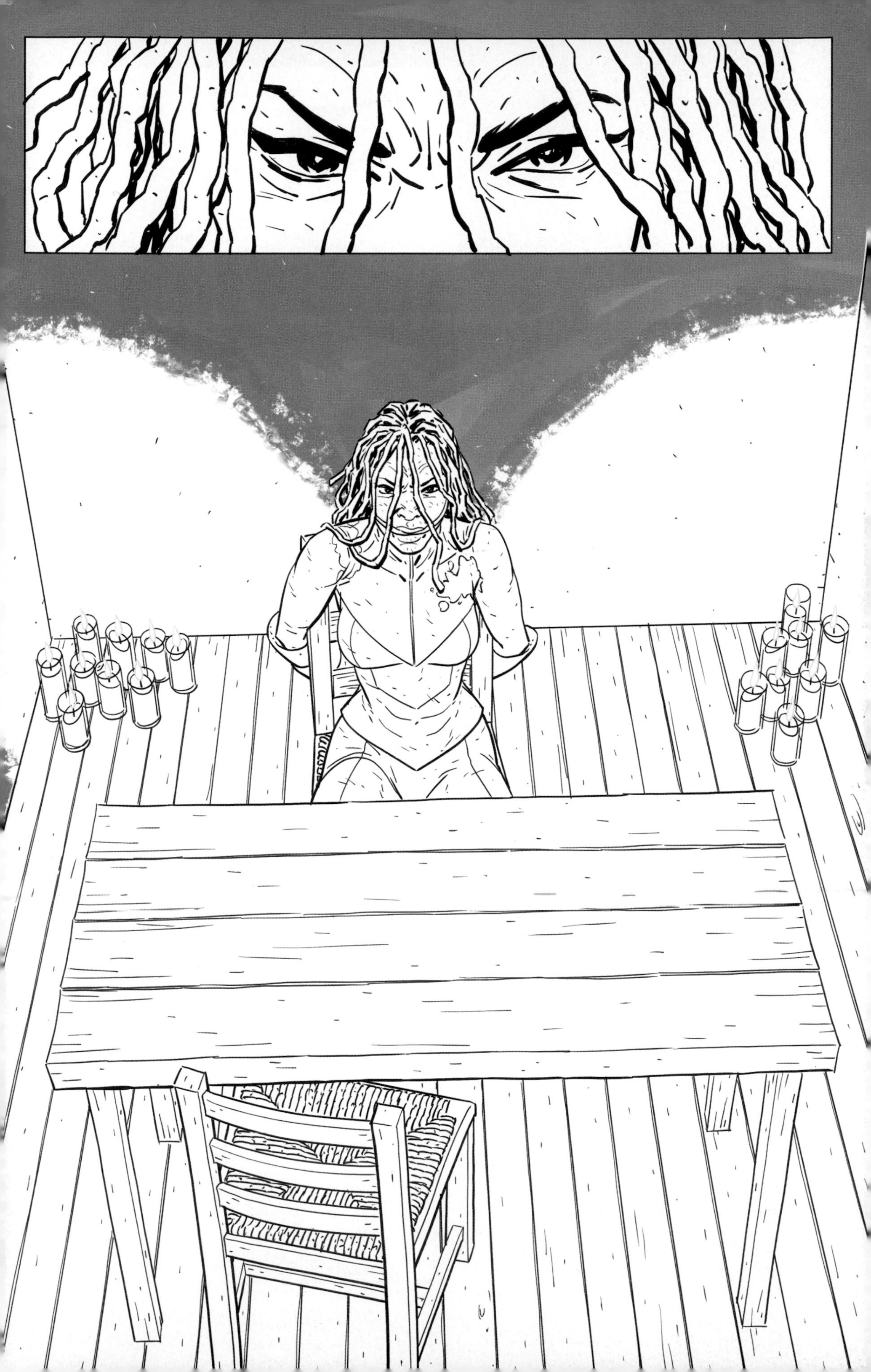

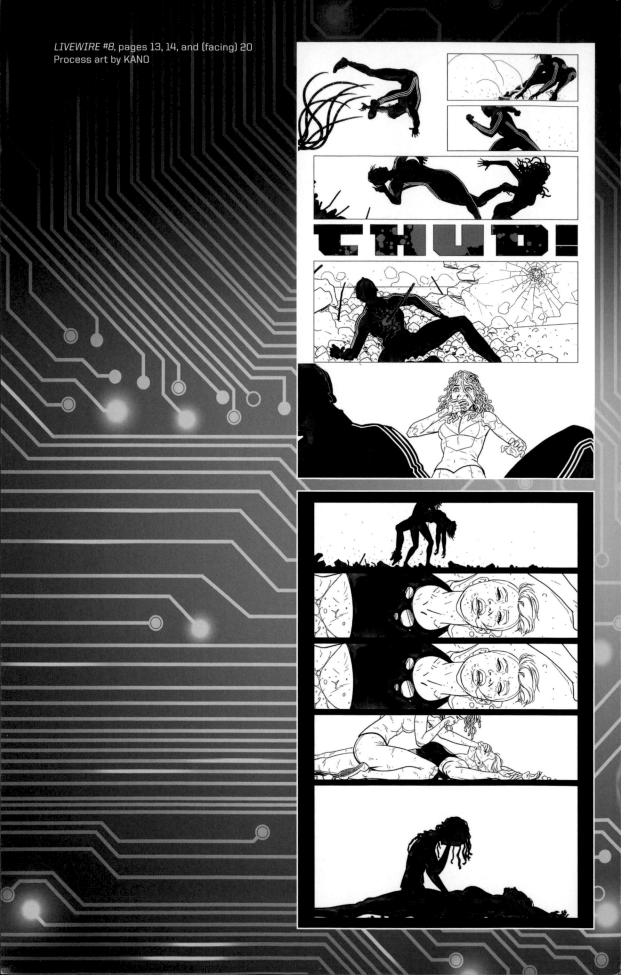

LIVEWIRE #8, pages 13, 14, and (facing) 20
Process art by KANO

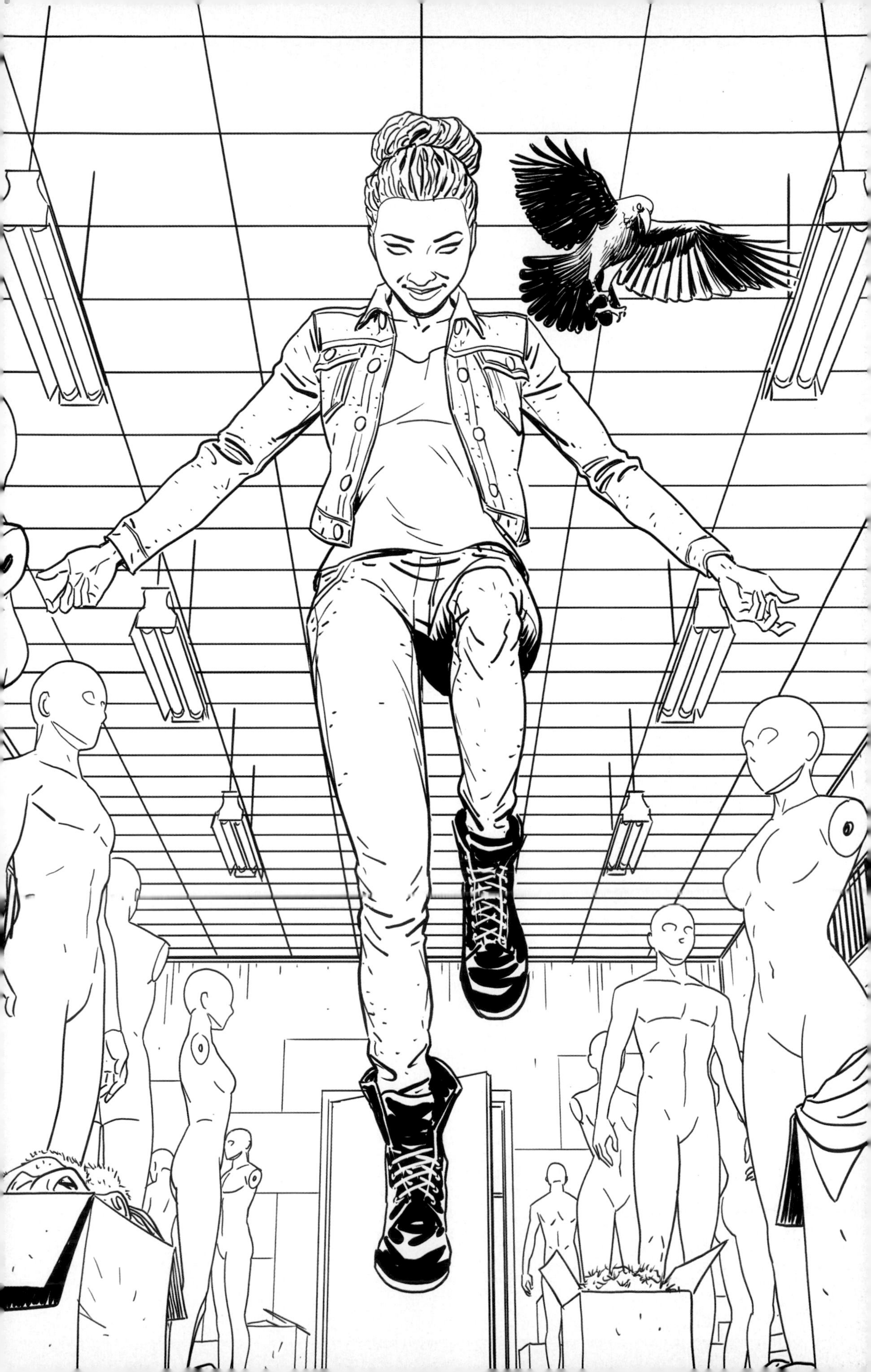

EXPLORE THE VALIANT

ACTION & ADVENTURE

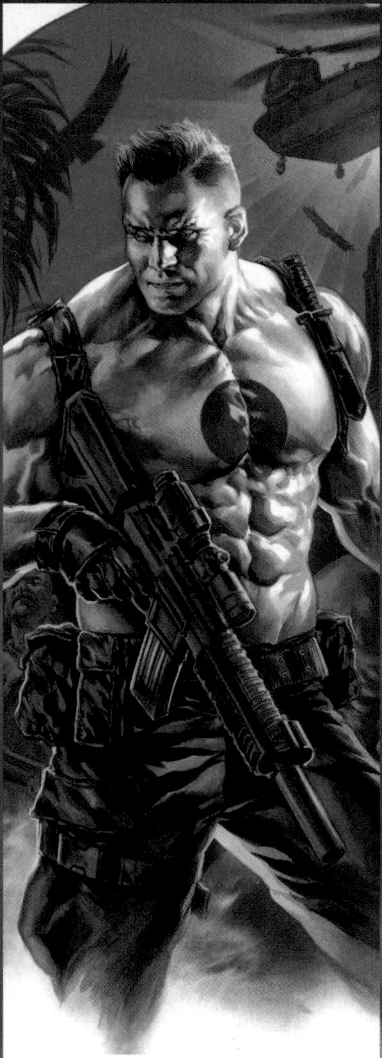

BLOODSHOT SALVATION VOL. 1: THE BOOK OF REVENGE
ISBN: 978-1-68215-255-3
NINJA-K VOL. 1: THE NINJA FILES
ISBN: 978-1-68215-259-1
SAVAGE
ISBN: 978-1-68215-189-1
WRATH OF THE ETERNAL WARRIOR VOL. 1: RISEN
ISBN: 978-1-68215-123-5
X-O MANOWAR (2017) VOL. 1: SOLDIER
ISBN: 978-1-68215-205-8

BLOCKBUSTER ADVENTURE

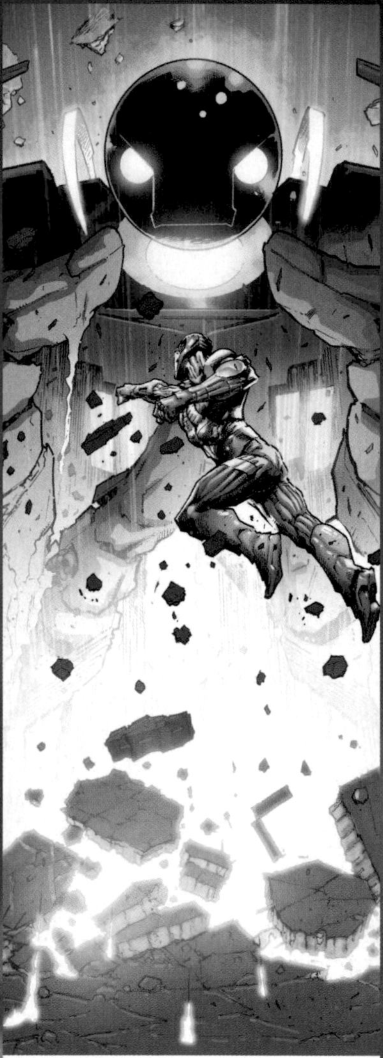

4001 A.D.
ISBN: 978-1-68215-143-3
ARMOR HUNTERS
ISBN: 978-1-939346-45-2
BOOK OF DEATH
ISBN: 978-1-939346-97-1
HARBINGER WARS
ISBN: 978-1-939346-09-4
THE VALIANT
ISBN: 978-1-939346-60-5

COMEDY

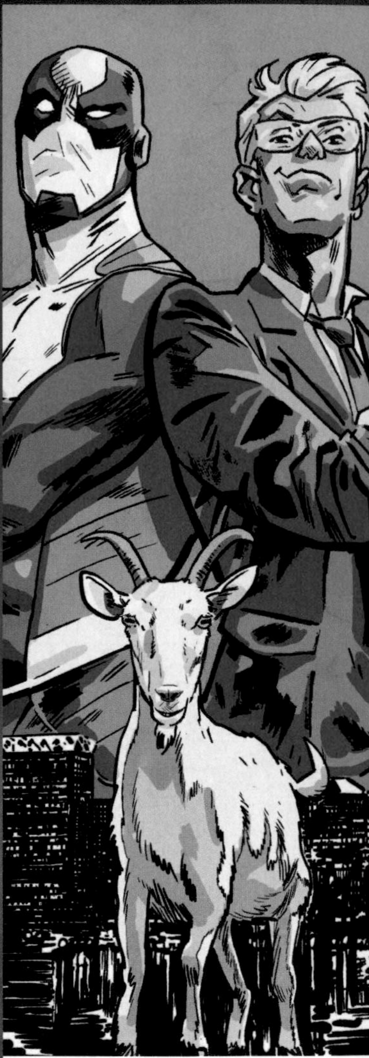

A&A: THE ADVENTURES OF ARCHER & ARMSTRONG VOL. 1: IN THE BAG
ISBN: 978-1-68215-149-5
THE DELINQUENTS
ISBN: 978-1-939346-51-3
QUANTUM AND WOODY! (2017) VOL. 1: KISS KISS, KLANG KLANG
ISBN: 978-1-68215-269-0

UNIVERSE FOR ONLY $9.99

HORROR & MYSTERY

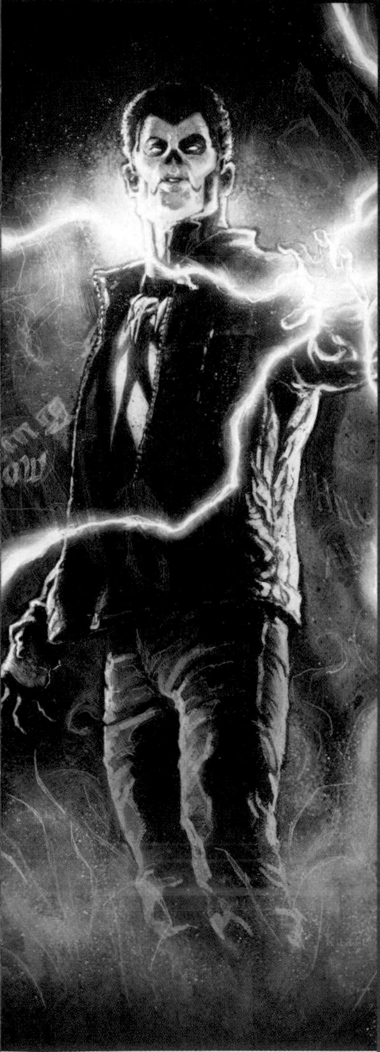

BRITANNIA
ISBN: 978-1-68215-185-3
THE DEATH-DEFYING DOCTOR MIRAGE
ISBN: 978-1-939346-49-0
RAPTURE
ISBN: 978-1-68215-225-6
SHADOWMAN (2018) VOL. 1: FEAR OF THE DARK
ISBN: 978-1-68215-239-3

SCIENCE FICTION & FANTASY

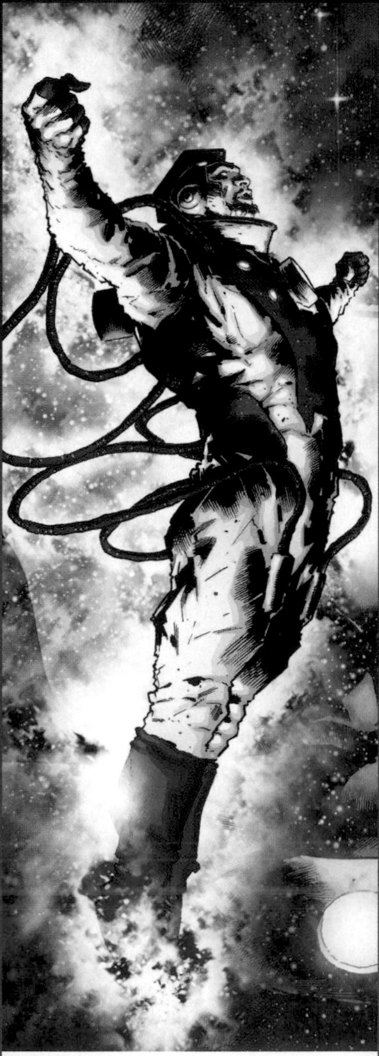

DIVINITY
ISBN: 978-1-939346-76-6
THE FORGOTTEN QUEEN
ISBN: 978-1-68215-324-6
IMPERIUM VOL. 1: COLLECTING MONSTERS
ISBN: 978-1-939346-75-9
IVAR, TIMEWALKER VOL. 1: MAKING HISTORY
ISBN: 978-1-939346-63-6
RAI VOL. 1: WELCOME TO NEW JAPAN
ISBN: 978-1-939346-41-4
WAR MOTHER
ISBN: 978-1-68215-237-9

TEEN ADVENTURE

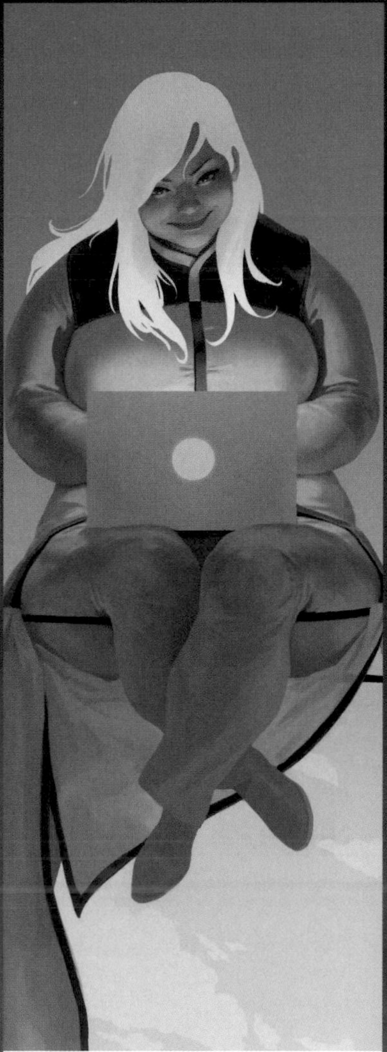

FAITH VOL. 1: HOLLYWOOD AND VINE
ISBN: 978-1-68215-121-1
GENERATION ZERO VOL. 1: WE ARE THE FUTURE
ISBN: 978-1-68215-175-4
HARBINGER RENEGADE VOL. 1: THE JUDGMENT OF SOLOMON
ISBN: 978-1-68215-169-3
LIVEWIRE VOL. 1: FUGITIVE
ISBN: 978-1-68215-301-7
SECRET WEAPONS
ISBN: 978-1-68215-229-4

Discover the entire Valiant Universe of titles at VALIANTENTERTAINMENT.COM/ALL-SERIES/

LIVEWIRE

VITA AYALA | TANA FORD

VALIANT

VOLUME THREE: CHAMPION

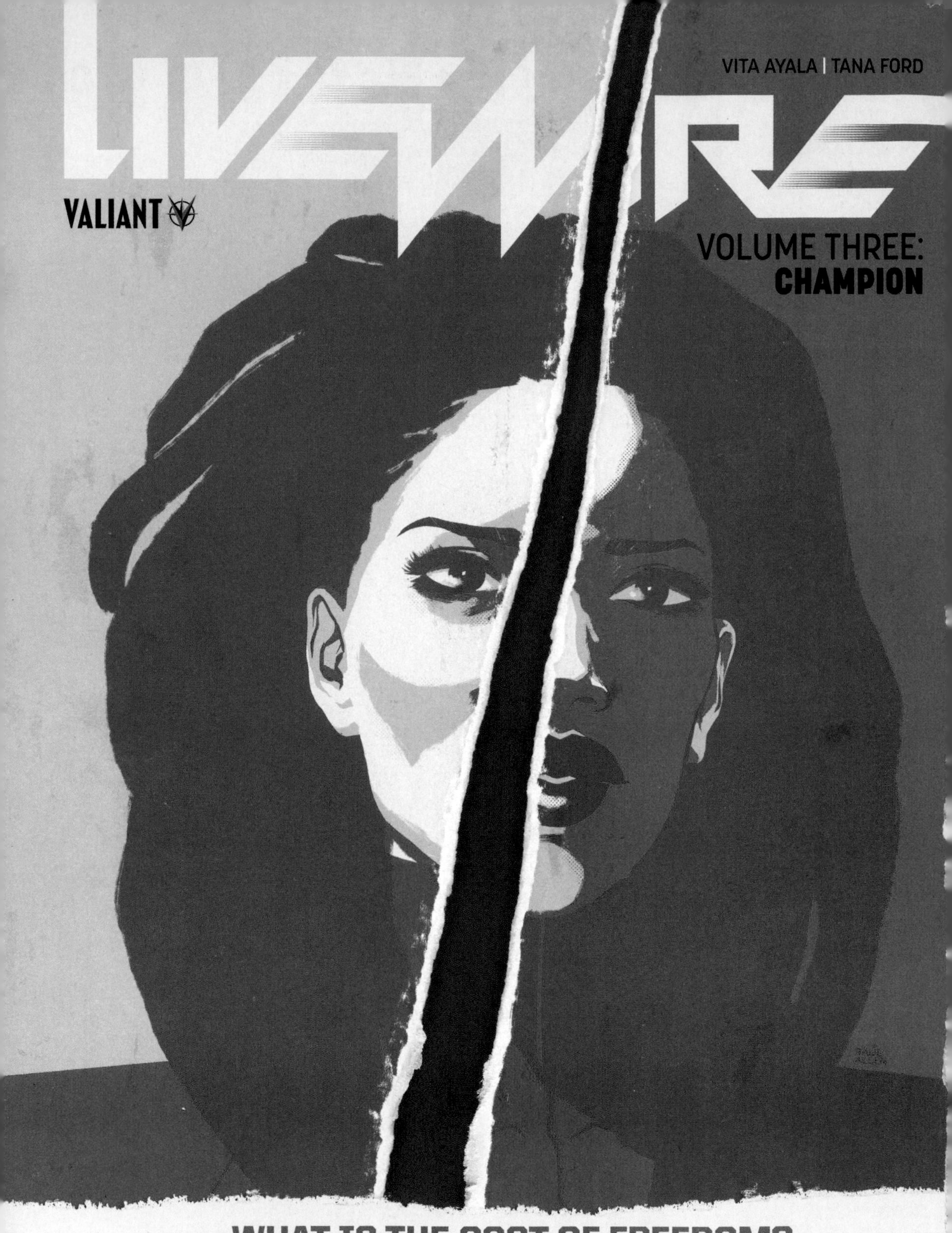

WHAT IS THE COST OF FREEDOM?

Wanted fugitive Livewire has been on the run for months from the authorities for shutting down the country's power in an effort to protect people gifted with powers. Will a shocking offer to go public from a renowned local politician pull Livewire into a political spotlight?

Valiant's breakout heroine fights to clear her name in the next electrifying volume from rising stars Vita Ayala (*Prisoner X*) and Tana Ford (*Avengers*)!

Collecting LIVEWIRE #9–12.

TRADE PAPERBACK
ISBN: 978-1-68215-354-3